Repealed

'An indispensable and compelling read, showing how feminist organising changes law and changes activists.'

—Máiréad Enright, Reader in Feminist Legal Studies, University of Birmingham and a founding member of Lawyers for Choice

'A call-to-arms in the on-going global fight for abortion access and reproductive justice.'

—Bríd Smith TD, People Before Profit

Repealed

Ireland's Unfinished Fight for Reproductive Rights

Camilla Fitzsimons
With Sinéad Kennedy

Foreword by Ruth Coppinger

PLUTO PRESS

First published 2021 by Pluto Press
New Wing, Somerset House, Strand, London WC2R 1LA

www.plutobooks.com

British Library Cataloguing in Publication Data
A catalogue record for this book is available from the British Library

ISBN   978 0 7453 4428 7   Hardback
ISBN   978 0 7453 4427 0   Paperback
ISBN   978 0 7453 4431 7   PDF
ISBN   978 0 7453 4429 4   EPUB

This book is printed on paper suitable for recycling and made from fully
managed and sustained forest sources. Logging, pulping and manufacturing
processes are expected to conform to the environmental standards of the
country of origin.

Typeset by Stanford DTP Services, Northampton, England

Simultaneously printed in the United Kingdom and United States of America

The history of this movement really needs to acknowledge all the people involved nationwide that helped get the Eighth Amendment repealed. Not just the figureheads. Local people in local areas helped this to pass.

I would love to say much more but I have to get the children to bed!

Member of ARC and Parents for Choice (2020)

Contents

Tables

Abbreviations

AAC	Anti-Amendment Campaign
AACW	Abortion Action Campaign West
AIMS	Association for Improvements in Maternity Services
ALRA	Abortion Law Reform Association
AMRI	Association of Mixed Race Irish
ARC	Abortion Rights Campaign
ASN	Abortion Support Network
AWG	Abortion Working Group
BPAS	British Pregnancy Advisory Service
CAP	Contraceptive Action Campaign
CARASA	Committee for Abortion Rights and Against Sterilisation Abuse (US)
CO	Conscientious objection
DUP	Democratic Unionist Party
EMAs	Early medical abortions
ET	Educate Together
HIQA	Health Information and Quality Authority
HSE	Irish Health Service Executive
GSOC	Garda Síochána Ombudsman Commission
ICBR	Irish Centre for Bio-Ethical Reform
ICCL	Irish Council for Civil Liberties
IFPA	Irish Family Planning Association
ILGA	International Lesbian, Gay, Bisexual, Trans and Intersex Association
IWLM	Irish Women's Liberation Movement
IWU	Irish Women Unite
LMC	Bereavement support (formerly Leanbh mo Chroí)
MASI	Movement of Asylum Seekers in Ireland
MERJ	Migrant and Ethnic Minorities for Reproductive Justice
MRC	Migrant Rights Centre
NARAL	originally in 1969, National Association for the Repeal of Abortion Laws, then National Abortion Rights Action League, and later the National Abortion and Repro-

	ductive Rights Action League. Now known as NARAL Pro-Choice America (US)
NCCA	National Council for Curriculum Assessment
NCCWN	National Collective of Community Based Women's Networks
NIHRC	Northern Ireland Human Rights Commission
NUI	National University of Ireland
NWCI	National Women's Council of Ireland
P4C	Parents for Choice
PLAC	Pro-Life Amendment Campaign
PPSN	Personal public service number (social security number)
RSE	Relationships and sex education
ROSA	Reproductive Rights against Oppression, Sexism and Austerity
SARRA	Sligo Action for Reproductive Rights Access
SAZs	Safe access zones
SIPTU	Services Industrial Professional and Technical Union
Sol-PBP	Solidarity-People Before Profit
SPUC	Society for the Protection of Unborn Children
START	Southern Taskgroup on Abortion & Reproductive Topics
TD	Teachta Dála (Member of the Irish Parliament)
TENI	Transgender Equality Network Ireland
TERF	Trans exclusionary radical feminism
TFMR	Termination for Medical Reasons
TfY	Together for Yes
TRAP laws	Targeted regulation of abortion providers laws
UNHRC	United Nations Human Rights Council
USI	Union of Students in Ireland
WRCG	Women's Right to Choose Group

Acknowledgements

There were so many people who authored this book. Thanks to Sinéad Kennedy, not just for her contributions, but for her tireless efforts for as long as I can remember. Thanks to Melisa Halpin, Helen Guinane and Sinéad Redmond, Paula Dennan, Laura Fitzgerald and Emma Quinn, Emma Campbell, Ailbhe Smyth, JoAnne Neary, Helen Stonehouse, Emma Hendrick, TFMR, START, Emily Wazak and Cristina Florescu, TENI, Limerick Feminist Network, SARRA, Fingal Feminist Network, Abortion Action Campaign West, and Emma Carroll and Ciara McGuane who created 'In Our Shoes'. There are many others too who answered the phone and replied to emails and allowed me to bounce ideas off them. Thanks to the artist Maser who made his iconic 'repeal' image available for others to use and which has been adapted for the cover of this book. And to Paula Geraghty who has been filming and sharing street activism for decades. To my editor Neda Tehrani, thank you. I learned an enormous amount from your astute observations, and suggestions for change. Thanks also to the team at Pluto Press for their work, and the copy-editor, Jeanne Brady.

Thanks to those who read early drafts: Sinéad, Jerry, Meliosa, Declan, Sarah, Brian, Anna and Conor, and to Bernie who was involved in the early stages. Oisin Kelly was often on hand for questions about the workings of the Dáil. Thank you to Ruth Coppinger, a tireless fighter and inspiring feminist and socialist.

Finally, to the thousands of ordinary activists who so heroically gave so much of themselves – we did it!

Foreword

Ruth Coppinger

'Without struggle, there is no progress'
Frederick Douglass

The referendum to repeal the Eighth Amendment will go down as a seminal event in Ireland's history. A major movement from below won a vital health and civil right, inflicting the most serious defeat on the Catholic Church in a country where it once held sway. For women and anyone who can become pregnant, the significance of winning this bodily autonomy in your country can't be overstated. Years of taboo, years of expense, years of secret, illegal journeys were over.

Such was the reduced power of the Church, it took no active part in the 2018 abortion referendum. This was incredible, given that the Church had been so central in 1983 in inserting the amendment in the first place and so central to the suppression of women's rights and reproductive freedom for a century.

The decisiveness of the referendum result points to a massive paradox, with the Church still in control of so much of the country's health and education systems, underlining that there is huge unfinished business for women's rights in Ireland.

Though a small country, repeal in Ireland also had international repercussions, being cited by Latin American activists as inspiration for pushing forward their abortion rights campaigns, particularly in Argentina.

The forces that brought about victory for abortion rights in Ireland must be given their rightful place in history. That is an important contribution of this book. Because as soon as the repeal mountain was climbed, there was a race to stick a flag on the summit and claim the victory. Politicians from government and opposition parties, who'd resisted calls for a referendum for years and who'd voted down repeal Bills, now quite literally jumped on the bandwagon/stage at Dublin Castle to take the plaudits.

These parties were either late converts and inactive in the actual canvass (Fine Gael), a majority No (Fianna Fáil), or, in the case of Sinn Fein, had taken a late repeal stance for abortion in very restrictive circumstances. These parties got plum media slots for the Yes side, yet had no record on abortion rights. The Labour Party, which did have a tradition of opposing the Eighth Amendment, had nonetheless held back a referendum, with Joan Burton as Tánaiste claiming the public had 'no appetite' for repeal and the party voting against repeal bills in 2015 and 2016.

These things matter, not just for a correct record, but also for making clear to anyone embarking on campaigns in the future how change actually comes about. Change has never come from the gift of establishment politicians, but from movements creating irresistible pressure from outside Parliament. Rights are won, not granted. As the black abolitionist Frederick Douglass said: 'Without struggle, there is no progress.'

Rather than a quiet revolution, a loud and persistent movement, led by young people, women and LGBT+ people, waged a five-year battle forcing the establishment to change course and then, particularly from 2015–16 on, pushing them to go much further than had ever been originally envisaged, winning abortion not just on the very restricted grounds that had been the normal discourse, but winning the right to abortion without having to give a reason up to 12 weeks.

Winning repeal wasn't about politicians going on journeys, something that became a well-worn cliché as establishment politicians explained their changed stance to voters. It involved protests, meetings, marches, the telling of personal stories, political art and so much more to bring politicians on those journeys. And as with any social change, from the right to vote to the right to form unions, it involved many people not just challenging the law, but sometimes breaking it.

As both a newly elected TD and an activist, I had the unusual position in 2014 of introducing a law into Parliament while also openly breaking one at the same time. I moved the first stage of a Bill to Repeal the Eighth Amendment in September and a month later was an organiser of the Abortion Pill Train that illegally imported abortion pills from Belfast.

An aim of this and the subsequent abortion pill buses (conducted by ROSA, the socialist feminist group in conjunction with Women on

Web, the international doctor-led agency who supplied them) was to promote safe medical abortion as an option for those who desperately needed it or couldn't travel. The other was tactical: by increasing use of the pills, it reinforced for politicians that any restrictive law post-repeal would be futile as it would be flouted. Availability of abortion pills was later cited as a 'gamechanger' for members of Parliament changing their positions and supporting the 12 weeks law. Funnily enough, none of them highlighted the necessary acts of civil disobedience that led to them being able to do this!

In this context, the role of Women on Web and other telemedicine agencies who bravely provided abortion pills in Ireland must be marked. They continue to take huge risks to save the lives and health of pregnant people anywhere in the world without access to safe legal abortion. Actions around abortion pills in order to change the law have subsequently become an important tactic, for example, in South Korea in August 2018, when 125 women swallowed the pills to signify the 125 women doing so illegally every hour in that country.

All those who faced criminality by providing information, phone numbers, funds for terminations, abortion pills and much else deserve huge credit.

If anything can be marked as a qualitative turning point in the struggle for repeal it is the tragic and horrific death of Savita in late 2012. Yes, many had criticised the Eighth Amendment and taken noble stances at various points in its 35-year existence. But it was not an active movement to actually repeal the amendment. Even after the death of Savita, tactical errors led to most of the leadership accepting a meagre legal change that fell very far short of repeal and wouldn't even have helped Savita. This set repeal back some years and belied a conservatism then existing that didn't grasp both the depth of change in attitudes taking place and the potential to go further.

The repeal sentiment that particularly burgeoned from 2016 in Ireland reflected an awakening of consciousness taking place worldwide among women and young people. A global feminist mass movement was developing around issues such as abortion rights, sexism and, most especially, against gender violence – from the Ni Una Menos (Not One Woman Less) movement against femicide and machismo in Latin America to the phenomenon of #MeToo. This was shown by the 'I Believe Her' protests that spontaneously sprang up in Ireland in March 2018 following the Belfast rugby rape trial at the same time as the repeal referendum campaign was about to start in earnest.

The roots of this growing feminist consciousness lie in a system that has raised the aspirations of women and girls, but then resoundingly shatters those hopes and can't meet those needs. That is why the new feminist movement is much more anti-capitalist. As a system, capitalism prioritises profit for a few and relies on inequality and division to survive – thus racism and sexism are part and parcel of it. Rigid gender roles and the nuclear family suit the system well: it would collapse without the unpaid carework women are conditioned to do and the disproportionate domestic burden they continue to shoulder, even when employed outside the home. The best the system can offer is summed up by the gender pay 'gap' which the World Economic Forum of billionaires tells us will now take 136 years to close at the current rate of progress – with decades added because of Covid.

In the pandemic, we see women are heroically battling on the frontlines and in essential jobs in health, education and retail. Yet the position of women is being set back by Covid, as they shoulder the responsibility of homeschooling, endure shocking increases in violence from abusive partners in lockdown and are three times more likely to lose their jobs.

The sacking of the Irish Debenhams department store workers is one example. The multinational retailer took the opportunity afforded by the pandemic to cut its losses, close subsidiaries and shops and shed its workforces, jettisoning redundancy agreements in the process. In response, the mainly female workforce protested, struck and occupied for over a year, usually acting without much support or approval of their union leadership. The resilience, self-organisation and determination these women workers have shown speaks to the radicalising of women that's taking place. It reminds us that women have always played a role in social change in Ireland, but have often been written out of the narrative.

The global gender revolt demands a zero tolerance of sexism in all forms, and the issues of sexual/gender violence or of bodily autonomy and abortion rights are often the most mobilising. This is because they go to the very core of oppression. That 83 per cent of women restrict their public movements due to potential violence and that 97 per cent of young women are sexually harassed came to be publicly discussed following the murder of Sarah Everard in London in 2021, which also led to widespread protests despite Covid restrictions and a brutal police response.

Capitalism promotes the objectification of women, the commodification of women's bodies, a macho culture of entitlement, and widespread victim blaming. Its whole philosophy is the strict classification of people in order of value. It legitimises coercion and violence by those who have power against those who have least. This applies to wealth and resources, but also within personal relations. Violence against women and gender non-conforming people will be a huge political issue as a new generation refuse to accept it as an inevitability. The same intolerance of oppression was seen when young people in particular made Black Lives Matter the biggest social movement in the US beginning in 2020, according to the *New York Times*.

Among the most inspiring days in the battle for repeal was International Women's Day in 2017. In the daytime, a 'strike for repeal' was called by a new ad hoc group of activists. Walkouts took place in colleges and by some workers and the main bridge in Dublin city was occupied, bringing traffic to a halt. That evening thousands took part in a march called by the repeal Coalition, with many school students clearly attending their first ever march. What strike for repeal showed was the way in which young activists were borrowing and lending tactics being used internationally, in this case, from Poland, and pointing to mass, collective struggle and strikes as the means of achieving change. The traditional tactics of the strike and of mass action are likely to be seen as absolutely necessary for the new global feminist movement to be successful.

It's ironic that a system that claims to be the ultimate expression of democracy has thrown up political figures at the helm in several large countries including the US, Russia, India and Brazil, who are arch-misogynists as well as being racist, homophobic, anti-environmentalist and anti-worker. These leaders have, at times enabled, encouraged and used the far right and elements of fascism. Right populism is becoming another frontier that all who want to fight misogyny will have to contend with.

Such developments are leading a new generation to conclude that the type of feminism needed is one that challenges all inequality and privilege. A young generation, in Ireland and globally, is seeing unaffordable housing, casualisation and environmental destruction as all that's on offer. The experience of repeal, as well as victorious campaigns against the water charges and for marriage equality (see Chapter 1), will be looked back on as examples of where change to the status quo was brought about by movements from below.

The newly independent Irish state of a hundred years ago was economically weak, unstable and poverty-ridden. The political parties that came to power leaned on the Church for authority and support, outsourcing education, health and control of women and the poor to Catholic religious orders. That legacy is far from dealt with. Abortion rights was an important battle. We should take the hugely positive lessons from repeal, as we go on now to fully separate Church and State.

…I've had to fly a few times in the last year. I always wear my repeal gear through the airport. People are still travelling as not enough GPs have signed up, the issue with the God Squad outside hospitals and GP surgeries. Women in Direct Provision, Traveller women, women experiencing domestic violence I fear are still not catered for and of course poverty and young girls. Lots done, lots more to do. Consent still an issue in hospitals.

Former Canvasser (2020)

Prologue

I'm not normally a fan of *The Late Late Show* but that night was an exception. I'd probably had a bit too much wine. That, coupled with the emotional rollercoaster of the previous few months all added to my nervousness as I sat on the sofa willing David McCullagh to read out the results of the exit poll clutched tightly in his hand. 'Breathe' I thought, 'it'll be too close to call.' But it wasn't. Four to one in favour of repeal in my hometown of Dublin. Outside the capital, up to 65 per cent had voted repeal. I began to feel a little lighter, a little freer and overwhelmingly proud to be Irish. I picked up the phone to call Anna, my daughter who although too young to vote, had been campaigning every evening. That night she'd chosen Demi Lovato at the 3 Arena over a night in with her Mum. She was on her way home, sandwiched between other tired concertgoers on a packed Luas. 'It's a landslide yes' she shouted, to the excitement of surrounding passengers.

I was 13 years old when the Eighth Amendment was inserted into the Constitution of Ireland. I proudly pinned a silver 'precious feet' lapel of two baby feet to my school uniform which showed my support for the amendment. I was against killing unborn babies, and why on earth would I have been anything else? I never connected a constitutional ban on abortion and its impact on the lives of women to my mother's situation at home raising nine children whilst enduring constant putdowns from a domineering husband. She'd stopped working on her wedding day because of the marriage bar. Her job was to be a wife and a mother. Nuala Fennell once described lives like these as 'a nightmare of unremitting pregnancy'.[1] Rosita Sweetman called it 'drowning in babies'.[2]

After I left school, I spent a year in a private secretarial college, then trained as a nurse which led to very different overseas adventures. First to Romania as the 'white saviour' rescuing Ceausescu's abandoned children, then to Saudi Arabia where I witnessed, and somewhat experienced, severe limitations on the rights of women. Despite specialising in HIV/AIDS care, I'd had enough of nursing by the mid-1990s and wound up running women's groups in an empty social housing unit in North Dublin. I co-facilitated with a local woman who could relate better to the lived experiences of other women in the group. I worked hard to be open about the advantages I had enjoyed in my life so that together we could unravel the gendered, class-based circumstances of our lives. Inevitably, many conversations focused on pregnancy, pregnancy loss and the challenges of parenting. We rarely talked about abortion. When writing this book, certain memories flooded back, such as an argument with a social worker who wanted contraceptive coils to be mandatory for all women on drug treatment programmes. Another woman I will call Julie was working towards visitation rights for her children, who were in state care. She was pregnant again and was distraught to be told, by a different social worker, that this child would also be taken into care. That was in 1999.

Outside of work I joined a left-wing revolutionary party in the late 1990s that openly supported abortion rights. I learned a huge amount from other women involved, such as Melisa Halpin, Marnie Holborow, Goretti Horgan, Brid Smith, Mary Ryder, Mary Smith and many others. I was much less active in the 2000s when my children were young, but I always made time to heckle anti-abortion crusaders camped outside Dublin's GPO with their giant-sized graphic photographs of foetuses. I remember, as if yesterday, hearing about the death of Savita Halappanavar.[3] Since 2013, I have built for and sometimes stewarded ARC's (Abortion Rights Campaign) annual March for Choice. In 2015, and by that stage an academic at Maynooth University, I designed consciousness-raising educational materials for ARC called 'Women's Reproduction and Rights'. I'm not in a political party now, but I canvassed for the socialist Ruth Coppinger in the 2016 and 2020 general elections and joined ROSA around then, a socialist feminist grassroots organisation you'll read more about in this book. Since the referendum I've been volunteering with ARC on their Policy and Advocacy Policy group, but most of my activism has been the fieldwork and secondary research that underpins this book. Hopefully, it's a useful resource.

I have always been an activist. We waited 35 years to get here so I feel it's my duty to do all that I can.

I have also been affected by the Eighth so it's also very personal.

Mayo-based canvasser (2018)

1

Introducing the Real Heroes

On 26 May 2018, in the historic surroundings of Dublin Castle, the then Taoiseach (Prime Minister) Leo Varadkar took to a hastily erected stage and faced a packed audience. The mood was electric. He proudly praised the nation for comprehensively voting by a two-thirds majority to remove Article 40.3.3 (or the Eighth Amendment) from the Irish Constitution. This amendment controversially equated the life of the foetus to the life of the woman, upholding an archaic anti-abortion regime by stating: 'The State acknowledges the right to life of the unborn and, with due regard to the equal right to life of the mother, guarantees in its laws to respect, and, as far as practicable, by its laws to defend and vindicate that right.'

To get around this, up to 15 women travelled overseas each day to terminate pregnancies, mostly to England. Others illegally bought pills online which they took without medical supervision. If they were caught, they faced up to 14 years in prison. Since January 2019, the need to travel for an abortion has mostly, although not completely, been eradicated. Abortions are now allowed in all circumstances in the first 12 weeks of pregnancy. After this, they are available in 'exceptional circumstances' such as if the life or health of a woman is at risk, or where it can be guaranteed that a baby would not survive more than 28 days.

As Varadkar basked in victory, he described the result as the culmination of 'a quiet revolution', continuing: 'We have voted to look reality in the eye, and we did not blink. We have voted to provide compassion where there was once a cold shoulder, and to offer medical care where once we turned a blind eye … Our democracy is vibrant and robust and can survive divisive debates and make difficult decisions.'[1]

Varadkar's Health Minister Simon Harris was also in Dublin Castle. He made sure to mingle with the crowd and obliged the many journalists who were keen to catch that winning soundbite. Poignantly, he referenced the many women forced to travel for abortions: '... today we are saying take our hand, we want to look after you in our own country ... a stigma has been lifted from Irish society ... we will now get on and we will legislate for women in our own country.' In the background, the crowds chanted 'Simon, Simon, Simon'. This was quite the sea-change. Just six years earlier, Harris had crossed swords with the Irish pro-repeal movement when he 'liked' a Facebook post by an anti-abortion activist. When he was challenged, he quickly clarified this was done by mistake, but he made sure to lodge his objection to any future change in the law.[2]

Varadkar thanked some of his colleagues by name. Senator Catherine Noone had chaired the Dáil (Irish Parliament) all-party Committee on the Eighth Amendment of the Constitution. Although she had done a competent job, this committee had watered down recommendations from a 2017 Citizen's Assembly which had voted in favour of abortion access on socio-economic grounds and where there is a foetal anomaly that isn't necessarily fatal. Varadkar acknowledged the aforementioned Simon Harris and his party's campaign coordinator, Josepha Madigan, who had been appointed just two months earlier. He then thanked both the Citizen's Assembly (who you'll read about in Chapter 4) and 'those involved in the civil society campaign who have been working on this issue for many, many years'.

But there was a hollowness to his words, and activists who fought long and hard for this day might be forgiven for raising an eyebrow at the prominent position these politicians were keenly occupying. What really happened is that in the months before the referendum, pro-repeal groups set aside repeated rejections by the political establishment and welcomed them into the fold. As recently as 2016, Fine Gael and most members of Fianna Fáil had voted down a Dáil bill that would have eased restrictions. That same year, Varadkar's government revised Dáil standards to prevent political slogans in Parliament after six Solidarity-People Before Profit TDs donned the black-and-white REPEAL jumpers designed by Anna Cosgrave that symbolised the movement. In October 2017, just seven months before the referendum, the Fianna Fáil Ard Fheis (annual conference) voted to oppose any attempts to 'diminish the constitutional rights of the unborn'. The motion was passed by a significant majority and welcomed with a round of applause.[3]

In reality, the true architect of change was a 35-year-long grass-roots movement that was mostly organised by women. The repeal movement involved different players at different times including the Women's Right to Choose Campaign and the Irish Women's Abortion Support group of the 1980s, as well as the Dublin Well Woman Centre, the Women's Information Network, the Pro-Choice Campaign and Action on X. There's been Migrant and Ethnic Minorities for Reproductive Justice (MERJ), Termination for Medical Reasons (TFMR), Doctors for Choice, Lawyers for Choice, Parents for Choice, The Artists Campaign to Repeal the Eighth Amendment, Reproductive Rights against Oppression, Sexism and Austerity (ROSA) and the Abortion Rights Campaign (ARC), many of which were still together in 2021. The human rights organisations Amnesty Ireland and the Irish Council for Civil Liberties (ICCL) were also active on the issue, and the Union of Students in Ireland and the National Women's Council of Ireland (NWCI). The Irish Family Planning Association (IFPA), which is a reproductive health provider that first opened its doors in 1969, have always campaigned for safe, legal abortion access. Because abortion was also prohibited in Northern Ireland, it too had grassroots activists, most notably the Alliance for Choice, formed in the 1990s by left-wing activists, civil society organisations and trade unionists. There were allies in Britain too, including the Abortion Support Network (est. 2009) which provided financial support and accommodation to many people who travelled. In 2013, these groups joined forces as the Coalition to Repeal the Eighth, convened by Ailbhe Smyth.

The repeal campaign was also driven by certain left-wing independent TDs, political parties and organisations including the Workers Solidarity Movement and more recently the alliance Solidarity-People Before Profit (Sol-PBP). In 2013, members of the Socialist Party established ROSA. This brought an anti-capitalist analysis to debates about abortion and started a conversation within socialist parties about their tactics in trying to win repeal. Members of People Before Profit and the Social Democrats were also amongst those involved in the set-up of local 'pro-choice' groups around the country, some of which remain active today. Some socialist TDs also made use of their role in the Dáil. In 2012, independent TD Clare Daly sought to legislate for fatal foetal abnormality. Two years later, in September 2014, Ruth Coppinger, a

Socialist Party member and high-profile activist since her student days introduced a private member's bill calling for a referendum to repeal the Eighth in tandem with the impending vote on marriage-equality. She challenged the then Tánaiste (Deputy Prime Minister) and leader of the Labour Party Joan Burton, who three months earlier stated there would be no referendum in the lifetime of the government in which she was a senior member. This was despite Labour claiming to be pro-choice since 2003. 'What an insult,' Coppinger stated. 'My generation of women, those of child-bearing age most affected by the Eighth Amendment, never got an opportunity to speak on it when it was originally passed. Their lives are dictated by a provision on which they had no say.' She then turned her attention to Varadkar who was health minister at the time and who had also ruled out a referendum. She challenged his recent assertion that the Catholic Church should not be brought into the issue and continued:

> It was the Catholic Church and a range of Catholic groups which lobbied and pressured for this amendment in 1983. No other religion … The past is a different country. The Catholic Church does not now enjoy the support it once did. However, the political establishment still seem determined to give it inordinate power and influence over health, education and other spheres of people's lives, particularly women.[4]

When the referendum was eventually called in January 2018, the tentacles of the grassroots repeal movement came together as 'Together for Yes'. From March through May 2018, this broad-based coalition became the face of a 35-year-long movement. Together for Yes united seasoned campaigners with those new to the struggle; and civil society organisations with once-reluctant politicians, as it sought to articulate a united voice. There were a number of high-profile U-turns, as politicians scrambled to catch up. Micheál Martin, the current Taoiseach and leader of Fianna Fáil declared his support for repeal in January 2018, which was a controversial move within his own party. Three weeks before the May vote, 31 Fianna Fáil Oireachtas (Parliament) members proudly posed together for a photo calling for 'No'. There were also divisions within Fine Gael – in fact, Varadkar was one of the last to decide he was pro-repeal. Others never shifted. Just a week before polling day, former Taoiseach John Bruton was the face of the #ToFarForMe hashtag, a last-minute attempt to steer the electorate away from what was an inevitable win for repeal.

Two days after the celebrations in Dublin Castle, three left-wing TDs – Brid Smith and Ruth Coppinger of Sol-PBP, and Clare Daly of Independents for Change – were amongst those to address the Dáil. These women not only acknowledged but understood the bottom-up nature of the movement. Each had played a significant role in what they knew was anything but a quiet revolution. Coppinger said she never doubted the electorate would deliver on repeal claiming 'the battle was not winning the referendum; the battle was getting a referendum granted from the Dáil over the past five years.' She took aim at her colleagues courting media attention and continued 'there is a danger we could see a re-writing of history to the effect that politicians going on a journey delivered this change. Actually, it derives from a grassroots movement that has built up, especially since the death of Savita.' In an equally impassioned speech, Daly also referenced years of struggle and again turned the mirror on the politicians around her, warning them against self-congratulating platitudes. 'This has been an uphill battle', she said:

> A boulder has been pushed up a hill for decades and no one here was behind it. Let us be honest about it for once. No one was involved. In fact, a lot of people here were sitting on that boulder, making it even more difficult for those outside who wanted to push for change. Others, of course, decided to jump ahead and claim some of the glory once the boulder was at the top of the hill and about to go down the other side, even though they had done none of the pushing.[5]

This book draws from testimonies of activists who did push that boulder, who came together in solidarity to form a collective roar that fought back against Ireland's repressive attitudes to reproductive rights. In the spring of 2018 and before any votes were cast, I gathered testimonies from 304 busy canvassers across each of Ireland's 26 counties.[6] Over 90 per cent were knocking on people's doors distributing leaflets, merchandise, voter registration forms and, where they could, striking up conversations with so-called 'undecideds'. The majority (60 per cent) also set up stalls outside shopping centres, train stations and other places where the public congregate. Teenagers (from 16 years old) who were too young to vote formed alliances with pensioners (65+) who had lived most of their lives under the shadow of the Eighth. Unsurprisingly, 81 per cent of canvassers were women. Most (59 per cent) had never canvassed before. This didn't stop high levels of activity – in fact, three-quarters of these 'repealers' were canvassing 2–3 times per week and one in five were out every day. Many wished they could have done even more, but their jobs, a lack of transport and care commitments got in the way. One-third (34 per cent) of these activists only got involved when Together for Yes was formed joining forces with more seasoned campaigners. 'I've been doing this for 35 years!' one remarked. From another, 'I've been active on the issue for 35 years' and again 'I've felt strongly about this issue since 1983. I was only 15 at the time and obviously couldn't vote and couldn't campaign either, as I grew up in a rural area.'

The reason these activists raised their heads above the parapet was, more than anything else, because they passionately believed that a person should be able to access abortion on their home soil without shame or stigma, whatever the circumstances. As one person lamented, 'this is one of the most important referendums of my time.' Some people pointed to the Eighth's role in maintaining inequality. As a case in point, this person got involved 'because I care deeply about this issue', continuing 'the Eighth Amendment is an absolute barrier to an equal and just society. It creates a big divide in Ireland as not everyone can afford or is allowed to travel. Removing the Eighth means creating a safer space for women in Ireland and contributing to an equal society.' At times, people felt a weight of history on their shoulders: 'I feel that the issue is incredibly important, and I would be so upset if I hadn't done everything I could to help get a yes in the referendum. Women have been treated horribly in this country – the Eighth is just one part of that – but it's a part we can do something about.' And another: 'I felt a sense of responsibility. I felt I owed it to a) those women who died, been harmed or been shamed by the Eighth and b) those women who have been fighting for reproductive rights since 1983 and before.' They are right to point out Ireland's long history of interfering with women's reproductive lives, which not only denied people the right *not* to have children, but also the right to *have* children. As is now well established, thousands of women and girls were incarcerated in a network of Church-run institutions where their babies were often taken from them.

One in ten activists had either travelled for an abortion or had bought pills online. Sometimes this was simply stated: 'personally affected', 'I had an abortion', or 'because I had an abortion and feel strongly that it should be available in Ireland.' Others shared troubling stories. One woman wrote, 'I feel very strongly about this issue. I went to the UK for an abortion in 2001. I had a terrible experience and when I came back to Ireland. I had to be admitted to a maternity hospital in Dublin for surgery.' A different person upsettingly shared, 'I had a son with a foetal fatal abnormality and could not afford to travel … I never want anyone to be forced into giving birth to death.' Others (5 per cent) had helped someone else procure an abortion; for example, 'I know people who have had to travel, I booked flights for one girl years ago who didn't have a credit card.'

Of the 19 per cent of canvassers who were men, their motives were much the same, including personal experience. This man shared:

At first, I really struggled with being a man and talking to women about such a sensitive issue, but the more I went out talking and canvassing the more comfortable I became. I have a personal experience of having to travel to the UK with my ex-girlfriend when we were both 17 (21 years ago) and to say it has stayed with me is an understatement.

Some men referenced wives, daughters and female friends. Others wanted to encourage other men to vote. But the issue of repeal appeared less emotive – in fact, 13 per cent did not give a clear reason for getting involved, compared to only 3 per cent of women.

This book also draws from testimonies I gathered in January 2020. This time, 405 former canvassers shared their memories of the campaign, their thoughts on abortion services today, and their levels of activism two years on.[7] As before, many people described being part of the repeal movement as life-changing. When this activist wrote 'I don't think I realised how special it was', she captured how many people looked back on the frenzied pre-referendum period. She continued: 'The mood was electric, it was only towards the referendum date that I truly recognised it as a history-making exercise … The movement was so inclusive and by the end I knew I would have been welcomed, even if I didn't have all the answers all the time.'

For many, this had been a long haul. One woman remembered, 'It was very exciting to be involved in a campaign that I have dreamed of most of my life; at 59 years old it was one of the most exciting things I ever took part in.' Another reminisced:

> The immediate camaraderie was fantastic … When canvassing etc. we were in it together. I am fast friends for life with many women I canvassed with in Dún Laoghaire. We shared the extreme highs and lows. Took the abusive bastards calling us murderers, the strangers hugging us in gratitude … I'm crying just remembering it all. Many of us became political together and still work together on that basis.

This woman was one of 16 per cent of people who disliked canvassing and found starting conversations with strangers about how they would vote was the most difficult aspect of being part of Together for Yes. Who can blame them? Standing at a neighbour's doorstep and wondering what sort of reception you would get was an unenviable task. Canvassers did not know if they were interrupting important family time or, worst of all, would be greeted with hostility and even banished from the door. This was a justifiable concern. When I asked about the biggest challenge, 32 per cent spontaneously named antagonistic encounters with people who were against repealing the Eighth Amendment. Many shared stories of unpleasant, often frightening altercations. One woman wrote, 'The negativity you get from extreme no voters, being cursed at and called a murderer on a public street does take its toll after a while.' Another young canvasser in Dublin described her main challenge: 'When I get home after a morning of being called a "baby killer" I find it very hard to switch off and stop thinking about it.' Although these stories were reported across genders, younger women were more likely to be targeted, something I witnessed first-hand when canvassing with my own teenage daughter.[8] This man, canvassing in Kildare, also talked about seeing younger voters being picked on: 'Seeing the emotional impacts of some of the bad responses on some of my fellow canvassers has been difficult to witness … such instances have tended to be younger women (18–25) being on the receiving end of aggressive responses from men in the 40+ bracket.'

A CHANGED IRELAND

Mostly however, canvassers were thanked for the work they were doing. Much groundwork had been done for these doorstep interactions in the years beforehand. By 2018, Ireland was in many ways, unrecognisable from its quite recent past. Once one of Europe's most conservative and religious countries, churchgoing had steeply declined, meaning most people would not have known about the Catholic Church's letter which called for a 'No' vote and was read to parishioners in early May 2018. There had also already been progressive change through the ballot box when in 2015, Ireland was the first country in the world to introduce same-sex marriage by popular vote. Again, this did not happen because of an enlightened government, but because of the efforts of gay-rights activists and their supporters. The marriage-equality movement had also faced decades of opposition from those who argued that the sanctity of marriage was for mixed-gender couples only. United under the umbrella of 'Yes Equality' it too grew from the grassroots and from those most affected by prohibition. LGTBQI+ couples and their supporters leaned on personal stories to ensure their issue would not be overshadowed. Together for Yes's strategy copied much of what had worked for Yes Equality; the umbrella operation that, three years earlier, had led the referendum campaign for same-sex marriage. They too united disparate civil society and campaign groups and effectively showcased a small, tiered leadership model.[9] These were just some of the many tactics replicated when 'pulling apart the book written on the marriage equality campaign … to examine their modus operandi', to quote Deirdre Duffy, the Together for Yes campaign manager.[10] Being part of Yes Equality was the motivation for some people canvassing for repeal. This young activist explained:

> After the Yes Equality referendum, our canvassing group met up in the home of our canvass leader, for a dinner-and-celebration-and-goodbye. With tears in my eyes, I thanked the organisers for making the campaign so easy to join; for opening the doors and allowing us inside, to be part of this experience. There was a huge generosity

there, and trust. I was – and I am – grateful. As we finished our speeches, one of the organisers said: 'Next, we tackle the Eighth Amendment'. I took that to heart.

People also took to the streets seeking change. At the same time as activists were canvassing, thousands protested in Dublin, Belfast, Cork, Galway and Limerick in response to the not-guilty verdicts of the rugby players Paddy Jackson and Stuart Olding, and their friends Blane McIlroy and Rory Harrison at the now infamous Belfast rape trial. Under the banner of #IBelieveHer, protesters raged against a judicial system that allowed the complainant to be cross-examined for eight days and have her blood-stained thong entered as evidence. They also objected to the misogynistic attitudes of these high-profile sportsmen; their mistrust and hatred of women was revealed to the world through WhatsApp messages they shared with each other. To quote this activist speaking in 2020, 'I have no idea how to rid the country of misogyny but it runs incredibly deeply.' In November 2018, there were also #ThisisNotConsent marches in Cork, Galway; Limerick and Dublin, again in response to a thong being produced as evidence in a rape trial involving a 17-year-old girl in which the alleged perpetrator was acquitted. These protests made international news. That same month, Dublin-based Google workers joined thousands worldwide in a coordinated walkout against sexual harassment in the workplace, an action which not only won concessions from management but also began a process of unionisation that linked their demands to decent pay and wider safety and dignity in the workplace.[11] Irish people had been protesting on other matters too. In 2011, we had our own Occupy Movement and, in 2014, a highly successful anti-austerity right2water campaign of mass mobilisations and collective non-payment forced the government to abandon plans to introduce domestic water charges. These campaigns were not detached from each other; rather, the same people were often involved. Steph Hanlon, one of the founders of Carlow for Choice explains, 'We were long-time activists who campaigned during the water charges movement, the marriage referendum, are now active in Extinction Rebellion ... we originated in 2017 due to the struggle for abortion; however, during that time we've lobbied for other issues i.e., housing, childcare, trans rights, etc.'

As is common in social movements, those canvassing for repeal reported a strong sense of community and cathartic release. In fact, the camaraderie people experienced in 2018 was the most frequently cited positive (57 per cent) aspect of being involved. There were multiple references to a 'community spirit' and many statements like 'I feel like I've found my tribe':

> The political climate in Ireland can often make you feel helpless. Canvassing lessens this feeling. I'm relatively new to the area I'm canvassing in, and it has connected me with people in the community of a like mind. I feel more part of the community as a result. Finding out my immediate neighbourhood is overwhelmingly yes made me feel more at home there.

Nearly everyone (95 per cent) thought joining forces as Together for Yes was the right decision. Comments like 'I think it is important to have a solid message coming from one organisation that represents diverse smaller organisations' recurred many times.

These people were not leaders, and they are not household names but unless their story is told, others will claim they orchestrated constitutional change. The following activist describes her memory of Dublin Castle which is very different to how Varadkar must have been feeling:

> I felt so demoralised, on the day … I was pissed-off from the minute I got to the count centre and Fine Gael walked up to me and they were like 'what's the numbers?', and I was like 'What do you mean what's the numbers? Who were you? They weren't on a canvass … Then when you just seen politician, after politician, come into Dublin Castle. And I was like, where is Ruth [Coppinger], and Brid [Smith] and Gino [Kelly] and Richard [Boyd Barrett]. They were the ones out knocking on doors every single night.

Another activist said, 'I was concerned that Fine Gael would reap the rewards of repeal in spite of dragging their feet on the issue for so long.' She was not wrong. When celebrating their 87th anniversary in 2020, Fine Gael angered many activists by listing 'repealed the Eighth Amendment giving women the right to choose' as one of their key achievements. It also ruffled some feathers when Deirdre Duffy announced her candidacy for Fine Gael in the 2020 election and implied they were responsible for repeal.[12] This book refutes this and reclaims a tremendous victory for the repeal movement, locating the locus for change in the decades-long struggles that came before it.

However, amidst an outpouring of positivity, many canvassers reported some drawbacks with the campaign. There was a strong sense that, in its final months, Together for Yes adopted a Dublin-centric outlook. This wasn't the only concern. A lot of people were unhappy with the campaign's medicalised tone that over-relied on stories of tragedy that focused on the 'hard cases'. Some believed that this fuelled a problematic narrative about 'good abortions' and 'not-so-good abortions' and gave centre stage to certain doctors despite feminist concerns about patriarchal and paternalistic attitudes within obstet-rics. Some wondered about a presumption that there was a sizable, silent middle-ground of conservative voters to win over. This didn't always match the overwhelming positive feedback many reported. For example:

> I only canvassed in my town; I was 70 then. I got a shock when first out, as I knew straight away, we were going to win by a landslide, which I conveyed to the team. I had been a team leader in Marriage Equality Referendum and knew this would be a higher Yes vote from canvassing both … In my case I had to bring my wife's sister to the UK. Her husband threatened to kick the fucker out of her. She had three miscarriages, so he was good at it, so it was personal for me.

Some were unhappy about a tight hierarchical structure within Together for Yes, that they believed had shut the door on some loyal campaign-ers in order to forge new alliances with liberal feminist organisations and political parties that did not represent, or indeed understand, the grassroots nature of the movement. A number of concerns were raised about an obliteration of working-class and migrant voices, and there was disquiet about a negative narrative about abortion pills that fuelled myths some groups had worked hard to debunk.

It seems fair to wonder so what? Who cares if there were internal disagreements within what was ultimately a successful operation that achieved its ultimate aim? As della Porta and Rucht put it, why should we care about 'the chats, discussions and conflicts that presumably occur in similar ways as in any social group'?[13] Surely all that matters is a campaign's public appearance and its ultimate impact on society? But della Porta and Rucht believe that we *should* care; that it helps to look backwards, even when on the side of victory, so that we can critically evaluate our performance and better equip ourselves for future struggles. We always knew there would be more work to be done. When I talked to her in 2021, Ailbhe Smyth, the convener of the Coalition to Repeal the Eighth and co-director of Together for Yes said, 'I mean, the day after the referendum was the day that we started to have to do the hard work of making sure that women could actually access abortion in this country.'

Certainly, things are much better. The Eighth is gone and abortions are now legally available, mostly as early medical abortions (EMAs), where drugs are prescribed to induce miscarriage. However, the overwhelming feeling two years after repeal is captured by this activist's remark: 'Look it's miles better than what we had but we still need to do so much more.' Despite the best efforts of activists both before and after the referendum, there are many problems with Ireland's law. Abortion is still criminalised despite repeated objections from legal and medical experts. This means a friend or family member who helps someone buy pills faces up to 14 years in prison. The same criminal sanction applies to doctors who prescribe pills one day after an arbitrary, but strictly enforced 12-week period, that is often impossible to accurately calculate. Or doctors who misjudge the point at which a woman is ill enough to legally qualify for care after 12 weeks, or who perform an abortion without being able to certifiably guarantee a baby would not live beyond 28 days. This creates a significant chilling effect for doctors that interferes with their clinical judgement when they are making complex medical decisions. Ireland's law has a mandatory 3-day wait period that disproportionately affects poor people, migrants, those living with violence, or with heavy care-loads, who can't take time off work, as well as people with disabilities and those with irregular periods, which can sometimes be a symptom of addiction or other health concerns. This terrible law is made even worse by the fact that it has not translated into services. Just 10 per cent of GPs have signed up to the government's scheme, and only 10 out of 19 hospital-based maternity services are offering full abortion services.[14]

One activist bemoaned 'Living beyond the pale, we are still very much forgotten and have little or no access to abortion.'

Many activists blame persistent vigil-type demonstrations outside providers' entrances. This practice, imported from the US and on the rise in the UK,[15] began as soon as legislation was passed. As people enter maternity services for all manner of reasons, hard-line anti-abortionists often crowd the streets outside, praying loudly and brandishing rosary beads, crucifixes and even mini-coffins. Activists who participated in this book were angry with the government for breaking their promise to create exclusion zones that would make these demonstrations illegal. Instead, our laws support conscientious objection in public services which not only preferences a falsely personified foetus, but it also then honours the values of the conscientious objector over the rights of the pregnant person. There are ongoing problems in Northern Ireland too. Although abortion was decriminalised in 2019 and guidelines were approved in 2020, services had still not been properly commissioned by late 2021.

There are consequences to these limits. In 2019, the first year that abortion was available, 6,666 pregnancies were legally terminated, most (6,542) before the 12-week cut-off. However, in that same year, the UK statistics on abortion for England and Wales reported an average of one person each day still giving an Irish address. A similar picture emerged in 2020 when, although 6,577 legal abortions were carried out in Ireland, 194 people gave an Irish address in clinics across England and Wales.[16] The Abortion Support Network (ASN) still supports around five people each week and continues to fundraise across Ireland and the UK for accommodation and travel costs. The ASN have helped international students and refugees who were falsely told they did not qualify, people with a catastrophic but not fatal foetal anomaly, people who were simply too busy with childcare and eldercare to make appointments far from home, and people who were given false information by so-called 'rogue' agencies or anti-choice GPs.[17] This message, published by the ASN, is reflective of a fairly typical scenario:

Hi, I need to travel to London next week for an abortion, but I have problem with money. I took abortion pills in Ireland which didn't work and then I was 13 weeks. So, my GP said I have to go to England. The costs will be way more than I can afford so I was hoping you can help me. My passport expired so I have been waiting for the new one and I am now 16 weeks. Please help me.[18]

Activists were also unhappy about the transphobic language in Ireland's legislation, where anyone other than a cis woman falls outside of the law's frame. The absence of gender-neutral language that would have catered for non-binary people and that would include the needs of trans men wasn't an oversight, rather government ministers rejected calls from across the Dáil to be trans inclusive. This omission compounds a long history of mistreating trans and non-binary people, who face an additional risk of transphobic and homophobic reactions from a medical establishment that can be cruel and judgemental, sending a strong message about acceptance, belonging and value. Bringing these factors together, one Cork-based activist captured how many feel two years on, when she wrote:

I'm angry that so many promises were left unfulfilled. I think the government thought they could just give us the bare bones and delay the rest (Safe Access Zone legislation, free contraception, better RSE [relationship and sex] education in schools) until people forgot about it. It's hard watching time pass and excuse after excuse. Regarding the legislation we have, we need to remove the 3-day wait, ensure adequate rural provision, provide better access for migrant, undocumented and refugee service users and make the language trans-inclusive. We're going to have to work hard to keep these issues alive for the [2021] review.

Two-thirds of canvassers were still active two years on and most of their focus was on improving Irish law. The same cannot be said for those in political circles. Despite many people being still denied local services the Minister for Health Stephen Donnelly claimed in March 2021 that 'termination of pregnancy services have bedded in relatively smoothly to date and are becoming a normal part of the Irish healthcare system, in line with Government policy.'[19] As Helen Stonehouse and JoAnne Neary, the current co-conveners of ARC put it in 2021: 'There is a distinct perception among some members of the media and the wider public – as well as the politicians – that the work is done. We're working on changing that.'

THOSE CANVASSING TO RETAIN, NOT REPEAL

Of course, not everyone was happy with the referendum result – one-third voted to keep the Eighth Amendment, a pattern that mirrors public opinion in the UK.[20] Their views were not only supported by some Oireachtas members but were encouraged by the counter-canvassing groups 'Love Both', which is part of the Pro-Life Campaign, and 'Save the 8th', which is tied to the Life Institute and have strong links to Youth Defence. There were others too like the Irish Centre for Bio-Ethical Reform (ICBR) which caught the public's attention when, just before the referendum, they displayed giant-sized graphic images outside one Dublin maternity hospital. This act was thwarted by a group called 'Radical Queers Resist', whose counter-demonstration covered the images with rainbow flags. Then, of course, there is the Catholic Church, the lead player in the international anti-abortion movement.

Although prefaced on the notion of protecting life and supporting women, it is important to confront the arguments of the anti-abortion movement head on – a movement that is at times obsessed with women's morality, sexuality and autonomy more broadly. This begins by debunking their simplest of arguments: that the right to life of 'the unborn' should supersede the right to body autonomy for the pregnant person. This narrative – that a fertilised embryo has the same rights as a person – is upheld through carefully crafted scientific opinion that seeks to pinpoint when life begins. Anti-abortionists argue that life begins at conception and back this up with claims about foetal pain and in-utero images of 'babies' apparently smiling, clapping, or sucking their thumbs. Ending a pregnancy, they argue, robs this foetus of a future. But just because something has the potential to develop into something else, does not mean we must treat it as equal to what it may become. A foetus only exists because of the life of the body that carries it. By keeping debates in the territory of 'the fertilised embryo', the self-titled 'pro-life movement' deliberately divert attention away from the situational circumstances of a person's life and the reality of an unwanted pregnancy. They also widely exaggerate post-abortion remorse and ignore the fact that the most common feeling after abortion is relief.[21] This does not mean that people take the decision lightly or that pro-choice advocates are callous about a choice that is often the least worst option from a number of negative outcomes.

There are other contradictions too. While the anti-abortion movement spew rhetoric about the sacredness of the unborn, they often stay silent on other reproductive violations, such as adoptions without consent, forced sterilisations, or when welfare laws police and punish childbearing and rearing. They rarely champion adequate services for people with disabilities and their families. Instead, they seize the disability narrative, regurgitating figures on foetuses with disabilities who have been aborted, with a particular emphasis on Down's syndrome. They then cynically recruit people with disabilities to champion their cause, but do little to address the many barriers people with disabilities face in exercising their own reproductive freedoms. In the case of catastrophic disability, they never talk about the quality of life for the child, or the wider infrastructural conditions for the family left to care for them. Many of those who are against abortion also oppose anything but a subservient role for women, whose principal purpose is to procreate within a heterosexual, monogamous family unit. As a case in point, the Iona Institute, a Christian organisation and a key player in the Irish anti-abortion movement, is against divorce, same-sex marriage and parenting, non-faith-based relationships and sexuality education and public funding for contraception.

BEYOND PRO-CHOICE/PRO-LIFE BINARIES

One of the successes of the anti-abortion movement has been its capacity to contain discussions in the legal domain, meaning many activists fight tirelessly to maintain already inadequate laws. Ideally, there would be no laws. Abortion, as well as all reproductive health-care services, would be available as needed and without the weight of moral arguments. Not everyone realises that there is evidence of abortions in historical texts of Catholicism, Judaism and some versions of Islamic doctrine.[22] For many years, ending a pregnancy before 'the quickening' (i.e., the first time foetal movement is felt) did not pose a particular ethical concern. In Ireland, Pauline Jackson's work has shown that abortion, and historically infanticide, have long been a central experience in the lives of women.[23]

To understand how reproductive rights became so embroiled in medical and legal discourse, it helps to briefly examine a history of abortion or, more accurately, a history of its regulation. One of the earliest Western example of its criminalisation was in parts of the US in the 1820s. Elizabeth Kissling explains how criminalisation was implemented in order 'to protect women from being poisoned by dangerous abortifacient drugs sold by unscrupulous vendors', and not to protect the foetus.[24] It was only in the late 1800s and early 1900s that people, mostly male doctors, began to object for other reasons. Beverly Thompson believes this was part of their own professionalisation, as they sought to discredit and ultimately criminalise female midwives and healers.[25]

Abortion became illegal in Ireland in 1861 as part of the United Kingdom and Great Britain's Offences Against the Person Act. But while abortion might not have been talked about much in the late 1800s and early 1900s, it was happening. Some doctors were quietly terminating pregnancies when this would save a woman's life.[26] We also had our own network of back-street abortionists and many hundreds, if not thousands, of women tried to induce a miscarriage in their homes. According to research by Cara Delay, they didn't resort to wire hangers or crochet needles as is commonly percieved; rather, they tried physical harm methods, engaging in extreme manual labour or ingesting purgatives or pills, so they would be less likely to end up in hospital which could alert the Gardai (police).[27] It would be the 1960s and 1970s before legal tides would move in the opposite direction. The UK Abortion Act of 1967 was one of the first laws passed, although this did not extend to Northern Ireland. And so began a steady stream of women travelling in their thousands each year. Sheldon and Wellings describe this act as 'a product of the moral climate and clinical realities of the 1960s, when widespread backstreet abortions resulted in significant maternal mortality and morbidity'.[28]

Although it took some activists by surprise when Together for Yes adoped a liberal, medicalised approach as their campaign message, historically speaking this wasn't unusual. Doctors were central to the legalisation of abortion in the UK. It made sense to consult them. Abortion was a much riskier surgical procedure in the 1960s than it is today, and a person needed to recuperate afterwards. However, at the same time as the Abortion Act was being debated, doctors were quite seperately emerging as an elite profession. The influential social critic Ivan Illich believes their capacities were over-hyped as part of the industrialisation of health care; a process where its prime interest would become profitability.[29] According to Sally Macintyre, public statements by British doctors, both for and against abortion 'were not based on "clinical medical grounds" but on political, moral and quasi-sociological grounds concerning which, it can be argued, the medical profession has no more competence to be heard than other members of the community'.[30]

There were feminist voices too, most prominently the Abortion Law Reform Association (ALRA), which was backed by the National Council of Women, the Women's Cooperative Guild and the Family Planning Association. These second-wave feminists asked important questions about patriarchy and exposed the dire circumstances of women living on low incomes who were caring for multiple children in poor housing and often with violent husbands. But most ALRA members were of 'the professional, middle classes', as were the women they represented.[31] They were less impacted by socio-economic factors that may lead a person to end their pregnancy. Their conditions also meant they trusted in institutions that not only mirrored but maintained their social status and were less reticent about giving control to doctors. It would be 1970 before an autonomous British left-wing, consciousness-raising movement convened at a Women's Liberation Conference at Ruskin College in Oxford. Dorothy McBride Stetson describes how this more radical group criticised the central role the medical profession had been given, and demanded free abortion and contraception.[32] But the die had been cast in the Abortion Act 1967, a legal framework that cemented the belief that abortion must be sanctioned by doctors and would be a criminal offence when performed outside of legally defined circumstances. History would repeat itself in the US, when state-wide laws were introduced in response to the US Supreme Court 1973 ruling in *Roe v. Wade*. There were already laws in some states and opposition had been building in what Kissling describes as a professional network of doctors from which 'Pro-life' campaigns could be organised. Although these groups shrouded themselves in medical arguments on when life begins, she argues 'From the vantage point of the twenty-first century, racist and anti-feminist messages are easy to read in some early anti-abortion campaigns.'[33] These fledgling anti-abortionists were heavily supported by the Catholic Church, despite Alesha Doan pointing out how leaders from Jewish and Protestant orthodoxies supported actions to direct women to safe, legal services.[34] In the end, it was determined the decision could only be trusted alongside expert medical guidance, something the anti-abortion movement lobbied hard for.[35]

Once again, feminist voices such as the Society for Humane Abortion (est. 1961) worked tirelessly to educate the public on abortion rights and which would evolve into NARAL pro-choice America. There were radical voices too such as the Committee for Abortion Rights and Against Sterilisation Abuse (or CARASA, est. 1974), a multi-ethnic, mostly Latino coalition that challenged feminists who defended abortion as a single-issue campaign. Elena Gutiérrez explains how CARASA argued low-income and working-class women could not secure reproductive rights, demanding decent pay, welfare rights and subsidised childcare as a prerequisite to reproductive freedom.[36]

FROM RIGHTS TO JUSTICE

What CARASA were modelling was an approach that turns an individualistic perspective on its head and argues against a pro-choice/pro-life dichotomy where those *against* argue the rights of 'the unborn' should supersede that of physical autonomy, and those *for* seek to protect a person's bodily autonomy. This individualist pro-choice perspective can, at a glance, seem unproblematic. Our bodies are our own and the right to exercise personal sovereignty trumps the rights of a falsely personified 'unborn'. The Eighth Amendment violated this right, and the law needed to be changed. As one canvasser put it 'Reproductive rights and bodily autonomy are fundamental principles ... and I want to fight for them in every way that I can.' But there are problems with this singular approach that not only ascribes substantial authority to the medical and legal professions, but it also ignores the challenges millions of people face in securing their human rights and well-being.

A reproductive justice perspective merges 'reproductive rights' with 'social justice', and moves the pendulum far beyond the right to safe legal abortion. Laws are fundamentally important, but they don't address the factors that can make a person vulnerable to pressures that influence reproductive decisions, such as financial poverty, access to contraception, multiple care responsibilities, the violence and coercion they endure, or their precarious migration, work, or housing status. A Reproductive Justice Framework was first formulated in the US by a group of black women who came together in 1994, calling themselves 'Women of African Descent for Reproductive Justice'. They were tired of liberal feminism's failure to take note of the situations working-class women of colour were regularly facing, and sought a much broader interpretation of reproductive health care and well-being. Some of the women involved went on to establish SisterSong, a feminist collective that is still synonymous with reproductive justice.

In her manifesto for activism, SisterSong co-founder Loretta Ross outlines three core principles at the heart of a reproductive justice approach: the right not to have children through birth control, abortion or abstinence; the right to have children under the conditions we choose, and the right to parent in safe, healthy environments, all alongside sexual autonomy and gender freedom.[37] A Reproductive Justice Framework typically draws a distinction between *reproductive health* services including sex education; *reproductive rights* which relates to laws that prevent or support access to reproductive health, and *reproductive justice* – which refers to a much broader movement that illustrates fundamental and consolidative structures such as social class, migrant background, dis/ability, ethnicity, and/or sexual orientation.[38] These intersecting features overlap and combine to create very different experiences for people. Loretta Ross, Lynn Roberts, Erika Derkas, Whitney Peoples and Pamela Bridgewater Toure are clear about the fact that this justice-based framework accounts for other social oppressions as well as race. They equally alert us to 'the misappropriation and co-optation of RJ by those who ignore the realities of abuses of power and institutionalized inequality that circumscribe the reproductive experiences of vulnerable people'.[39]

These are the ideas that underpin this book that, across eight chapters, reclaims a tremendous victory for Ireland's grassroots reproductive rights movement. The canvassers you will meet were not the centre of attention in Dublin Castle, but they take the stage here as I draw lessons from the highs and lows of the campaign and frustrations with the political establishment's failure to honour the spirit of the 2018 result. I also draw from interviews with key pro-repeal activists and other stakeholders. Their voices are blended with secondary research, my own experience as a pro-repeal activist and my analyses as a critical feminist researcher. To begin, I will address the extent to which reproductive rights continue to be violated in Ireland, not just in access to abortion, but along the much wider continuum a reproductive justice model entails.

A great many middle-class/wealthy white Irish women are happy to leave poorer, non-white or Traveller women behind and align with right-wing parties. There is a great deal of exploitative female landlords, business owners, senior executives. This shows the limits of liberal feminism.

Activist (2020)

2

Reproductive Oppressions in Ireland

The first time Amara's heart sank was when she was being shown around the Dublin Hospital where she would give birth to her first child later that day. A midwife had met her and husband Eyob (both pseudonyms) in the lobby. As she accompanied them to the ward, she pointed out some important markers along the way. Amara was 25, professionally qualified and from North Africa. She is dark skinned and was wearing what she describes as 'a small Hijab'. She and Eyob had moved to Ireland just two years earlier in 2017. There was another couple with them too. As all five trekked through the hospital, Amara could not help but notice that the midwife hardly acknowledged her. 'She only talked to the Irish couple,' she explained, 'and walked with them. She ignored us completely. I don't know if she meant to be racist or if it is just a coincidence, but it made me feel uncomfortable.' The 'coincidences' would continue – in fact, within an hour she had her second unpleasant encounter, this time with the admitting doctor. Amara was worried about a hereditary condition that had made her cousin sick. She had questions about the risks to her baby. She was also worried that her English 'wasn't that good' and was afraid that important information might get lost. She did not want to use the hospital's interpreter. This was basically an anonymous, often male, voice on the end of a phone, therefore a process that would not capture the nuances of what she wanted to say. Her fears were realised in the most painful of ways. 'The doctor didn't take it seriously,' Amara shared, 'she was so rude and sharp with me … so it was a very negative experience. She treated me like I am an ignorant woman coming from a Third World country.' Things didn't improve much throughout her stay and, overall, Amara didn't understand a lot of what she was being told. In the end, she had a forceps delivery and was discharged a couple of days later. When I asked her about how we might make things better she answered:

Muslim women are just women of a different background ... And we are not ignorant, we are the same as any other woman in the world who wants a great new Mom experience, and we would like to be treated with respect. Sometimes we can feel the 'I am talking to an ignorant person' look inside the physician's eyes.

This story comes from extensive research I collaborated on about the experiences of Muslim women in Irish maternity settings.[1] Amara's story was not uncommon – it was typical of many Muslim women's time in hospital. People reported persistent negative attitudes, mistrust, misconceptions about religious markers and erroneous assumptions about birthing preferences and pain tolerance. Some healthcare workers (who were mostly white) also participated in this research, although it was more difficult to recruit them. They often agreed that racism is a problem and could pinpoint discriminatory practices in some colleagues. But they were less able to turn the mirror on themselves and look at how their own actions helped to create an institutional environment that perpetuates racial injustice.

Improving maternity care for women like Amara is just one of the many ambitions of a reproductive justice approach that emerged in the US some 27 years ago. The model created by the Women of African Descent for Reproductive Justice, and that they continue to develop, offers a framework for assessing whether a person's reproductive rights are being met and for acting when they are not. Everyone has the right to be healthy enough to become pregnant and to have full control over when, and with whom, this happens. But this can only be guaranteed if someone has a decent standard of living with access to food and medicines and where they do not live with sexual coercion and assault. People should also receive appropriate relationships and sexuality education that emphasises consent and removes stigma from sexual expression. The right to contraception is also vital. If pregnant, there should be free, non-judgemental pre-natal care or access to abortion without shame or stigma. There should be options about where and how a person gives birth, including at home, and with a support person of their choice. People also have the right to give birth without medical coercion and obstetric violence and to adopt their own style of parenting. Children should be able to live in a safe environment. This includes having a roof over their head, access to public services, freedom from pollutants and a life free from violence and harassment including by the State. Importantly, reproductive justice also protects the right *not* to have children in the first place, challenging the patriarchal belief that this is the social obligation of women. When someone decides not to have a child, they shouldn't be looked at with either suspicion or misplaced sympathy; rather, this right should be respected, and their reasons should not be undermined.

REPRODUCTIVE RIGHTS AND THE CAPITALIST PATRIARCHY

Rather than treating reproductive choices in isolation, a reproductive justice approach brings politics into the room. Nancy Fraser suggests that when second-wave feminist demands for broad reproductive freedoms (amongst other freedoms) took root, this coincided with a much more influential policy shift away from Keynesian welfare protections for citizens towards free-market neoliberal principles that revolved around protecting the interests of the market. Rather than wealth 'trickling down', growing gaps in income inequality are now well documented.[2] Harsh austerity and bank bailouts have deepened the chasm between the haves and the have-nots, meaning many people must work harder just to stand still, never mind improve their living standards. Ireland is a good example of neoliberalism at its purest. Repeatedly, both Fianna Fáil and Fine Gael, with their minor coalition partners, have advanced clear neoliberal policies that have created what Kieran Allen describes as 'a free enterprise paradise' that offers light touch regulation and tax breaks for the rich, and that always favours the interests of big corporations over its citizens.[3] Allen also describes Ireland as the poster-boy of EU austerity, where neoliberal politicians have convinced their privileged global peers that people can suffer the pain of severe cuts so we can keep attracting overseas investors. As trade unionism falters under the weight of co-option and falling membership, Ireland has become a breeding ground for low-paid precarious employment and weak labour protections that mostly impact women and children.[4] As this economic model has become ever more entrenched over several decades, this also deepens the exploitations that are integral to its survival. Neoliberalism was not invented from a green-field scenario but rather from a capitalist model that was built on racism and sexism.

Reproductive injustices are deeply embedded in capitalism's racist history – in fact, one of the first actions of the US Reproductive Justice Movement was to call out the depth of white supremacy within the capitalist mindset. In the US alone, disease was deliberately spread within Native American populations, enslaved women were brutally raped and forced into marriage to increase the slave population, and a state-sanctioned eugenic programme forcibly sterilized an estimated 60,000 women of colour.[5] Ireland has a different historical context to the US and many other European countries, including the UK. Most (although by no means all) inward movement that has diversified Ireland has been more recent and a result of global labour market trends, as increasing numbers of people moved to Ireland from European, African, Asian and Middle Eastern countries. The result has been a rapidly growing indigenous non-white population. But we have always had an indigenous Mincéir population who have endured shameful levels of anti-Traveller discrimination that denies their equal rights to health, education, housing, employment and identity.

Many Irish women have also endured significant oppression as a result of capitalism's reliance on gender inequality for its survival. We are led to believe that caregiving and cleaning up after everyone else comes naturally to women; a myth that contributes to high levels of exploitation within the largely feminised industries of social care, childcare and hospitality, where mostly women often work long hours for low pay. The perceived 'virtuousness' of these roles justifies not paying them at all for the domestic work that they do within the home. This division of labour, across public and private realms, sends out a strong message that a woman's main role is to give birth to and raise children, ultimately reproducing the workforce – something capitalism relies on, yet works hard to avoid paying for.

Much reproductive health care has been complicit in maintaining the patriarchal control that is necessary for capitalism's survival and today's doctors also work within neoliberalised, deeply individualised healthcare systems. Most people seeking abortion only ever deal with a general practitioner (GP), the majority of whom are committed to treating people well. But this doesn't change the fact that GPs are ideologically bound to a disease model of health that often unnaturally separates our bodies from our minds and that significantly underplays the impact of our living conditions on our health. Contraception, pregnancy, abortion and childbirth weren't always under the control of doctors. As recently as the 1960s, many women gave birth in highly feminised community settings and in the company of midwives. There were fatalities though, both for mothers and babies (including my own grandmother and uncle). Although these occurred often because of poor public health standards and the effects of poverty more broadly, the female-led practice of midwifery was frequently blamed. By degrees, maternity care was moved under the control of male, hierarchal obstetric settings. These environments were often covered in religious iconography, with the Catholic Church exercising significant control over Irish maternity services. To give a rather stark example, Archbishop John Charles McQuaid was a frequent visitor to the National Maternity Hospital in the 1960s. This was not a social call – rather, he had a direct say in deciding if a woman could have a caesarean section, a procedure that could limit future pregnancies.[6] The alternative he could push for was the barbaric act of symphysiotomy where a woman's legs were tied in stirrups and her symphysis pubis ligament was severed.

Today, deference to medicine, patriarchy and the cost-cutting philosophy of neoliberalism, come together powerfully to ensnare women within a system that often places little value on the pregnant person's experience outside of a pathological lens. Obstetric coercion and violence are endemic and, although the Eighth Amendment was often blamed for increasing medical compliance, not much has changed since its repeal. This is because, whether practiced by men or women, obstetrics is often rooted in a misogynistic obsession with women's reproductive power. To quote Heather Cahill, women are largely viewed as 'essentially abnormal, as victims of their reproductive systems and hormones' where pregnancy is 'inherently pathological – a clinical crisis worthy of active intervention'.[7] Many examples within everyday obstetric practice demonstrate this, but interference during childbirth deserves particular scrutiny. First of all, women are commonly instructed to give birth in an unnatural, horizontal position, something only introduced in the last 200 years and never backed by sound medical research.[8] With the support of technology, their 'care-giver' then routinely subjects them to a raft of sometimes humiliating and very unpleasant procedures such as vaginal examinations, sweeps and routinely breaking their waters. In 2019, a UN special report on mistreatment in reproductive health services affirmed what many women instinctively know to be true, that much 'obstetric care' is actually a form of violence against women.[9] The UN criticised active management practices that are common in Ireland, such as artificially speeding up labour and expecting women to deliver within a certain timeframe. Encouraging women to prepare birth plans in advance compounds the problem, as this creates an illusion of choice in an environment of escalating intrusion. When plans 'fail', many women blame themselves. All the while, requests for natural birthing are dismissed and alternative treatments are denied. Many people who have given birth in an Irish maternity hospital can relate to what I've written here.

There has also been increasing criticism about the rising number of caesarean sections without a clear justification as to the reason why this surgical procedure is carried out. Caesareans can effectively prevent maternal and baby mortality; however, the WHO have described growing rates worldwide as 'a major public health concern', arguing that beyond a certain threshold, elevated surgical intervention may increase maternal and perinatal morbidity because of 'short and long-term risks that can extend many years beyond the current delivery and affect the health of the woman, the child and future pregnancies'.[10] Caesarean rates in Ireland have risen sharply in the last twenty years, recorded as 34.3 per cent of all births in 2019, including over 50 per cent of first-time births in one maternity unit.[11] Factors that contribute to growing caesarean section rates are complex and include maternal demand. Whilst a person should have the right to choose a caesarean, choice is again a limiting paradigm. There are many compounding factors surrounding the birthing experience that start long before a person presents in labour and are a culmination of the pathologising of natural birth at a deep cultural level. There is nothing to suggest that things will change anytime soon; instead, a Janus-face stance persists where Ireland's national maternity strategy evokes language that prioritises natural methods, whilst its hospitals create environments where interventions are a normal way to give birth. Sometimes healthcare workers (mostly midwives) set up alternative community schemes and home-birth options. But these are often chronically underfunded and offer restricted access. With little choice but to work in hospitals, research by Keating and Fleming found midwives are often unhappy about the interventions they participate in, but are constrained by the obstetrics of active management protocols and constant time-pressure.[12]

Obstetric violence in the extreme has also been underplayed or simply dismissed. Between 1974 and 1998, the obstetrician Michael Neary was employed at the Catholic-run Our Lady of Lourdes Hospital in Co. Louth. Without sufficient consent, he sterilised 129 women through caesarean hysterectomy immediately or soon after they gave birth. Neary also performed a higher than average number of episiotomies, a procedure where a woman is cut between the vagina and anus. He explained his behaviour away by positioning himself as the hero who saved lives or prevented women facing problems with hypothetical future pregnancies. Whilst many staff remained tight-lipped, a report by Sara Burke details how victims 'spoke about how Neary would joke about stitching them up tightly and "providing a play pen for their husbands", other women who were his patients said they pleaded with him not to carry out a hysterectomy on them but he went ahead and did it anyway.'[13] When details of a review into his practice was published in the *Irish Times* in 1998, some of his victims learned for the first time that their hysterectomies were unnecessary. Neary was placed on administrative leave and eventually struck off the Medical Register in 2003. No criminal charges were ever brought and he retired on a state pension.

The medical profession has also looked to the judiciary on particular occasions to deny women their birth preferences. In 2013, Waterford Regional Hospital sought a High Court order to carry out a caesarean section without consent. Whilst the hospital claimed the woman was 13 days overdue, she disputed this by as much as 3 weeks. Before the case was called, the heavily pregnant woman reportedly 'relented' and agreed to the procedure. The Irish health service tried again with a different woman in 2016. This time, Ms B wanted to have a vaginal birth for her fourth child after three caesarean sections. Doctors sought a court order claiming there was a risk her uterus might rupture. They requested 'the court to authorise the use of "such reasonable and proportionate force and/or restraint" to perform surgery upon Ms B against her will'.[14] The judge denied the order, despite acknowledging the Eighth Amendment gave independent rights to the foetus. As part of this ruling he stated:

If Ms. B was not pregnant, the performance of invasive surgery upon her, against her will, would be a gross violation of her right to bodily integrity, her right to self-determination, her right to privacy and her right to dignity ... This Court does not believe that the increased risk which she is undertaking for her unborn child is such as to justify this Court in effectively authorising her to have her uterus opened against her will, something which would constitute a grievous assault if it were done on a woman who was not pregnant.[15]

One of the starkest examples of what can happen when patriarchal attitudes within health care collide with the neoliberal ideals of privatisation and cost-cutting is the ongoing Cervical Check Scandal. In 2018, the Irish public became aware that 206 women who had been diagnosed with cervical cancer had previously received incorrect negative smear-test results whilst participating in the state's Cervical Check screening programme. These tests had been subcontracted to private US laboratories who used different quality benchmarks. As one angry activist put it, 'The cervical check scandal meant women were sacrificed to save a few quid by cheap outsourcing to shitty lab services.' The controversy only came to light when Vicky Phelan sued one of the offending US laboratories. When she went public, it became clear that the Irish Health Service Executive (HSE) hadn't told most of the women affected, forcing the HSE into a rapid process of disclosure. An independent enquiry by Dr Gabriel Scally exposed what he described as entrenched misogynistic and paternalistic views within the medical profession – attitudes most repugnantly captured in one consultant's comment to one deceased woman's family that 'nuns don't get cervical cancer.'[16] Despite a promise from the then Taoiseach Leo Varadkar that no woman affected would have to go to court, Ruth Morrissey, a terminally ill woman from Limerick was forced into the High Court to seek compensation. She won her case but in 2020, the State, along with US laboratory Quest Diagnostics, appealed the ruling to the Supreme Court. They lost. Four months later, Ruth Morrissey died without a public apology from either the State or the HSE. Afterwards, her husband spoke openly about the trauma of watching her sick and in pain being cross-examined in the highest court in the land, a damning indictment if one were needed about what happens when neoliberalism and patriarchy intersect. Ruth was just one of a number of women, or their families, who continue to seek justice through the Irish courts. In 2020, the cervical check survivor group '221+' withdrew their support for a government-led tribunal of enquiry, claiming they had been repeatedly betrayed by broken promises that they would participate in agreeing the terms of reference in advance. Vicky Phelan described the government's actions as 'a slap in the face' for the women affected.[17]

REPRODUCTIVE UNFREEDOMS

Some women enjoy significant reproductive privileges over others, and it is important to be up front about this. Notwithstanding the non-homogenous nature of any group of people, there is a clear need to shine a light on the experiences of migrant women in Ireland, many of whom, even those with overseas qualifications, work in low-paid, unstable jobs, including as carers in the private homes of middle-class families.[18] This has knock-on effects on their capacity to have and raise children, as the decision to end a pregnancy, although at one level deeply personal, is also fundamentally shaped by political, social and economic contexts. Where migrants with precarious low-paid work and/or poor living conditions do proceed with a pregnancy, international research suggests they are more likely to give birth prematurely, their babies statistically have lower birth weights and there are more neonatal admissions that in the general population.[19] African women living in Ireland have a higher perinatal mortality rate and double the number of stillbirths than their Irish-born counterparts.[20] Overall, women of colour are up to four times more likely to die in pregnancy or childbirth,[21] and some commentators have speculated that this figure could be higher, as maternity deaths can go unreported or are misclassified.[22]

In 2010, Bimbo Onanuga, a 32-year-old Nigerian woman, died in the Rotunda Hospital when the birth of her stillborn baby was medically induced using an unlicenced drug. The inquest into her death ruled 'medical misadventure'. The hospital's Master (chief obstetrician) Sam Coulter-Smith denied telling Ms Onanuga's partner that she died 'due to a series of mistakes'.[23] Medical misadventure was also the cause of death when an Indian woman, Savita Halappanavar, died in 2012, after she was denied an abortion while actively miscarrying. The circumstances and impacts of her death will be discussed in more detail in Chapter 4. Savita's death sent shockwaves through Ireland and stirred many people into action. For example, a canvasser told me 'I first began marching after Savita died. My sister was at the same stage of pregnancy as her and it hit me pretty hard. I remember feeling absolutely terrified. It still fills me with dread.' The same verdict, medical misadventure, was returned at inquests into the deaths of Dhara Kivlehan (2010), Nora Hyland (2012) and Nayyab Tariq (2021). In 2016, Malak Thawley died on an operating table in Holles Street Hospital when her aorta was accidentally torn during surgery for an ectopic pregnancy. The operation was performed by a second-year registrar and the consultant was not initially onsite. The coroner's verdict was, again, medical misadventure. Following pressure from her family and some opposition TDs, Simon Harris (then Minister for Health) ordered an independent inquiry into her death. But Holles Street objected and successfully blocked the inquiry in the High Court. Given these litany of tragedies, Ronit Lentin's description of ethnic-minority migrant women who enter into Ireland's maternity services as 'm/others', subjugated within a system that privileges white bodies, is justified.[24]

Being pregnant or parenting can be extremely difficult for people who are not legally supposed to be in Ireland. This is because our public healthcare system requires 'ordinary residency', which mostly means legal residency. Without a social security number (PPSN), an undocumented person can be denied such basic services as long-term illness benefit, health care for children and, of course, abortion. There are international protections for an obstetric emergency including childbirth, but not for antenatal and post-natal care. This is not advertised and often people simply don't know how or where to access health care, especially within a system that over-relies on familiarity with the English language. Mostly, people worry that if they do come forward, this will alert immigration authorities and they will be deported. As a result, women have presented for the first time in labour meaning hospitals have no medical history of their pregnancy. Rachel Reid of the Migrant Rights Centre (MRC) explained that, at the moment, there is a 'firewall' between the Departments of Social Protection and Immigration meaning a person can apply for a social security number (PPSN) and their details will not be passed to immigration authorities. This agreement was put in place during the Covid-19 pandemic and applies to healthcare services. 'It's a grey area,' Rachel explained, 'it's important that the firewall continues after Covid to ensure that there is no barrier for people to access maternity care in the future.'

There are also many challenges for migrants who have arrived in Ireland seeking international protection and are housed in Ireland's much-criticised for-profit system of Direct Provision. Just like prison, a person in Direct Provision needs permission to be away from their reception centre overnight. They must also survive on an allowance of just €38.80 per adult per week and €29.80 per child. These factors combined can push abortion services out of reach where a person requires two appointments, three days apart and where the closest GP is miles from their reception centre. When an asylum-seeker gives birth in hospital, they often endure stigmas. One woman I talked to described how 'one of the doctors was questioning me about my life as an asylum-seeker and she was saying that I am so lucky to have money without work. She says to me that she works like a donkey and has to pay tax. I cried a lot that day.'[25] Things often don't improve when forced to bring up children in this substandard accommodation. Zoryana Psych, who spent six years in a Direct Provision reception centre and who writes extensively about this, described to me what this was like:

As a first-time mother, I felt very isolated, without family to support me. In the Direct Provision centres, there is nobody to help – whether physically or emotionally. Going twenty times per day upstairs/downstairs to get a meal, or a cup of tea, you need to bring your baby with you, as no kettles are allowed in the rooms. There was no food that I felt like eating, as all food was plain and grey, like the days lived in Direct Provision. I breastfed both of my children, and was very lucky in that sense, as I did not need to beg the management for extra portions of baby milk if there was not enough to feed. There was no food to support the weaning process either. One friend gave me a steamer, and I quietly steamed vegetables bought by another friend – during the night, on the window board. My heart was pounding in my throat to the sound of the opening corridor doors, from fear of being caught by management or security and be reported to the immigration authorities ... Room check-ups could be carried at any time, and the door could be open at any time, stripping away any right for privacy. After a very quick knock, the door would be unlocked too fast, purposely not giving you the time to come to terms with what is happening. No agency cared how I managed to bring up my children through the times in DP, how I have tried to keep them healthy – physically and mentally. I felt invisible and non-deserving.

Every day, while in the DP system, I felt like I was failing – as a mother, as a woman, as a wife. Relying on others for six long years took away my independence and made me a dependant being, without any will over mine, or my children's lives.

Asylum-seekers are also not allowed legally to work in Ireland until they have been resident in a Direct Provision centre for six months. After this, they are often employed in the worst jobs for the least money, even when they have overseas qualifications. Many who are legally granted the right to stay in Ireland remain in cramped reception centres because it is practically impossible to find a place to live in Ireland's exorbitantly priced private rental market.

For people with disabilities, they have had to endure a culture of ableism that privileges able-bodied people, casting them as more valuable members of society. Historically, disabled people were forced to live in large institutions and there is evidence of eugenics practices in Ireland.[26] There is still constant discussion surrounding disabled people's right to have children without due regard for individual capacities and circumstances. There is also long-standing research that shows parents with psychiatric disabilities are at greater risk of child welfare systems that revoke visitation and/or custody rights.[27] In the post-repeal period, the Re(al) Productive Justice: Gender and Disabilities research project was created from within the Centre for Disability Law and Policy at National University of Ireland (NUI) Galway.[28] Re(al) Productive Justice described to me their work as 'to make visible the experiences of disabled people in Ireland seeking reproductive justice'. They adopt the reproductive justice framework drawn up by SisterSong that 'consider[s] reproductive justice to be the system in which persons have the right and supports to choose to have, or to not have, a child and to parent one's children'. The Re(al) Productive Justice team assert 'services and information on reproduction need to be accessible to person with all types of disabilities', and explain:

Disabled people are often denied the right to make reproductive decisions, including decisions about fertility, contraception, pregnancy, childbirth and parenting. Following the Repeal campaign in Ireland in 2018, it was felt by the research team that the conversation about reproductive rights ignored some key elements for more marginalised groups.

When sharing preminary findings from their oral histories project in 2021, researchers Jenny Dagg, Maria Ní Fhlatharta, Aine Sperrin and Eilionóir Flynn describe repeated violations of the reproductive rights of people with disabilities, including long-term use of contraception without adequate consent and coercive practices that enforce sterilisation.[29] They also recount violations in pregnancy and childbirth, such as hostile attitudes and threats that children would be removed from their care. In one example, an expectant mother with a physical disability was told by a public health nurse that her case was 'going to become a child protection issue' unless certain agreed systems were in place before the child was even born. Another woman, this time with an intellectual disability who sought interpreter supports during ante-natal visits, discovered this triggered a pre-emptive report to child protective services.

Reproductive justice approaches also recognise ongoing violations of reproductive rights for LGBTQI+, transgendered and non-binary people. Same-sex couples often endure homophobia relating to their capacity to parent and face legal hurdles in being named on their own children's birth certificates. Many trans-folk are denied adequate healthcare services and endure growing levels of stigma despite their right to a birth certificate in their chosen gender, as set out in the Gender Recognition Act (2015). A similar UK law is often thought to be the flashpoint for the contemporary rise of trans-exclusionary discourse, or trans-exclusionary radical feminism, as it is commonly called, and whose adherents are labelled TERFs. Trans-exclusionary discourse relies on biological essentialist views of womanhood where only a cis woman is considered female. The Irish writer Graham Linehan, a white cis male, is amongst those who have touted outlandish claims of predatorial behaviour by trans women in female-only spaces. He was eventually banned from Twitter in 2020 for repeated violation of the platform's rules including comparing puberty-blockers to eugenics.

Éirénne Carroll, CEO of the Transgender Equality Network Ireland (TENI) describes to me the current state of affairs:

Over the last five years we have seen a steady increase in transphobic rhetoric and a parallel rise in violence against trans people. For example, from 2016 to 2020 the total number of transgender people murdered internationally rose from 295 to 350. That is an 18 per cent rise where the victim is identified as transgender, these numbers could be much higher. Since 2016 there has also been an exponential rise in organisations and activists that convene around attacking and dismantling transgender rights and equality legislation. The International Lesbian, Gay, Bisexual, Trans and Intersex Association (ILGA) also reports that in the last year alone transgender rights and protections have stagnated or regressed in 50 per cent of European states. Transgender people not only are advocating for their civil rights, they are also fighting movements that are building to remove support for transgender people from the wider LGB rights movements. In particular in Ireland and the UK organisations and exclusionary activists have targeted trans women online, sought to expose their personal details, and support movements that malign trans women. Transgender people right now are seeing the ravages of a pandemic continue to impact safe housing, adequate employment and community engagement. They are also facing a wider cultural conversation unfold that denigrates their rights, bodies, and acceptance. As such transgender people have valued the wider work of intersectional feminists that continue to remind us all that feminism has always been driven from the most marginalised among us, and from intersectional work. If we want to see a decrease in violence and harassment, feminists and feminist movements that are intersectional will be key.

The integrative nature of oppression was starkly illuminated when, in 2018, Sylya Tukula, a transgender woman in her thirties, died in a male-only Direct Provision centre in Galway that she was forced to stay in by immigration authorities. Following a state enquiry into her death, she was cruelly buried in an unmarked grave without her friends in Ireland being informed. The Movement of Asylum Seekers in Ireland (MASI) have repeatedly raised concerns about the treatment of Tukula both in life and death, and continue to criticise the manner in which other deaths have been handled and how data on deaths in Direct Provision is not published. A reproductive justice approach encourages proactive demands for economic justice, comprehensive, non-judgemental health care and a freedom from violence and discrimination for trans people.

WHEN THE COURTS AND COPS ARE NOT YOUR FRIEND

So why do so many of us allow things to tick along like this despite the way millions of people are so clearly disadvantaged by a highly unequal distribution of wealth and a globalised system that not only tolerates but perpetuates ableism, racism, sexism and class-based discrimination? Part of the reason is that capitalism is not just an economic model; rather, it is held together by a complex web of myths and strategies that trick us into thinking that there is no alternative to it. Progress might be slow, we are told, but eventually we will get there. We are also told that gender equality is inevitable. All women must do, is *lean in*, as Sheryl Sandberg so famously suggested, and infiltrate the spaces where men continue to hold much economic, legal and political power. This individualist outlook involves eulogising the achievements of privileged women as proof that the glass ceiling can be broken. Calling on us to 'smash the patriarchy', the neoliberal feminist turns a blind eye to the impact of capitalism on millions of women, by ignoring situations where the State is the perpetrator of harm and where criminal justice and welfare systems actively control reproductive freedoms.

Angela Davis, an abolitionist feminist, has written extensively on how the prison-industrial-complex relies upon a privatised model that fills prisons with people from poorer backgrounds, people with addictions and mental health problems and people of colour, mostly for minor misdemeanours. These prisons then profit off the fruit of their unpaid or low-paid labour.[30] Ireland has mostly resisted privatising its prison system, but there are other parallels in terms of Davis's assertion about the characteristics of state punishment that 'both reflects and further entrenches the gendered structure of the larger society' and controls women through the overuse of strip-searches, and other invasive practices.[31] The reproductive healthcare prisoners receive is often woefully inadequate and there are clear violations of the rights of people of all genders when they are locked up for long periods of their fertile lives. The numbers of women in prison is growing throughout the world, including in Ireland. Most of Ireland's female prison population are from backgrounds of financial poverty, homelessness, addiction, or family breakdown.[32] Shockingly, Traveller women are 18–22 times more likely to be imprisoned than their settled counterparts.[33]

There are other ways in which the criminal justice system polices reproductive freedom, including when it criminalises abortion. This does not stop abortions happening but instead forces people into unsafe situations. Although current Irish laws are yet to be put to the test, women in Northern Ireland have, in the past, had to contend with criminal charges for procuring unsanctioned abortions. In 2016, a teenager who was unable to raise enough money to travel to Britain was found guilty of illegally performing an abortion on herself for which she received a suspended sentence. Siobhan Fenton describes how 'in desperation she ordered pills online and performed an abortion. Her flatmates found out when they discovered foetal remains and bloodstained clothes in their kitchen bin. They then reported her to the police who arrested her.'[34] In 2019, a woman was acquitted just before her court date after five years of legal wrangling over obtaining abortion pills for her 15-year-old daughter who was in an abusive relationship.

Another example of state-sanctioned reproductive injustice is within Ireland's foster care service, which is one of the largest care systems in Europe. Although presented as a neutral, child-centred service, the vast majority of children in care are from low-income families, one in four have a disability, and Irish Travellers and children of African descent are seven times more likely to end up in care than the general population.[35] In 2013, two Roma children were forcibly removed from their respective families over concerns that they were not biologically related. At the time, international news channels were obsessing over a blonde-haired child who was taken away from the Roma family she was living with in Greece on suspicion that she was being trafficked. As it turned out, she was there because of a private arrangement between families. Prompted by sensationalist reporting of that case, a neighbour of the first Irish family affected telephoned a journalist who then phoned the Gardaí. After a surface-level identity check, they called to the house and took a 7-year-old girl from her parents. The second case again started with a public tip-off that led to a distraught 2-year-old boy being taken from his mother and placed in emergency foster care. Both children were returned within a couple of days. A subsequent report by the Children's Ombudsman, who assessed each case separately, criticised An Gardaí Síochán for ethnic profiling. These might be considered as extreme examples, but many low-income, migrant and working-class women constantly worry that coming into contact with social services could lead to their children being taken from them. In 2020, a HSE report into a cluster of suicides amongst young women in South Dublin found previous experience of negative attitudes when they sought help left women reluctant to engage with public supports, despite significant financial stress and challenges in housing and domestic violence.[36] Women on welfare are being watched. During the first year of coronavirus lockdowns, investigative journalist Aoife Moore uncovered a discriminatory system of unannounced social welfare inspections that policed the behaviour of women on single-parent welfare benefits. Women described how inspectors rummaged through their belongings looking for evidence of a male partner and questioning them about their personal relationships. These visits left many of those affected feeling 'small and worthless', but unable to make a complaint because they feared losing their welfare payment.[37]

Reproductive justice advocates also point a finger at police brutality. The global reaction to the murder of George Floyd galvanised an already active US Black Lives Matter Movement that was started in 2013 by three black women – Alicia Garza, Patrisse Cullors and Opal Tometi – who were concerned about the safety of their children following inaction after the death of the teenager Trayvon Martin. To be abolitionist is no longer considered a particularly radical viewpoint and many people now accept that the police frequently enact extreme levels of violence against racialised and working-class people even when they are not resisting or fighting back. Ireland is no different. Across a series of podcasts called 'Policed in Ireland' (launched in 2020), Vicky Conway and her guests uncover practices similar to universal policing methods across the globe. 'Policed' exposes targeted stop-and-searches of people (often children) from certain communities, high levels of surveillance and brutality on African Irish and Irish Traveller communities, extreme policing of sex-workers, ineffective protections for domestic violence victims, prejudice towards working-class people and the inapproproriate detention of people with mental health problems. According to the sociologist Lucy Michael, the Gardaí have done little to address the behaviour of many of their employees. They have inadequately resourced their diversity unit, ineffectively trained their staff and resisted demands to implement a human rights framework.[38] Sometimes obvious displays of discrimination break through Irish newscycles. In 2019, Traveller representative groups expressed outrage when a video surfaced of Gardaí mocking Mincéirs. The following year, a Traveller man videoed his own stop-and-search where a female garda confiscated new toys from the boot of his car even though he insisted these were Christmas gifts he was hiding from his children. He later shared the video on YouTube along with receipts for the toys.

Migrants and Ethnic Minorities for Reproductive Justice (MERJ) have been a central force in exposing the normalisation of these sort of policing practices and have been to the fore of the Irish Black Lives Matter movement. In June 2020, they partnered with MASI and Black Pride Ireland[39] to protest in Dublin City centre. MERJ also took a lead in demonstrations against the death of George Nkencho, a young black man from Dublin with a history of mental illness who, in 2020, was shot dead by Gardaí despite being armed only with a knife. At the time of writing, the Garda Síochána Ombudsman Commission (GSOC) are investigating the shooting, while the Garda who shot Nkencho remains on duty. MERJ have also been to the fore of grassroots organising on anti-carceral approaches through a series of dialogic, consciousness-raising workshops called 'Beyond Carceral Feminism'. They continue to develop their ideas on alternative approaches to looking to the state for solutions.

If we accept that a person's financial stability and job security has very real impacts on their capacity to have and raise children, we understand why a reproductive justice approach is expansive enough to include the need to fight against often state-sanctioned erosions of working standards. When workers at the retail outlet Debenhams were made redundant in the spring of 2020, their employers broke a 2016 agreement to pay them two weeks' redundancy plus two weeks' ex-gratia per year of service. They protested outside of Debenhams stores across Ireland and remained there for over a year. Things came to a head in April and May 2021, when Gardaí forcibly removed picketers by physically lifting them to one side of the street so that trucks sent by the corporate giant KPMG could enter stores to retrieve stock. Reports circulated of up to 60 Gardaí sometimes being involved in manhandling the mostly female ex-employees and their supporters, some of whom were in their sixties and seventies. Opposition politicians from Solidarity-People Before Profit objected to the role of the police in the Dáil.

Whilst the Gardaí have defended their actions as in the execution of a court order obtained by KPMG, many people have raised questions about using Gardaí resources to support one side over another in a legitimate industrial relations dispute, particularly at a time when a simultaneous internal Gardaí investigation found over 3,000 domestic violence 999 calls were deliberately cancelled by members of the police force. Women's Aid described this failure to respond as of 'deep concern',[40] but likely not terribly surprising given Women's Aid's previous reporting of mixed and negative experiences with Gardaí responding to domestic violence. These included 'police officers being rude and women feeling that they were not being taken seriously, Gardaí not trying to locate the perpetrator at large, women being given incorrect information and Gardaí minimising the abuse and the risk posed by the perpetrator.'[41] In the first known action of its kind, Gardaí did manage to find the resources to charge ROSA activists for breaching Covid regulations when, in March 2021, they organised a small, socially distanced outdoor protest that called for action against an exponential rise in levels of violence against women during the Covid pandemic.

The Eighth Amendment clearly violated people's right to abortion on domestic shores and its abolition was a fundamental prerequisite to the emancipation of people. But, as this chapter has shown, concentrating on abortion's singular focus can obscure wider reproductive inequality that is not just a part of the Ireland of today, but was stitched into the fabric of our past. The next chapter will explore Ireland's abysmal historical record on reproductive oppression that dates back to the foundation of the State.

This issue has bothered me for a long time. I had a termination when I lived in Holland during my studies, never once did I feel shame until I moved back to Ireland. There is such a long history of injustice against women in this country, women should not be second-class citizens. We should have the basic human right to body autonomy. Just sick of the church and State controlling women.

Canvasser (2018)

3

Ireland's Dark History of Injustices Against Women

Camilla Fitzsimons and Sinéad Kennedy

Before looking forward, it makes sense to look back and ask why, in 1983 and at a time when there was a tide of pro-choice reforms happening across Europe, did Ireland become the first country in the world to introduce a constitutional ban on abortion? This situation cannot be separated from an environment where a cosy coalition between the Catholic Church and the State resulted in a cultural environment where the ideal for an Irish woman was to be married, a homemaker, fertile and largely silent. Interlocking systemic abuses of women, girls and their children, who were enslaved in now-notorious institutions that were mostly run by religious orders, would come together to help create a culture where a small but dedicated anti-abortion movement with the backing of the Catholic Church gathered sufficient traction to direct an allied government towards calling a referendum to insert the Eighth Amendment.

In 1922, the 'Irish Free State' was established. By degrees, the monogamous, Catholic, patriarchal family would become its fulcrum. The original vision for this emancipated republic didn't include patriarchal subservience; in fact, equality for women was one of its founding principles. Article 3 of the 1922 Constitution stated, 'Every person, without distinction of sex, domiciled in the jurisdiction of the Irish Free State ... shall enjoy the privileges and be subject to the obligations of such citizenship.'[1] This aspiration was however short-lived, as was the 1922 Constitution itself. Instead, the newly formed independent but conservative State adopted Catholicism as one of its principle regulating ideologies. As historian Marianne G. Valiulis puts it:

Catholicism triumphed in the Irish Free State because it: (1) promised stability and order; (2) provided a justification for independence; and (3) reinforced the gender stereotypes which the 'conservative revolutionaries' carried with them and which seemed necessary for the new State to flourish.[2]

In the decades following political independence, the Irish State's project of national identity formation became synonymous with its identity as a Catholic country. This was mostly embodied in two ways: a desire among Catholic clergy to prevent the use of contraceptives, and a related need to affirm the virtue of large families protected by the sanctity of marriage.[3]

The new State's patriarchal, Catholic ideology was quickly reflected in its attitudes towards women. Their role in the fight for liberation was erased from mainstream history; the actions of Cumann na mBan (the Women's Council) and such freedom fighters as Elizabeth O'Farrell, Eva Gore-Booth and to a lesser extent Countess Markievicz were relegated to the margins. The role of the Irish Women Workers' Union (est. 1911) was also underplayed. This union did not just secure important workers' rights, it sought to improve people's living standards more broadly, including high infant mortality and high levels of disease.[4]

The introduction of a series of legal measures erased women from public life, including the Juries Bills of 1924 and 1927 which encouraged women to 'opt out' of jury service. The Civil Service Amendment Act of 1925 and the Conditions of Employment Act of 1935 restricted women's capacity to work, forcing many to remain in the home.[5] A number of harsh legal reforms were also introduced. Through the banning of divorce (1925) and the sale and importation of contraception (1935), women's sexuality was channelled into childbearing within marriage and the family home.

The alliance between the Catholic Church and Irish State culminated in a second Irish Constitution (1937), a deeply conservative document that privileged both the institutions of marriage and the family, leaving no doubt that the role of women was not in public or the workplace, but within the home. The family it imagined was (and remains) highly gendered where the 'special' role of women within the private home is elevated as an ideal. Article 41, entitled 'The Family' states:

1. 1°The State recognises the Family as the natural primary and fundamental unit group of Society, and as a moral institution possessing inalienable and imprescriptible rights, antecedent and superior to all positive law.

    2°The State, therefore, guarantees to protect the Family in its constitution and authority, as the necessary basis of social order and as indispensable to the welfare of the Nation and the State.

2. 1°In particular, the State recognises that by her life within the home, woman gives to the State a support without which the common good cannot be achieved.

    2°The State shall, therefore, endeavour to ensure that mothers shall not be obliged by economic necessity to engage in labour to the neglect of their duties in the home.

As the prominent pro-choice activist Ruth Riddick observed, the terms 'woman' and 'mother' are understood interchangeably in this Article, as is demonstrated by the rhetorical shift from 2.1 to 2.2.[6] The identity constructed for Irish women is thus solely in domestic terms where 'women were mothers, women were wives.'[7] Early drafts of this second Constitution were met with significant opposition from some women's groups. A campaign was organised by the Women Graduates' Association and the Joint Committee of Women's Societies and Social Workers. Along with the Irish Women Workers' Union, they sought amendments and deletions of offending articles.[8] While some allowances about electoral and employment rights were won, these concessions were not enough to prevent the Constitution from instilling a legalistic and cultural environment that forced women into the home. However, as Maria Luddy notes, it was 'significant that the campaign was undertaken at all' and that it was essentially the last 'high profile feminist campaign until the revival of feminism' in the 1970s.[9]

The result was that by the late 1930s the Church's patriarchal and paternalistic 'special position' extended far beyond close working relationships with politicians and touched virtually every aspect of Irish life. As Valiulis explains, 'women's political, economic and reproductive rights' were 'so severely curtailed so as to make it clear and explicit that women were indeed barred from claiming for themselves a political subjectivity, a public identity.'[10] Most women endured multiple pregnancies whilst labouring under difficult conditions in the home.

Thousands of working-class women who continued to hold low-paid menial jobs, such as in domestic service, farm labouring, or in sewing and cigarette factories,[11] managed both spheres often at great personal cost. Girls lucky enough to stay in Ireland's Church-run schools after primary level were taught how to cook, clean and be good housewives. Women were to reproduce the next generation of the family, and indirectly, to reproduce the nation itself.

THE INCARCERATION OF WOMEN

We now know the extent to which the vision of the stable traditional family so cherished by Catholic Ireland rested upon a particularly brutal system of containment where women and their children became what the journalist Conall Ó Fátharta describes as 'little more than a commodity for trade amongst religious orders'.[12] Where a woman or girl did become pregnant outside of marriage, this was humiliating for her family. Many mostly middle-class women fled to England, often returning childless. Poorer women and many from rural communities weren't so 'lucky'. In her must-read book *Republic of Shame* (2019), Caelainn Hogan details the full horrors of Ireland's incarceration of 'fallen women' through an interlocking system of Mother and Baby Homes and Magdelene Laundries. It is difficult to know the exact numbers affected. The Coalition of Mother and Baby Home Survivors estimate 35,000 women and girls went through nine Mother and Baby Homes between 1904 and 1996, but believe this is a conservative estimate because many records are incomplete or unreliable.[13] Under the so-called 'shield' of the Catholic Protection and Rescue Society of Ireland, thousands of these women were subject to forced profitable, often overseas, adoptions.[14] The Coalition estimate at least 6,000 children died in these homes, sometimes from malnutrition. Many were also subjected to unsanctioned vaccination trials. In 2014, one such institution, the Bon Secours Mother and Baby Home in Tuam, Co. Galway hit the headlines when a local historian called Catherine Corless claimed that up to 800 children had died and that their remains had been dumped in a septic tank. Corless's work resulted in a 2017 government-commissioned investigation into the affair which confirmed this grim reality.

It is also estimated that between 1922 and 1996 as many as 30,000 women were imprisoned under slave-like conditions in highly profitable, Catholic-run Magdalene Laundries.[15] The culture of secrecy around these laundries was at times deafening. The State was not a passive bystander – rather, Gardaí regularly 'arrested' and returned women who escaped from these institutions despite no legal grounds for holding them.[16] In 1941, Bloomfield Laundry lost out on a lucrative military contract to the Magdalen Asylum in Donnybrook. This was a catalyst for the 1945 laundry strike initiated by the Women's Workers Union, which is credited with winning important rights for all workers across Ireland. These laundry workers were undoubtedly experiencing significant hardship, but many did not question how working conditions in the Magdelene system allowed them to compete as they did.

When a government inquiry was eventually commissioned, the Report of the Inter-Departmental Committee to Establish the Facts of State Involvement with the Magdalen Laundries, 2013 (known as the McAleese Report) forced the State to acknowledge that they were accomplices. The then Taoiseach Enda Kenny apologised to women who had spent time in the Magdalene laundries. However, the report was largely viewed as inadequate and received criticism from many quarters. The United Nations torture watchdog said it lacked many elements of a 'prompt, independent and thorough' investigation.[17] Four of the religious orders who ran the laundries issued statements which only succeeded in compounding the pain and anger experienced by many survivors. As Hogan argues:

> [Although] expressing regret for any hurt the women may have experienced in their institutions ... they added caveats about the laundries being a product of the times, or about the nuns providing a refuge in good faith. They would not commit to making any contribution towards the State's multimillion-euro redress scheme, despite several requests by the government.[18]

In response to the McAleese Report, a survivors' group, Justice for Magdalene (est. 2003), published a counter-report that criticised the McAleese inquiry for excluding the 796 pages of testimony submitted to the inquiry team, of which 'not one syllable' appeared in the final report.[19] Almost two decades later, the same problems were identified in the long-awaited report from the Commission of Investigation into Mother and Baby Home and Certain Related Matters, which was published in 2021. Again, the report caused outrage amongst survivor groups and the public at large, with accusations of gaslighting on a mass scale by dismissing or minimising survivor testimonies of abuse. Many public protests were held despite Covid-19 public health restrictions. Calls for the report to be set aside grew considerably when Mary Daly, one of the three members of the commission, chose to address an academic community at an online Oxford University event despite repeatedly refusing to meet with survivor groups and even Oireachtas members. Irish journalists, academics and some survivors logged onto the call and reported on the event. Writing in the *Irish Times*, Jennifer Bray described how in the seminar's chat function, one survivor who had been interviewed by the commission shared how here personal testimony was captured within the report in a way that was 'littered with inaccuracies and misrepresentations which changed the context and accuracy of her story'.[20] Again intersectionalism played its part. The Association of Mixed Race Irish (AMRI) have brought their concerns about the treatment of children of colour to the United Nations Human Rights Council (UNHRC) claiming that the Commission of Investigation in Mother and Baby Homes fundamentally failed to investigate institutional racial discrimination within these homes and also industrial schools. AMRI are not only seeking recognition for the additional discrimination these children experienced, but an assurance that current care structures will review its systems so as to prevent further racism.[21]

Just like Mother and Baby Homes and Magdalene Laundries, the industrial schools AMRI refer to held a strong anti-working-class bias. From the 1920s through 1970s, children as young as age 5 were sent to these religiously run industrial schools with a generous capitation grant on their heads.[22] Again with the support of the judicial system, these 'schools' targeted children living in poverty, sometimes rounding them up on the streets where they were likely getting a break from overcrowded tenement housing. Some were put before the Children's Court because they 'might' commit an offence, others were found guilty of missing school, begging, or were locked away because of a perceived lack of guardianship.[23] Once incarcerated, they were severely brutalised and neglected. Their parents on the outside were denied the right to rear their own children.

These historical events weigh heavy on the conscience of many Irish people and shape our identity to this day. When one Wicklow activist shared her reason for canvassing to repeal the Eighth Amendment, she put it like this: 'Between the Magdalene Laundries, child trafficking, the disgusting treatment of babies in Tuam and Mother and Baby Homes elsewhere, symphysiotomies, and the cervical smear scandal, Ireland has treated her women abysmally. We have had enough.' Another canvasser described her motivation starkly when she wrote 'I couldn't sit by and allow old, religious men to control women's bodies any longer. Anger. Pure anger made me get involved.' The State is yet to investigate the parallel incarceration and abuse of women through state-run psychiatric services.

SECOND-WAVE FEMINISM

By the early 1970s, women began organising to demand and achieve greater economic, social and political independence; they started to remain in education for longer, assumed occupations traditionally understood to be the preserve of men, socialised in pubs, played sports and acquired economic independence, allowing them to rewrite conventions about appropriate behaviour for women.[24] In 1970, the Irish Women's Liberation Movement (IWLM) was founded by a group that included Máirín de Burca, Mary Anderson, Moira Woods, Marie McMahon, Rosita Sweetman, Nell McCafferty, Margaret Gaj, Mary Maher, Mary Kenny, Nuala Fennell, Mary Sheehan and June Levine.[25] In her book *Feminism Backwards*, Sweetman describes the actions of the IWLM in 1971–72 including the publication of their manifesto *Chains or Change* and their appearance on 'The Late Late Show' which Ailbhe Smyth described:

On 6 March 1971, when the controversial TV chat show, 'The Late Late Show', devoted an entire programme to the Women's Liberation Movement. The effect was electric. The I.W.L.M. women on the panel raised hitherto unspoken issues and taboo topics for women (indeed everyone) in Ireland on a range of social and sexual matters – unmarried mothers, working mothers, the 'helpless dependency of the Irish wife,' the miseducation of girls, social conditioning and so on … The issue of liberation had been well and truly raised and placed on the social and political agenda. Women's silence would never be quite as absolute as it had been.[26]

Their most famous feat was when they took the train from Dublin to Belfast and bought condoms which they proudly displayed to the waiting media when they returned. The stunt served feminism well, as powerful images of women waving condoms in the air were beamed into living rooms across Ireland.

In 1972, Maura O'Dea Richards set up 'Cherish', which not only supported women parenting alone, it challenged the stigma of single parenthood. Cherish successfully lobbied for the unmarried mother's allowance and was instrumental in eradicating the status 'illegitimacy'.[27] In later years, O'Dea Richards expressed regret that Cherish never scrutinised conditions within the Mother and Baby Homes and Magdelene Laundries.[28] In 1974, Women's Aid was established, bringing the previously taboo topic of domestic violence into the headlights. Irish Women Unite (IWU) also formed in 1975 and stayed together for around 18 months. Linda Connolly and Tina O'Toole describe this group as 'the main catalyst for the formation of the Contraceptive Action Campaign (CAP) in 1976, the first Rape Crisis Centre in 1977 and the first Women's Right to Choose group in 1979'.[29]

More moderate strands of feminism would ultimately take centre stage, a process that began with the Commission on the Status of Women (est. 1972) which was an umbrella group of middle-class, feminist organisations.[30] This commission presented findings from their deliberations to the State and invited other groups to join them in establishing a national women's organisation. This would later become the National Women's Council (1995), a key organiser in Together for Yes and still the leading liberal feminist organisation in Ireland. Some women did set up alternative groups in working-class communities, especially in Dublin, and often in partnership with left-wing feminists working in universities. These local leaders were not against the NWCI's demands for equal pay and conditions, but this agenda simply did not relate to their lives. Instead these 'women's community-based education' groups merged radical feminist ideas with a simultaneous 'popular education' movement that sought to unpack dimensions of patriarchal power and problematise the distribution of wealth in society.

When the Women's Right to Choose Group (WRCG) began meeting in 1979, abortion was not a political issue in Ireland, and it was neither understood nor prioritised as a critical feminist issue in the way that the women's movements in Europe and North America had. The 'right to choose' position was discussed and debated in some left-wing sections of the movement, but more dominant liberal sections decided that a focus on abortion would be problematic, risking a conflation of contraception with abortion. As a result, only a few left-wing women's organisations like the WRCG considered abortion a critical feminist issue.[31] The reality of abortion in Ireland was rarely discussed; yet it was a real, if unacknowledged, aspect of women's lives. Between 1968 and 1983, at least 30,560 Irish women travelled to Britain in order to obtain an abortion, with the number climbing steadily year by year,[32] a fact that was largely and conveniently ignored by the campaign to introduce the anti-abortion constitutional amendment. These official figures were published annually (by the Department of Health in England and Wales) and then reported without comment in Irish newspapers. In 1979, the Dublin Well Woman Centre was established to aid women with crisis pregnancies, including the option of a referral to an British abortion clinic. The WRCG set up the Irish Pregnancy Counselling Centre and began agitating around the issue of abortion by holding public meetings and seminars, writing articles and speaking to the media. In 1981, they published a pamphlet *Abortion: A Choice for Irish Women*, advocating abortion as a necessary choice for women; this pamphlet became one of few sources of abortion information at a time when this was tightly regulated and subject to the 1967 Censorship of Publications Act.[33]

THE 'PRO-LIFE' AMENDMENT CAMPAIGN

The rise of a highly resourced, well-organised anti-abortion movement in Ireland is best understood as a conservative counter-movement designed to oppose the emerging liberalisation of Irish society. Their agenda was, from the outset, much broader than opposition to contraception and abortion, which journalist Fintan O'Toole describes as just 'one front in a wider religious war'.[34] Conservative forces had already attempted to mobilise on a number of issues: they had organised against the formation of a multi-denominational primary school in Dalkey in 1976, arguing that it was a fundamental challenge to the Catholic dominance of the Irish education system. O'Toole describes how a group calling themselves the 'League of Decency' organised a series of public campaigns against 'immoral' TV shows and family planning clinics. They even opposed a small State grant that was given to the Dublin Rape Crisis Centre. However, their initiatives failed to receive the support they had hoped for; where they found the most traction was around the issue of abortion. The risk that abortion could be legalised was aggravated by the reasoning behind the US *Roe v Wade* Supreme Court ruling in 1973: that a constitutional right of privacy was 'broad enough to encompass a woman's decision whether or not to terminate her pregnancy'.[35] This sent shivers down the spine of Irish conservative circles who feared a similar case could arise in Ireland. These fears appeared to be confirmed when the Irish Supreme Court ruled in 1973 that 27-year-old Mary McGee had the right to access contraception after determining that married couples have the constitutional right to make private decisions on family planning.[36] The far right feared that abortion would be next and decided that the only way to make it impossible for the Supreme Court to extend this to include a right to end a pregnancy, was through a constitutional ban on abortion.

In 1981, the Pro-Life Amendment Campaign (PLAC) was established, an organisation that Ursula Barry described as 'a defensive reaction to the process of change which had gathered momentum during the 1970s'.[37] An important part of PLAC's tactics was to divert conversations away from the lives of women. Disclosing abortions, in public or private, is a powerful way to challenge stigma. In 1980, a radio documentary by the broadcaster and feminist Marian Finucane followed one anonymous woman on her journey to England. It was noted in 1983 in *Magill* magazine that 'the programme offered no opinions as to whether abortion was right or wrong. The woman herself didn't know. The listener, any listener, was made to sense that this was a very complex matter'.[38] The documentary served as an exceedingly rare counter-narrative to the dominant 'good versus evil' framing that was characteristic of the politics and the media. It also suited PLAC to contain the debate within a legalistic remit, an approach largely modelled on similar actions in the US, and their tactics won support from all the main political parties and the media.

In November 1982, the first draft of the amendment was prepared by a Fianna Fáil government under the leadership of Charles Haughey. Soon after Fianna Fáil lost power, but this did not dampen PLAC's efforts as, in February of the following year, a coalition government of Fine Gael and Labour revitalised the proposed amendment, altering the wording to appease concerns by the then Attorney General. The revision was then put to the people.

The Anti Amendment Campaign was established (in April 1982) to oppose the referendum. The campaign operated as a broad front to which organisations and individuals could affiliate. The grounds on which PLAC was to be opposed were encapsulated in the following five-point platform:

1. The proposed amendment would do nothing to solve the problem of unwanted pregnancies in Ireland.
2. The amendment would allow for no exception even in cases where pregnancy severely threatens a woman's health or where pregnancy results from rape or incest.
3. The amendment seeks to enshrine in the Constitution the teaching of one religious domination. Leaders of Protestant Churches and the Jewish Community have expressed grave reservations about the matter.
4. The proposed amendment will impede further public discussion and possible legislation on abortion.
5. At a time of severe unemployment, when one-third of the population is living on or below the poverty line, the proposed amendment is an irresponsible waste of public funds.[39]

By the time the referendum campaign began in earnest in the summer of 1983, the AAC would refine their focus toward the first, third and fifth points following a series of divisions between the left and more liberal sections of the campaign. It was clear from the beginning that the political terrain of the referendum campaign would be determined and dominated by PLAC. This created tension with the AAC, the source of which was not just between those who supported the right-to-choose position and those who did not; rather, the key differences that emerged were often questions of strategy and tactics, and were, as Gordon argues, the same type of differences that are found within any campaign which involves a coalition of different political forces from liberal to radical, tensions which would, as we will see, reappear in the Repeal campaign in 2018.[40] The political climate in which the AAC was operating was intensely hostile from the outset. While there was much political debate on the necessity of an amendment in a country where abortion was already illegal, there was little debate on the issue of abortion itself and why women need access to abortion.[41] The central tenet of the AAC campaign was that the lives of women would be put at risk (health was rarely mentioned) and although, as we will see, women would lose their lives, it simply did not carry enough weight at the time. Pauline Jackson, an academic and activist with AAC writes of the period:

> Most women had never discussed abortion in public – indeed, not outside an intimate circle of friends! None knew how to make a speech on the subject. None of the left-wing political parties would agree at first to join the campaign. It seemed for a time that every official legitimate political faction was going to support an amendment to the constitution to 'give an absolute right to life of the foetus.'[42]

There was an enormous anti-abortion sentiment on the ground and campaigners struggled. Shortly before the launch of PLAC, the Women's Right to Choose Group (WRCG) held a packed meeting in Liberty Hall, Dublin. The meeting was invaded by the anti-abortion Society for the Protection of Unborn Children (SPUC),[43] which was an offshoot of the British organisation of the same name. They shouted and abused the speakers. An attendee writes of her experience that night:

> For the WRCG this was a very unnerving experience. It made us realise that we were not going to be allowed to continue to operate unhindered. SPUC had been set up in Ireland in June '80 ... but until the Liberty Hall meeting, we had not actually experienced them in operation. We had tended to reject them as arch Catholic fanatics, but it was now becoming clear that they were very well organized and that their message had strong appeal. They were using the existence of our group to create the illusion of a serious threat against which the up-to-now latent anti-abortionism of Irish society need[s] to be mobilized.[44]

Women's experiences of pregnancy and abortion were nowhere to be found. In 1981, the journalist and activist Mary Holland became possibly the first woman to stand up in public and talk about her abortion. But no one stood up with her. In response, she received hate mail, was vilified in newspapers and condemned from pulpits around the country. Her then partner, Eamonn McCann, described what she had to endure:

> Mary was chair of the Anti-Amendment Campaign. She wasn't just shouted at in the street, she was followed into functions and subjected at close quarters to spittle-flecked tirades delivered into her face. At one gathering, she apologised for leaving early, explaining that she had to get home for a birthday party for one of our children. A red-faced pro-lifer was on his feet in a flash: 'The child you murdered won't be at that party.' Cue a chorus of jeers as she walked towards the door. Letters arrived not just at the *Irish Times*, where she worked, but at our home, wishing all manner of personal disasters upon her and promising hell-fire from the instant mortal life ended.[45]

Her treatment served as a clear warning to any woman considering taking a similar public stance. As a result, a woman talking about her abortion in public was an exceedingly rare event until the Repeal campaign emerged three decades later. As Medb Ruane concluded, in relation to Irish women and abortion, 'theological and legal arguments supplant the personal testimony of women.'[46] Indeed, even the word 'abortion' was largely absent from the debate, with both sides using the term 'the substantive issue'.[47] In the end, the referendum was passed by a 66.9 per cent majority, with a turnout of just 53.6 per cent. Reflecting on the intense campaign that delivered this outcome, Hug argues that the results reflected the fact 'that the vision of babies being killed in the womb was stronger in the minds of the Irish than the potential danger' that the meaning or presence of the Eighth Amendment in the Constitution would create for the lives of women living in Ireland.[48]

THE AFTERMATH

One important thing to understand about the Eighth Amendment is that it did not simply ban abortion; effectively, abortion was already illegal, in all circumstances. Ivana Bacik argues that the Eighth Amendment was 'uniquely misogynistic, in that it expressly sets up the right to life of both the pregnant woman and the foetus that she carries in conflict – anticipating that a time would come when somebody would have to decide between them.'[49] The weight of this reality is voiced by one canvasser's words: 'I find it very difficult to accept that a fertilised egg has the same constitutional right to life that I have.' As Fiona de Londras and Mairead Enright observe in their deliberately accessible legal study, at first glance the Eighth Amendment could appear 'innocuous or merely aspirational' and could have been interpreted in a variety of ways.[50] Instead, what we got was 'a near-absolute prohibition on abortion in Irish law' which, while certainly the intention of those who advocated for its inclusion, was not inevitable. De Londras and Enright suggest that had the Eighth been interpreted as 'protecting life in all its richness and depth' instead of just 'the bare condition of being alive', pregnant people may not have experienced the 'drastic intrusions' into their lives that became characteristic of abortion law in Ireland.[51] However, what transpired was an environment where the Eighth Amendment gave permission for misogyny to express itself as a national standard. It acted as a cultural marker of contempt, reminding women, lest they forget, that their place was within the monogamous domestic realm. Indeed, in the months and years after the referendum it began to feel like it was open season on women. This reality would be reinforced in 1984, by two tragedies that would have a lasting and profound effect on Irish society, sending a strong message to Irish women.

On 31 January 1984, five months after the Eighth Amendment was inserted into the Constitution, Ann Lovett and her new-born baby boy died alone in a grotto in Granard in Co. Longford. It was a cold, wet January day; Ann gave birth alone and then cut her umbilical cord with scissors; the baby had been strangled by the cord during birth.[52] Together they lay alone, exposed to the elements for around two hours before they were discovered by some passing schoolboys. It took another two hours for her to make it to hospital where she died twenty minutes later. Rosita Sweetman describes the night the news broke:

The story, titled 'Young Girl Died in Field After Giving Birth' was read out as part of the next morning's papers at the end of 'The Late

Late Show': 'Young girl dies in a field after giving birth, my goodness me …' said Gay Byrne, the show's host, then chucked the paper on the floor with 'Nothing terribly exciting there.' As an example of the male callousness of the time it was appalling, but as a newsman who prided himself on having his finger on the nation's pulse, 'Gaybo' couldn't have been more wrong. The death of Ann Lovett and her baby convulsed Ireland for months.[53]

Her death emphasised many stark contradictions at the heart of Irish society. Early reports suggested Ann had successfully concealed her pregnancy. As things unfolded, it became clear that many in Granard, including teachers at her school, were, at the very least, suspicious. This level of State and community neglect was not isolated; rather, it reflected the situation across Ireland, and society's capacity to ignore the plight of girls and women hit home for many people for the first time. A poem by her school friends, which Moira Maguire reprints, sums up the deep-felt emotions that surrounded this avoidable tragedy:

Oh my God what have we done
we killed our friend and now she's gone
it's only now we have deep regret
she needed help which she did not get
No one on his own is to be blamed
it's all of Granard should be ashamed
when she died everyone did cry and moan
but when she needed help, she was alone.[54]

Ann's 14-year-old sister Patricia took her own life three months later. Ann's death also had wider implications. Hundreds of Irish women, moved by what had happened, wrote anonymous letters to RTE Radio 1's 'Gay Byrne Show' describing their experiences of concealed and unplanned pregnancies. Overwhelmed by the sheer number of letters received, one entire programme was devoted to reading them out.

Then there was also the mistreatment of Joanne Hayes, or the so-called 'Kerry Babies Case', as it came to be known. This is the story of how the Irish State and its judiciary instituted a witch hunt against a young woman, Joanne Hayes, under the guise of a criminal investigation into the murder of a newborn baby boy whose lifeless body washed up on a Kerry beach in 1984. The infant was posthumously named 'baby John'. As is to be expected, an extensive Gardaí investigation followed; but rather than seek to uncover the truth, the police unnecessarily probed into the private life of Joanne Hayes. Hayes, who had nothing to do with the death of the infant, was experiencing a simultaneous personal tragedy where she concealed a stillbirth after giving birth alone and without medical care. She was unmarried, her family did not hold much power locally, and she was in a relationship with a married man, Jeramiah Locke. Knowing that she had been pregnant, the Gardaí questioned her. Although Hayes and her family originally confessed to baby John's death, this was under duress and they quickly withdrew their admission of guilt. Hayes cooperated fully with the inquiry and led police to where her own child was buried on the family farm. This however failed to prevent the Gardaí making outlandish claims that sought to link her situation with that of baby John, despite clear medical evidence that discounted any connection.

It was not long before media circles questioned the handling of the affair, forcing the State to establish a public tribunal into the Gardaí's conduct. But instead of objectively enquiring into police behaviour; it doubled down on an institutionally misogynistic narrative about Hayes that effectively put *her* on trial, even though she was not under investigation for any crime. A male-led, Church-influenced committee subjected her to intense questioning that probed into deeply personal aspects of her private life. The message was clear. Her relationship with Locke fell outside of the Catholic morality expected of Irish women and she was the sole culprit. In her book *A Woman to Blame*, Nell McCafferty described the events as medieval and one of Irish womanhood on trial. She speaks frankly about her discomfort as a journalist looking on when Hayes was subjected to intense questioning, including about her menstrual cycle, a previous birth, and her sexual history. McCafferty details how Hayes 'broke down repeatedly. Her tears and sobs and laboured breathing were a daily feature, an hourly feature and then a minute-by-minute occurrence as the interminable questions came at her in relays from the five legal teams gathered around her.'[55] Despite this, the tribunal continued.

People protested. The Tralee women's group sent single yellow flowers to Hayes, an action that quickly spread across the country.[56]

Local people also organised protests outside the tribunal and people travelled from other counties too. McCafferty describes one bus-load of protesters from Dublin made up of people from left-wing political parties, feminist groups, and KLEAR, a women's community-based education project. In summing up the overall attitude to women at the time, McCaffrey writes:

> A measure of his temperament and attitudes to women in the Kerry Babies case is the judicial pronouncement made at its end by Justice Lynch. He asked, 'What have I got to do with the women of Ireland in general? What have the women of Ireland got to do with this case?' He presumed to lecture Irish women on what he saw as their misguided support for Hayes in her agony, by sending her flowers and Mass cards. He found that the 'most wronged woman' in the matter was Mary Locke, the wife of Jeremiah Locke, the man who had fathered Joanne's babies. 'Why no flowers for Mrs Locke?' he asked. 'Why no cards or Mass cards? Why no public assemblies to support her in her embarrassment and agony? Is it because she married Jeremiah Locke and thus got in the way of the foolish hopes and ambitions of Joanne Hayes?' Mary Locke's reply to his query was simple, dignified and devastating for Lynch. She declared: 'Joanne Hayes was harshly treated.'[57]

The treatment of Joanne Hayes is a stark portrayal of misogynistic and patriarchal Ireland at its worst. This, McCafferty claims, sharpened the hearts and minds of many people in terms of the nation's treatment of women. It was January 2018 before Joanne Hayes received an apology from the State. In December 2020, 26 years after the tribunal, she was awarded damages by the High Court and a declaration that all accusations against her and her family were unfounded.

The cases of Ann Lovett and Joanne Hayes were just two of the most tragic and high-profile cases of the period, but many other women suffered stigma and discrimination through an unofficial nexus of State and religious authority. In 1984, Garda Majella Moynihan, who was unmarried at the time, gave birth to a baby boy. The father of the child was another garda. In her book *A Guarded Life*, Moynihan revealed how she was charged with breaching An Garda Síochána's disciplinary rules, for having premarital sex with another guard, and for having a child outside of marriage and then coerced into putting her baby up for adoption. It later transpired that Archbishop Kevin McNamara advised the Garda Commissioner Larry Wren not to sack her for fear this might 'open the flood-gates to England'. In 2019, Majella Moynihan received a public apology from the Garda Commissioner Drew Harris.

In August 1982, Eileen Flynn was fired from her job as a teacher at the Holy Faith Convent in New Ross, Co. Wexford. She was sacked because she was an unmarried mother and was living with the baby's father, a separated man, Richie Roche (divorce was illegal in Ireland until 1996). Two months after the birth of her son, she received a letter that referred to complaints from parents about her lifestyle and of her open rejection of the 'norms of behaviour'. It also reminded her of the 'scandal' already caused.[58] Flynn refused to accept her sacking and took a case to be reinstated in her post but lost her unfair dismissal case at the Employment Appeals Tribunal and at the Circuit Court. Refusing to accept defeat, she appealed to the High Court on 8 March 1985. The case was heard by Mr Justice Declan Costello who would, seven years later, issue an injunction preventing a 14-year-old rape victim from travelling to Britain for an abortion. Rejecting Flynn's appeal, he wrote in a reserved judgment:

> I do not think that the respondents over-emphasise the power of example on the lives of the pupils in the school and they were entitled to conclude that the appellant's conduct was capable of damaging their efforts to foster in their pupils' norms of behaviour and religious tenets which the school had been established to promote.[59]

The Flynn case received major publicity and caused public debates about divorce and the role of the Catholic Church in State education that reverberated for many years to come. More than a decade later, Sister Rosemary Duffy of the Holy Faith Order wrote a letter to the *Irish Times* in an attempt to justify their actions: 'Eileen Flynn was dismissed because in the town where most of the pupils and parents of the school lived she openly and despite warnings to the contrary continued to live a lifestyle flagrantly in conflict with the norms which the school sought to promote.'[60] In response, Flynn reflected on the events in an interview stating:

At the time it was a very frightening situation for me. Look at it this way: I had a small child and my livelihood had just been taken away from me … People were terrified that there was going to be a witch-hunt, that my case would just be the first. Yes the school won, but it was a pyrrhic victory.[61]

By the mid-1980s, it was difficult not to conclude that Ireland was no country for women. These cases forced Irish society to cast a cold eye over Ireland's treatment of women, its attitudes to sexuality and the functions of the State, its Judiciary and the Gardaí.

GRASSROOTS FEMINISM UNDER ATTACK

In 1987, Ailbhe Smyth described the Irish women's movement as in crisis. It had failed to prevent the Eighth Amendment and had also failed to legalise divorce in 1986. Smyth pessimistically wrote:

It is difficult now for feminists in Ireland to avoid a sense of disillusionment and demoralisation – and therefore, a difficult period to write about with any degree of equanimity. We know now that the encounters of the 1970s over contraception, rape, equal pay were mere skirmishes, a phoney war, prior to the battles of the 1980s against the serried ranks of church and state, staunch defenders of the Faith of our Fathers and the myth of motherhood. The litany of defeats, and of victims – some known, the vast majority unnamed and nameless – is shocking.[62]

Throughout the 1990s and early 2000s, there was a strongly negative portrayal of feminism in popular culture. The journalist John Waters's valiant attempt to popularise the expression 'Feminazi' was part of a broader global male supremicist backlash, the repercussions of which penetrated much public discourse where even calling yourself a feminist became a challenge. Although Ailbhe Smyth had been optimistic that women's community education might hold firm on its radicalising potential, this was not to be the case; it too would be domesticated. Three factors contributed to the neoliberalisation of the wider community sector of which these women's groups were part of. This began with a rapid professionalisation process that coincided with State funding for the work from the early 1990s onwards. This shifted power away from its left-wing, working-class grassroots to often well-meaning, and also left-wing, but nonetheless middle-class professionals. Many held qualifications in teaching, nursing and social work, but lacked first-hand knowledge of the realities of living on a low income and did not deal with structural classism on a daily basis. Eleanor D'Alton, Mary Fenton, Helen Maher and Maeve O'Grady explain how local people were often side-lined:

> This situation came to a head in the early 1990s as development funding for anti-poverty work became available to disadvantaged communities. The activists who organised groups and submitted funding applications were then rejected for the paid community work jobs that were created, because the jobs went to applicants with academically-recognised qualifications. To add insult to injury, these same voluntary workers were expected to train the newly employed graduates.[63]

A second factor in the co-option of women's community-based education came in the guise of social partnership. Many, unmandated, often self-appointed, leaders most of whom fit the description above, were lured by the promise of a civil society-State partnership that mirrored Ireland's National Partnership Agreements of the time and promised to address local concerns. But partnership didn't work – instead it detracted from direct action and in the end delivered only tokenistic gains before collapsing in 2008, along with the Irish economy. The third neutering feature was a State-led drive towards a managerialist, outputs-oriented model of service delivery that included harsh austerity cuts and forced mergers, which were implemented from 2008 onwards without consultation. In 2009, 13 community development projects with an openly radical agenda were suddenly closed as their funding was withdrawn. The remaining 170 independent projects were forcibly absorbed into State structures, their assets were sequestered, and their independent boards of management were forcibly disbanded. These actions were justified by a government report which contended there was 'little evidence of positive outcomes for these [community sector] initiatives'.[64] Thirty thousand, mostly women, took to the streets in a 'Communities Against Cuts' march in Dublin organised with Ireland's largest trade union SIPTU (Services Industrial Professional and Technical Union). They carried placards that read, 'We never felt the boom but now we feel the bust' and 'Value people not banks.'[65] These demonstrations were ignored.

Some groups rejected government funding when their role was forcibly changed. Meitheal, a project led by community development and feminist principles of equality, participation and collective action, withdrew from their role as a 'support agency' to other projects when the terms of agreement changed to include a monitoring role. They stayed open and generated their own funding, but their capacity was hugely reduced. Equally Banúlacht (est. 1990) closed in 2012. In a letter to its supporters, it cited 'a number of factors that have combined to make it impossible to continue to do our work according to our feminist ethos', including a directive that State funding could not be used for campaigning or advocacy work.[66] Those that survived had to fundamentally tailor their work to meet government demands to deliver education for employability rather than education for critical consciousness.[67]

One space that did hold firm on a radical analysis was Ireland's militant left-wing revolutionary parties. Two parties dominated: the Socialist Workers Party (now part of People Before Profit) and the Socialist Party. Both consistently held a pro-choice position that they linked to the wider circumstances of people's lives. Goretti Horgan, a founding member of Derry Women's Right to Choose and an organiser for the Anti-Amendment Campaign, was and remains an important voice in Irish socialist feminism. Horgan had written the first edition of the 1982 pamphlet *Abortion: Why Irish Women Have the Right to Choose*, which was updated and re-published in 1988, 1992, 2002 and 2012.[68] As editor of the *Socialist Worker* newspaper (1982–92), she ensured there was always a strong feminist voice. The party's annual Marxism conferences also held public talks on abortion throughout the 1990s and 2000s, at a time when there was often silence on the issue. Similarly, the Socialist Party, of whom Ruth Coppinger is a member, were never shy about raising the issue throughout the 1990s and 2000s and had strong connections with student's union groups. However, the revolutionary left in Ireland has always been a small political space. In many respects, its influence has only been felt recently through the election of a number of TDs from both People Before Profit and the Socialist Party.

Second-wave feminism won significant reforms that improved the lives of many women. Compared to other European countries, Irish feminists were starting from a low base, thanks to the cosy, but brutal, coalition of Church and State that we have described. But its radical origins were tempered through the dominance of a more liberal discourse and a deliberate attack on more radical community-sector voices. However, green shoots of what would become the movement that repealed the Eighth were pushing through, as student groups and left-wing parties in particular almost immediately defied the sentiment of the Eighth Amendment by providing abortion advice and information. In response, conservative campaigners would switch their attention to blocking these actions, leading to a series of prolonged and expensive legal cases that would eventually be decided by the European courts. It would not be until February 1992, and the case of *Attorney General v X*, that the courts would make a specific judgment about abortion and the Constitution. This, along with other seminal cases discussed in the next chapter, would see public opinion change irrecoverably.

While I was active long before Repeal, it has been the proudest and most meaningful campaign I have taken part in. The feeling of the vast majority of voters supporting mine and all women and pregnant people's bodily autonomy was incredibly uplifting and regularly inspires me to keep fighting for full equality. To go from the Eighth Amendment being voted in the '80s to a massive movement and popular vote for Repeal shows that change is possible.

Activist (2020)

4

After the Eighth, the Slow Movement for Repeal

Sinéad Kennedy

So how did we get from a place where no referendum to liberalise abortion laws had ever been put to the Irish electorate in any meaningful sense to a campaigning hashtag – #RepealThe8th – becoming government policy? In the aftermath of the 1983 referendum, activists continued to campaign for abortion and to support women in need of abortion. It is important to understand the campaign to repeal the Eighth not just as a brief moment in Irish history but as part of a process – a struggle of continuity that ebbed and flowed over the course of three decades, culminating in the 2018 explosion of activism that features in this book.

1983–92: IN THE SHADOW OF THE EIGHTH

In the aftermath of the 1983 referendum and the surprise defeat of the 1986 divorce referendum,[1] emboldened by their victory, anti-abortion groups, in particular the Society for the Protection of Unborn Children Ireland (SPUC), turned their attention to banning abortion information and referrals. Not content with outlawing abortion in Ireland, they also wished to prevent women gaining access to information about abortion services in Britain. After the referendum defeat, pro-choice activists began to concentrate their efforts on ensuring that women in Ireland could at least find out how to travel for abortions. For those readers born into the age of the worldwide web where information is literally available at their fingertips via the Internet and mobile phones, it is important to remember how difficult, challenging and vital this activism was. Abortion information in Ireland was so tightly controlled that, following complaints from the Offices of Censorship of Publications, the women's magazine *Cosmopolitan* began publishing a separate Irish edition that substituted a blank page for the one where ads for abortion services would normally be printed, with a 'Publisher's Notice' explaining why. In May 1992, Easons, Ireland's largest magazine and newspaper distributor to retail newsagents, refused to sell and distribute copies of the British newspaper the *Guardian* when they arrived at Dublin Airport because the issue contained a full-page advertisement for Marie Stopes clinics, a well-known provider of abortion services in Britain.[2]

There were a number of abortion referral agencies operating in Ireland in 1983 offering non-directive counselling to pregnant women and providing women who chose abortion the contact details of clinics in Britain. In June 1985, SPUC initiated legal action against two of the main providers of pregnancy counselling in Ireland, Open Door Counselling and the Well Woman Centre. The attorney general subsequently joined the action and in December 1986, the High Court issued an injunction prohibiting both organisations from offering pregnancy counselling services, with Justice Hamilton arguing that it was illegal to provide information in Ireland about abortion clinics in Britain. The centres stopped providing the information but appealed the decision to the Supreme Court; their appeal was denied on 16 March 1988 on the grounds that this information could 'if availed of … have the direct consequences of destroying the … constitutional right to life of the unborn.'[3] The injunction was later clarified to prohibit the communication of the names, addresses and contact numbers of all abortion clinics outside the State. In response and in defiance of the injunction, pro-choice campaigners shifted tactics and began to concentrate on providing abortion information instead of counselling. Open Door Counselling established an emergency telephone hotline, Open Line Helpline, so that women could continue to access abortion information. The number was distributed throughout the country via fliers, stickers and graffiti on toilet doors in pubs, nightclubs and student unions. Activists would also gather outside the GPO in Dublin at weekends shouting the number of the helpline via the now infamous chant '6794700 – Women have the right to know!' In September 1988, on the strength of the Hamilton judgment, SPUC obtained an injunction against three student unions for including abortion information in their student handbooks. The handbooks contained detailed information about contraception, advice to support women deciding whether or not to have an abortion and, crucially, the names and addresses of abortion clinics in Britain. Student unions had been at the forefront of the struggle for reproductive rights in Ireland since the 1970s. The students' case would go from the High Court to the European Court of Justice, the Supreme Court and back again.[4] The case was not formally resolved until March 1997 when the judges accepted that abortion law had changed in Ireland following the X case (discussed below). As Chrystel Hug noted in one of the most detailed and comprehensive studies of that period, *The Politics of Sexual Morality in Ireland* (1999), these cases 'proved that an ordinary citizen can enforce the law as in Article 40.3.3 and deprive women in distress of the necessary information relative to their decision to terminate their pregnancy'.[5] Despite the restrictions on information, women continued to travel in their thousands to Britain every year. In fact, the numbers steadily increased following the 1983 referendum. In 1983, at least 3,677 Irish women accessed abortion in an English clinic; by 1992, that had increased to 4,254.[6]

1992: THE X CASE

The abortion debate appeared to have reached a political cul-de-sac in Ireland after the 1983 referendum and there was virtually no political appetite to revisit the topic. Pro-choice campaigners continued to campaign but in a deeply hostile environment and were largely exercised with ensuring that women could access information and travel to Britain. It was vital work but there was little space to advance the question of 'a woman's right to choose'. However, in February 1992, a case would hit the headlines that would fundamentally shift how abortion was understood in Irish society; that case became known as the 'X case'. It involved a 14-year-old rape victim who was known to the public only as 'Miss X'.[7] In February 1992, her parents attempted to take her to Britain for an abortion because the young girl insisted that she would rather end her own life than continue the pregnancy to term. The Gardaí were contacted by the girl's parents to see if foetal DNA could be submitted as evidence against her rapist, who was contesting the charges against her. The Gardaí sought legal clarification on the admissibility from the attorney general at the time, Harry

Whelehan (use of DNA evidence in legal cases was in its infancy). In response, Whelehan sought a High Court injunction against the girl and her parents, prohibiting them from leaving the jurisdiction for the duration of the pregnancy in order to ensure that the life of the foetus was protected. Granting the injunction, Justice Costello argued that the risk posed to Miss X's life by requiring her to continue the pregnancy was 'much less and of a different order to magnitude' than the risk to life of the 'unborn'.[8] When the story broke in the Irish media some days later, there was a public outcry with thousands of people taking to the streets in a series of spontaneous protests, expressing shock and horror at the treatment of the young woman and demanding not only that Miss X should be allowed to travel abroad for an abortion, but that she should also be allowed to have an abortion in Ireland. This was a dramatic shift in public opinion for a country that less than nine years previously had voted to enshrine the foetal right to life in its constitution. It also revealed that when Irish people were faced with the reality of abortion denial and its effects, they were prepared to allow women and girls to make their own decisions.

Miss X and her parents appealed the injunction to the Supreme Court and the Court ruled by a majority of four to one, to remove the injunction. In their judgment, the majority judges decided that abortion was legal in Ireland where a woman's life was at risk, including the risk of suicide. However, two of the judges noted that there was no legal certainty that it was legally permissible for a woman to travel outside of Ireland to access abortion. According to James Kingston, while the Eighth Amendment was not 'an absolute prohibition on abortion', it did mean that the State had an obligation to protect 'the right to life of the unborn by ensuring that pregnant women did not travel out of the jurisdiction'.[9] The X case and the legal ambiguity around the right to travel reinvigorated the pro-choice movement and opened up a space where campaigners could begin to articulate a pro-choice argument and get a hearing, even if that was not yet a political possibility in Ireland.

In response to the X case judgment and under pressure to appear to respond to the scale of protests around the case, the government agreed to hold a three-part referendum in November 1992 clarifying the legal position of abortion in Ireland. However, the referendum attempted to reverse the Supreme Court decision in two conflicting ways; first, it sought to introduce a new constitutional amendment that would exclude suicide risk as grounds for an abortion and, second, it attempted, constitutionally, to protect a woman's ability to travel abroad to access abortion even if those grounds were unlawful in Ireland. It also included an amendment making it constitutional to access information on abortion services that were available abroad. Despite the demands from an increasingly vocal and emboldened pro-choice movement, and a more liberal public, the government refused to even consider offering the electorate the opportunity to liberalise Ireland's abortion laws and instead sought to put the genie back in the bottle by asking the electorate to reverse the X case judgment. As far as politicians were concerned, the status quo held and Ireland's hypocrisy around abortion must continue; women living in Ireland were allowed to access abortion just as long as those abortions did not happen on the island of Ireland.

However, the electorate voted in favour of the most liberal regime available to them; they supported the right to abortion information and the right to travel abroad for an abortion, while opposing the government's attempt to remove suicide as grounds for an abortion. The X case would prove to be an important moment, not just in terms of the struggle for abortion rights in Ireland but also in terms of the wider struggle for social change in Ireland and confirmed one of the key fears of the Catholic right in Ireland; that the slightest concession to liberalism would cause 'the floodgates to open'. Indeed, within a year of the X case, the Fianna Fáil government of the day began an extensive programme of social reform. Undoubtedly, the passage of this reform was accelerated by revelations of clerical sexual hypocrisy and the sexual abuse of children, which destroyed the moral authority of the Catholic Church.

1992–2012: AFTER THE X CASE

The re-energised pro-choice movement that emerged in response to the X case found themselves frustrated. Undoubtedly, the X case created a sea change in Irish attitudes to abortion, but campaigners were met with a morass of political cowardice and indifference. In the run-up to the 1992 referendum, the government promised that if the electorate did not vote to reverse the X case, they would provide legislation to set out the terms under which life-saving abortion was permissible in Ireland. The failure of six successive governments to legislate created a legal vacuum that meant that doctors and healthcare providers were practising under the shadow of criminalisation, something that many doctors would only acknowledge publicly during the Repeal campaign. This failure to legislate would be a contributing factor in the death in 2012 of Savita Halappanavar (discussed in detail below).

In 1995, legislation on abortion information was finally introduced. However, the legislation was highly restrictive with access to abortion information tightly mediated and controlled; only doctors, advisory agencies and individual counsellors, could give information on abortions, the information had to be provided alongside information on parenting and adoption and could only be given in the context of one-to-one counselling. The Regulation of Information (Services outside the State for the Termination of Pregnancies) Act 1995 prohibited a doctor from making an appointment for an abortion in another State on behalf of their patient if the woman was experiencing serious health problems. Most problematic of all, doctors and clinics offering crisis pregnancy counselling were legally obliged to give women information on parenting and adoption and could refuse to give information on abortion. This resulted in the proliferation of so-called 'rogue pregnancy agencies'. The sole purpose of these rogue agencies was to prevent women from having abortions. Women reported being harassed, bullied, and given blatantly false information.[10] Five years after the X case, in November 1997, the same case was essentially rerun in the courts: the C case. This time the young girl at the centre of the case was a 13-year-old rape victim in the care of the State who required an abortion. Despite more protests and calls for political action, the status quo remained unchanged; women continued to travel abroad for abortions or carried unwanted pregnancies to term, and politicians maintained their moral high-ground.

In the aftermath of the X case, women were travelling in ever-increasing numbers for abortion in Britain and, with the advent of low-cost airlines, to other destinations such as the Netherlands. Pro-choice campaigners found themselves constantly in the position of having to react to the State's oppressive anti-abortion agenda. So, in 2001, in an effort to be pro-active on the issue, pro-choice activists worked with the Dutch charity Women on Waves,[11] which brought a ship with a portable surgery on board to Ireland with a plan to offer abortions to women in international waters. It was an important effort to break the log-jam of political indifference that surrounded the issue and while it generated much national and international media attention, it failed to mobilise a layer beyond reproduction healthcare professionals and dedicated pro-choice activists. As the historian Mary Muldowney, who interviewed many of the activists from that period, remarked:

> The event had very little impact on national sensibilities. Given that more than 300 women called the helplines organised by the Irish activists ... and that they were clearly prepared to go on board a ship to be taken to international waters for that procedure, the level of desperation evident in those cases was strangely unacknowledged.[12]

This assessment appeared to be confirmed by the government's decision to hold another referendum in 2002 in a second attempt to reverse the X case decision and remove risk of suicide as grounds for an abortion in Ireland. This was again rejected by the electorate, albeit narrowly. The status quo once again reigned supreme; Ireland pretended it was an abortion-free nation while exporting thousands of women each year to seek abortion care abroad.

However, the legal and medical uncertainty around abortion in Ireland, especially when a woman's life was at risk, ensured that it would continue to be a key political issue, with abortion cases hitting the headlines every couple of years with depressing regularity. In 2010, Michelle Harte became pregnant whilst receiving treatment for cancer, and was forced to travel to Britain for an abortion whilst severely ill. Although her doctors had advised her to terminate the pregnancy because of the risk to her health, the hospital where she was being treated refused to authorise an abortion on the basis that her life was not under 'immediate threat'. Harte therefore had to travel to access an abortion, delaying and interrupting her care. She died from cancer in 2011. The Eighth Amendment also resulted in the implementation of outrageous measures to preserve pre-natal life after a woman's death. In the highly publicised PP case in 2014, a woman who had experienced brain-stem death when she was 15 weeks pregnant was left on life support against the express wishes of her family. This was because a foetal heartbeat was present, and doctors were fearful of overstepping legal boundaries.[13] PP's family had to make an application to the High Court so that her life support could be turned off. The court described the measures used to prolong foetal life after the death of the pregnant woman as grotesque and granted an order to end them, but found that if there had been any chance of the baby being born alive then the somatic care would have been continued.

In 2010, three women (legally referred to as A, B and C) who had accessed abortions in the UK took a case against the Irish State within the European Court of Human Rights. The Court unanimously ruled in the ABC case that Ireland's failure to implement the existing constitutional right to a lawful abortion when a woman's life is at risk (in other words, X case legislation), violated a woman's right under Article 8 of the European Convention on Human Rights.[14] The State was obliged to respond but adopted its usual delaying tactics, avoiding the issue with callous indifference for two years, and acting only under pressure after another avoidable tragedy in October 2012 that pro-choice activists had sadly predicted: the death of Savita Halappanavar.

2012: THE DEATH OF SAVITA

Certainly, pro-choice activism continued to be evident in Ireland, but it typically involved small numbers of dedicated activists who organised largely in the face of political indifference and public apathy, while women who needed abortions continued to travel abroad or take the abortion pill illegally under the threat of a prison sentence. However, in 2012, a new phase in Irish pro-choice activism began; it would lay the foundations for one of largest political mobilisations in the history of the Irish State: the referendum to repeal the Eighth. In January 2012, abortion activists re-galvanised themselves to mark the twentieth anniversary of the X case judgment by calling for 'X Case legislation' to be introduced.[15] In April that same year, the independent TD Clare Daly put forward a Private Member's Bill to implement the X case judgment before the Dáil (Irish Parliament). The Bill was rejected with 110 TDs voting against it and just 20 TDs voting in favour. In September 2012, activists organised the first ever 'March for Choice', which mobilised several thousand people across the country. This march (which will be discussed more in Chapter 5) was particularly significant as it was the first time that the pro-choice movement in Ireland had mobilised significant numbers on an explicitly pro-choice agenda and not in response to another horrific case.[16] The majority of activists involved in the movement considered themselves to be pro-choice, but they had usually stopped short of mobilising around the explicit demand of a 'woman's right to choose' out of fear that it would alienate Irish society, which was generally understood to be very conservative on the issue. However later that year, a tragic event would challenge this conservative apathy and, unlike the 1992 X case, the desire for change that it created, became impossible to contain.

In October 2012, Savita Halappanavar, an Indian woman living in Ireland, presented to University College Galway Hospital with a miscarriage at 17 weeks. But the doctors treating her felt that due to the presence of a foetal heartbeat they could not treat her immediately, citing the Eighth Amendment as their reason for inaction. In severe pain, both she and her husband Praveen repeatedly asked for a termination but their requests were denied with one nurse, as was widely reported, telling the couple, by way of explanation, that 'this is a Catholic country.'[17] The delay proved fatal and Savita Halappanavar died of septicaemia on 28 October 2012. Her death provoked a wave of national and international horror at Ireland's punitive abortion regime, with thousands gathering in a silent vigil outside the Dáil once the story broke in the media. That same weekend tens of thousands marched in Dublin, with simultaneous demonstrations in all major town and cities across the country, all chanting 'Never Again'.

With the protests showing no signs of abating, the government found themselves under enormous pressure to act, with protesters calling not just for the introduction of X case legislation, but for a referendum for the Eighth Amendment to be removed from the Constitution. In order to appear to be acting, the government convened an All-Party Oireachtas Committee on Health and Children (January–May 2013) to investigate the implementation of limited abortion legislation. The end result was a highly restrictive piece of legislation called the Protection of Life During Pregnancy Act (PLDPA) 2013. The Act controversially created a differentiation between a physical threat to life and a threat to life due to a risk of suicide (mental health). Where the threat arises because of risk of suicide, three doctors – an obstetrician and two psychiatrists – would need to agree that her life is at risk. If this panel did not agree, a woman could be referred to a further panel of three doctors. This created a situation where a suicidal, pregnant woman could potentially be questioned by up to six doctors before she could access an abortion. The cumbersome and deeply problematic nature of the legislation was confirmed in the summer of 2014 in a case involving a young migrant woman. Ms Y, who was pregnant as a result of rape, became suicidal after being denied an abortion. Begging for the decision to be reversed, the young woman went on hunger strike. Instead of acceding to her request for the abortion that she was now legally entitled to under the PLDPA, an order to force-feed her was obtained from the High Court and she was eventually 'convinced' into continuing her pregnancy until the foetus was viable, at which point she was induced.[18] The political response fell far short of what was required to ensure women's safety, with politicians clearly demonstrating that they were more interested in making concessions to the anti-abortion lobby, inside and outside of the Dáil, than ensuring that women's lives, health and choices were respected and protected. The end result of the debacle around the PLDPA was that it further antagonised pro-choice campaigners, adding energy to this new phase of highly visible abortion rights activism that will be touched on below, then discussed in more detail in the following chapter.

2013–17: THE MOVEMENT TO REPEAL

The death of Savita Halappanavar and the unworkability of the PLDPA galvanised the pro-choice movement into an intense campaign that pressured the government into calling a referendum to repeal the Eighth Amendment. In 2013, a coalition of groups, activists, political organisations and NGOs came together to establish the Coalition to Repeal the Eighth Amendment in order to protect and respect women's lives, health and choices. The organisation would eventually represent over a hundred leading groups and organisations across Irish society. In 2016, a group called Strike for Repeal mobilised around a global demand for women to strike on 8 March, International Women's Day. Their actions inspired thousands of young people across the country to walk out of schools and universities and to shut down Dublin city centre for much of the day. By the time of the next general election in March 2016, it was clear that a national social movement for

'Repeal' had emerged that was capable of putting strong pressure on the next government to call a referendum. Responding to this growing pressure, in May 2016 as part of its Programme for Partnership Government,[19] the new minority government committed to establishing a Citizens' Assembly, which would be charged with making recommendations to the Oireachtas on the Eighth Amendment. Pro-choice activists were unsurprisingly sceptical about the Assembly, seeing it as a delaying tactic which would allow politicians to avoid having to act on this issue. It was undoubtedly designed to slow down the pace of change, but it did prove a useful exercise in that it allowed politically nervous politicians to see that the appetite for political change on abortion ran deep across Irish society.

The Citizens' Assembly had its first meeting in Dublin Castle on 15 October 2016, followed by a further five weekend sessions, between November 2016 and April 2017. Representative organisations and activist groups from both sides of the debate, as well as members of the public, were invited to make submissions. In total, the Assembly received well over 13,000 submissions, over 8,000 of which were online and 5,000 by post. Anonymous submissions were not accepted, except in the case of personal stories. All were made available to the public via the Assembly's website.[20] The Assembly also heard from a wide range of medical and legal experts and human rights groups, as well as campaigning and civil society organisations. Most significant of all, the Assembly heard from women – women who had had abortions, and from women who had decided to continue with their pregnancies. Following extensive discussions and deliberations, the Assembly recommended that Article 40.3.3 of the Constitution should not be retained in full and that it should be a matter for the Oireachtas to decide how to legislate on these issues. The Assembly members also made recommendations to the Oireachtas about what should be included in this legislation. It was clear from the final day of deliberations (23 April 2017) that the citizens were prepared to support more liberal options on abortions than they were offered by the Assembly.[21] The Assembly originally offered the citizens 40 options but under pressure from the citizens themselves they increased this to 65 after being challenged on the Assembly's insistence on creating an artificial distinction between mental and physical health and the failure to include socio-economic reasons as grounds for abortion. To summarise the findings from the Citizens' Assembly:

- **Ballot 1:** The members voted by a majority of 79 votes to 12 votes that Article 40.3.3 should *not* be retained in full.
- **Ballot 2:** The members voted by a majority of 50 votes to 39 votes for Option 2: Article 40.3.3 should be replaced or amended.
- **Ballot 3:** The members voted by a majority of 51 votes to 38 votes for Option 1: Article 40.3.3 should be replaced with a constitutional provision that explicitly authorises the Oireachtas to legislate to address termination of pregnancy, any rights of the unborn, and any rights of the woman.

Pro-choice activists, who had been arguing hard for the Eighth Amendment to be removed with no replacement, were initially deeply disappointed by the result of the third ballot. It appeared to open the door for the government to put forward a more restrictive amendment to replace the Eighth. However, in light of the subsequent fourth ballot it could be interpreted very positively: in order to avoid any confusion, the Assembly recommended to include an explicit constitutional statement declaring that abortion regulation does not belong in the Constitution and that it is the job of the Oireachtas to legislate for (progressive) change.

- **Ballot 4:** The specific recommendations are as follows.
  A woman shall be entitled to access an abortion:

  Up to 12 weeks
  - On request/without need to provide additional grounds

  Up to 22 weeks
  - In cases where pregnancy is a result of rape
  - On grounds of foetal diagnosis of serious disability
  - Risk to health (In a separate vote, members voted explicitly not to create a distinction to between physical and mental health).

  After 22 weeks/no gestational limits
  - On grounds of diagnosis of fatal foetal abnormality
  - Serious risk to health
  - Risk to life.

Ailbhe Smyth, convenor of the Coalition to Repeal the Eighth Amendment who addressed the Assembly and who would go on to become one of the co-directors of Together for Yes, summed up the experience of the Citizen's Assembly:

> It was clear that this Citizens' Assembly, which had started off neutral at best, had decided in their minds they wanted very liberal abortion legislation, including for socio-economic reasons. They wanted abortion to be available for the first fourteen weeks to protect women's health, without any qualification. They had listened carefully and did what they thought would respond to women's needs.[22]

Following the Citizens' Assembly, a 21-strong cross-party Oireachtas Committee on the Eighth Amendment (discussed more in chapter 7) was tasked with examining their recommendations.[23] In December 2017, the Committee recommended; that Article 40.3.3 (the Eighth Amendment) should be removed from the Constitution; that having an abortion in Ireland would no longer be a criminal offence; that abortion without restriction as to reason should be permitted up to 12 weeks, and that abortion with gestational limits set by medical best practice should be permitted for reasons of fatal foetal abnormality or risk to health, including the mental health, of the woman. These recommendations were then considered by the government in January 2018, which announced that a referendum to remove the Eighth Amendment would be held at the beginning of summer 2018. If successful, the government would move to immediately introduce abortion legislation in line with the recommendations of the cross-party Oireachtas Committee.

The years from 2012 to 2017 were a crucial period of strategic issue-definition, public education and awareness-raising, sustained political lobbying and wide mobilisation. Counter to the perceived liberal wisdom, the campaign for a referendum to remove the Eighth Amendment was not won because of pro-choice policies within mainstream politics; rather it came about as a result of a highly organised and political grassroots movement that was led largely by women. By the time the Citizen's Assembly made its recommendations on abortion to the Oireachtas, much of the groundwork to re-orientate the abortion debate to centralise women's experiences had paid off. The Citizens' Assembly was the first time in the history of the State's official engagement with the issue of abortion that a space was created to allow women's direct experiences to be heard, and these stories undoubtedly influenced the Assembly's decision. Also, during this time, foundations were laid, strategy formulated, research carried out, and relationships were built and consolidated, and would result in the creation of the umbrella organisation, Together for Yes to coordinate the national campaign to remove the Eighth Amendment.

2018: TOGETHER FOR YES

For core people working within the Coalition, it became increasingly clear that a successful campaign would require a centrally organised and national coordinated operation to drive forward a clear message and coordinated strategy in a manner similar to how the Marriage Equality campaign had led the 2015 referendum campaign for same-sex marriage. With this in mind, three organisations – the National Women's Council of Ireland (NWCI), the Coalition to Repeal the Eighth Amendment (Coalition) and the Abortion Rights Campaign (ARC) – came together in January 2018 to establish Together for Yes (TfY), a national civil society campaign to remove the Eighth Amendment. The idea was to create a broad and diverse campaign rooted in the experiences of women and their families and focused on achieving laws and services that responded to women's needs and to best medical practice. Collectively, the three organisations had a long record of accomplishment and public profile on the issue, as well as considerable campaigning and mobilisation experience. A determining factor in coming together was that each organisation committed to share human and financial resources, political know-how, organising and research capacity, and considerable grassroots and mobilisation support.[24] The three organisations spent a number of weeks working together to design an effective campaign structure led by three co-directors, one from each organisation: Grainne Griffin (ARC), Orla O'Connor (NWCI) and Ailbhe Smyth (Coalition). The co-directors subsequently asked the Irish

Family Planning Association (IFPA), which was probably the oldest organisation in Ireland campaigning for reproductive rights, to join the Together for Yes executive.

One of the first and most difficult tasks early on for the new campaign was to establish the campaign identity and to agree on a campaign name. Some had reservations about the name 'Together for Yes' and tried to come up with alternatives. 'Yes for Repeal' was a name that had been informally discussed among many different groups for many months, and had the support of many activists, particularly grassroots campaigners, as it connected with the work that they had done over months and years to make the referendum a possibility.[25] However, it was not a name that connected with people outside of pro-choice politics and others felt that this final stage of the campaign needed a new identity that was more inclusive of those who were not active or committed to the issue but still desired change. Together for Yes began to be the name that emerged; not just as a name but also as a concept that could be 'filled' and given meaning by people gathering around the campaign. The campaign also felt that the name could be used to build a broad-based alliance that stood '*for*' rather than 'against' something; it was an inclusive concept, allowing disparate groups and individuals to come together on this single issue.[26] The key decisions for the campaign was the question of focus. This was a referendum campaign where the question being asked was whether or not to remove the Eighth Amendment from the Constitution. It was clear early on to campaigners that this had to be the focus and would be the key to the campaign's success. The key challenge was to convince voters, some of whom would personally be against the idea of abortion, to support removing the constitutional ban on abortion and to allow women to make these decisions for themselves. From this, it followed focusing on the personal stories of women's and couples' own unmediated experiences were central to shifting and re-framing the narrative of abortion. It was this decision that would inform much of the campaign messaging and structure.

As a result, the messaging for Together for Yes focused on access to 'abortion care', rather than on pro-choice or reproductive rights messages. The campaign decided that by framing abortion as 'a healthcare need' and placing it in the context of women's health care more broadly, the referendum campaign could present abortion as a private matter between a woman and her doctor. The decision was influenced by focus-group findings, which showed that this was the framing which resonated best with those who were undecided. Multiple pieces of research confirmed that the electorate trusted just two groups of people to talk about abortion: women who have had an abortion, and doctors.[27] These ideas were then reflected in the poster and campaign slogan: 'Sometimes a private matter needs public support: Vote Yes.' As we will see in Chapter 6, this decision proved to be one of the more disputed aspects of the TfY strategy, particularly among those working and canvassing on the ground. This disquiet was also aired at the 'internal campaign organising day' which involved various groups and activists from around the country. However, despite these reservations, there was a sense among activists that a unified Yes campaign was absolutely necessary if the referendum was to be won, a decision supported by the canvassers who contribute to this book.

As the core campaigning argument of Together for Yes was that abortion was a healthcare issue, one that is fundamentally between a woman and her doctor, this resulted in positioning doctors and other health professionals' front and centre in the campaign. Doctors for Choice was an important advocate for articulation and alliance within the medical profession. It supported doctors to speak clearly about the issues, and to play an active role in the campaign. Individual doctors, including well-known gynaecologists and obstetricians, played a very significant role delivering the campaign messages, as did other healthcare personnel and providers, including the Irish Family Planning Association (IFPA). Again, not all canvassers supported this approach (see Chapter 6), but they were not the target audience. The second core campaign strategy was the use of stories. The Irish philosopher Richard Kearney has noted the importance and normative role of narrative in the development of a national identity. Narratives, he writes, create 'a distinctive sense of cultural self-identification and self-imagining in the guise of narrative voice or viewpoint' and thus serve to 'legitimate or delegitimate the political social and cultural tenure' of a community.[28] Drawing on the experience of Yes Equality during the Marriage Equality referendum campaign, the personal stories of women who had experienced abortion became a linchpin of the campaign's evidence-base, and a key driver of campaign strategy. It was felt that personal stories, rather than theoretical or abstract argument that largely characterised the 1983 referendum campaign, could reach people with their immediacy and authenticity, and were essential to grounding the credibility and integrity of the campaign. This strategy also chimed with the international #MeToo movement which also emerged in 2018 and saw women around the world tell their stories of abuse and harassment by powerful men.

Despite delivering one of the most significant referendum results in Irish history, the Together for Yes Campaign was plagued by external criticism, often disguised as advice from apparently well-meaning journalists who were almost exclusively male. As journalist Una Mullally wrote shortly after the May referendum victory:

> In revisiting much of the analysis that patronised the movement throughout the campaign I can only conclude that many (mostly male) commentators and journalists didn't actually know that much about the history of women's and feminist movements or how they organise, and didn't bother to learn about them.[29]

Mullally's assertion was encapsulated by two leading male political commentators – David Davin Power and Stephen Collins – who were both writing columns for influential daily newspapers. In the run-up to the public vote, Davin Power's 16 March 2018 column declared that the 'Repeal campaign will lose without a leader.' Clearly, he was oblivious to any form of democratic 'leadership' that did not involve a charismatic leading man. His analysis clearly ignored the women, young and old, who were blossoming into leadership roles in every town and community on the island. In a different column written by Stephen Collins immediately after the referendum, Collins demonstrated similar blindness when he credited the Taoiseach Leo Varadkar with masterminding the entire Repeal campaign. This was the same Leo Varadkar who had spent the previous three years shifting between a 'pro-life' and pro-choice perspective, in response to whatever way he considering the political wind was blowing. The fact that these political commentators felt confident in making these assertions despite the fact that TfY was led by three women co-directors, that the campaign director was a woman, that the campaign was powered by women leading in every corner of the country, says everything about the invisibility of women's activism in mainstream politics. These bad-faith criticisms were different to the good-faith post-repeal concerns raised by some radical feminists within the movement, who argued that some voices had been excluded from the campaign. Their observations have been constructively relayed alongside support for uniting as TfY and in the spirit of the continued struggle for reproductive justice that we are all part of and will be explored in the following chapters.

The repeal movement began in the shadow of the pro-choice defeat in 1983, with the X case in 1992 and was re-ignited around the tragic death of Savita Halappanavar. It started with what are sometimes referred to as the 'hard cases', cases involving rape, serious risk to health or cases of fatal foetal abnormality but it also quickly became about the everyday experiences of women who travelled abroad or took the abortion pill, because given their own particular set of circumstances, they simply did not want to be pregnant. For a country which had derived much of its identity from telling stories about women, the Repeal referendum afforded women a unique opportunity to tell their own stories. It energised and empowered generations of women across the country who led an unprecedented and unparalleled campaign for bodily autonomy. Understood in this way, perhaps the result of the referendum should be less surprising that it initially appeared.

The grassroots canvassing has been extraordinary, Dublin North-West has been run with the precision of a well-oiled machine ... If I miss a canvass session, I get sad because I miss the camaraderie and feeling of belonging, of being in this together.

Canvasser (2018)

5

No Quiet Revolution – The Grassroots Gather

Written with help from Paula Dennan from Kerry for Choice, Helen Guinane and Sinéad Redmond from Parents for Choice, Melisa Halpin from Repeal the Eighth Dún Laoghaire, Laura Fitzgerald from ROSA, Emily Wazak from MERJ, Rachel and Ruth from ARC, a spokesperson for Termination for Medical Reasons (TFMR) and testimonies from 304 activists.

In 2016, I interviewed Nicola (a pseudonym) about her job as a community worker. She had been working with a local community development project just around the corner from where she lived for around 25 years. Its ethos was 'to work with people as equal partners in their health so as to facilitate health opportunities for people who would not normally have access because of poverty and disadvantage'. It was mostly women who used the centre. 'We take our lead from the issues affecting their lives,' Nicola explained, 'it's about the collective over the individual and about trying to influence wider social change.' When I asked her to describe her work 'at its best' she answered, 'it's people taking ownership of issues and reaching a point of analysis that allows them to take action on their circumstances or at least understand their circumstances.' 'On a personal basis I am a socialist,' she tells me and elaborates: 'I believe intrinsically that people are equal, but that society fosters inequality through the class system of oppression. In my work I'm drawn to the methodologies of Paulo Freire who challenged the way knowledge is imparted and how hierarchy is created in our society.'

But Nicola was tired and pretty disillusioned. Although this is how she imagined her work and how the organisation outwardly described what they do, it is not what happened in the day-to-day. It used to be. Now they mostly recruited women for healthcare courses and each application involved a huge amount of labour-intensive paperwork. 'It's all about each individual now, getting them through the programme … we are fighting for our survival,' she shared and went on to say 'the whole sector is totally constrained. It is becoming increasingly difficult to challenge inequality on a societal level as we are so restricted by the value for money approach of funders.'[1]

I met Nicola two years after this interview during the 2018 repeal campaign. She was also a canvass leader with her local group. But despite the community group she worked for having a focus on women's health, canvassing was something she kept separate from her work. In fact, she was not allowed to talk about the referendum with the groups she worked with but rather was to remain impartial. When I looked into the reasons why, I learned that some women's community-based education groups had indeed been directed by their state-funded national oversight organisation, the National Collective of Community Based Women's Networks (NCCWN), to adopt a neutral stance, even though they were members of the National Women's Council of Ireland (NWCI). This separation of abortion rights work from the other work of a project was also common practice in other community -sector groups which were not part of the NCCWN. People have put forward different reasons as to why this happened. One justification is that most community groups were registered charities. Commenting on repeal would apparently breach the rules of the Charities Regulator, and they could be sanctioned. There was no guarantee this would happen but there was precedent. In the spring of 2018, the Project Arts Centre were forced to remove a 14-foot-tall red-and-white Repeal mural by the artist Maser on its outer wall, an action the Irish Council for Civil Liberties believe led to high levels of self-censoring within other groups.[2] A second reason is that although technically pro-choice, the NWCI and many of their members didn't pursue progressive, pro-active policies on abortion for many years. Community groups were also uncertain on the use of public funds because of a 1995 Supreme Court 'McKenna Ruling', which precludes their use to advance one side over the other in a referendum. It is also the case that, by 2018, there was a strong sense that the best way to maintain funding was to stay away from politics and keep your head well below the parapet. There was also no guarantee that all community groups were pro-repeal, especially given the close connections with religious groups that some enjoyed, and there was an unspoken reluctance to open what could be a divisive conversation. But for groups like the one Nicola worked for, remaining neutral was a quantum leap from their history of consciousness-raising political activism These once radical organisations that had been part of a feminist movement that responded to reproductive oppressions and the status of women more broadly had slowly and incrementally been absorbed into the neoliberal state agenda, where their core purpose was now individualised service delivery on a shoestring budget.

WE'RE NOT AFRAID TO TALK ABOUT ABORTION

When public opinion on abortion began to shift in 2012, nonprofit women's community-based organisations were thus limited in what they could do and were unable to respond in any meaningful way. Instead, a new layer of autonomous groups would emerge which would be free to decide on their own organisational structure and tactics. The untimely death of Savita Halappanavar was not the only controversy in 2012 that convinced many people that it was time to act. The mood in Ireland at the time was turbulent. People were feeling the pain of Ireland's fifth austerity budget which had been delivered in late 2011, and there was so sign of reprieve.[3] At the same time, high levels of political corruption were being uncovered through an expensive tribunal which was also being paid for by the Irish people.[4] In May, a BBC documentary accused Seán Brady, the most senior Catholic priest in Ireland, of ignoring sex abuse allegations against the pedophile Brendan Smyth that would have saved future victims. That same month, the Justice for Magdelenes group criticised the government for failing to act on the UN Committee Against Torture's condemnation of their role in detaining women and girls in Magdelene Laundries. There was even a referendum. Following an underwhelming campaign, just 50 per cent of the electorate turned out to ratify European fiscal policy measures that many people didn't bother to take the time to understand.

In February 2012, over two hundred people turned up to a public meeting in the Gresham Hotel in Dublin organised by key activists from Action on X and Choice Ireland to mark twenty years since the X Case. The meeting was chaired by Ailbhe Smyth and the speakers were independent TDs Joan Collins and Mick Wallace, journalists

Vincent Browne and Anthea McTierney, Fiona DeLondras, who would become a key activist in Lawyers for Choice, and Goretti Horgan from the Northern Ireland Alliance for Choice. According to long-time activist Alison Spillane, this meeting was different to other initiatives because rather than being reactionary, it was participatory and pro-active.[5] Anti-abortion activists likely smelt a shift in the air and, with funding from overseas, Youth Defence launched their 'Abortion tears her life apart' poster campaign in June 2012, misjudging the national atmosphere and the momentum that was building for a very different sort of Ireland. Their giant-sized, graphic billboard posters angered many, including Cathie Shiels and Sinéad Redmond who created an opposing Facebook page and organised a protest outside the Dail.[6] This was the beginnings of the Abortion Rights Campaign (ARC). The ARC's website explains:

> The seeds of the Abortion Rights Campaign were planted on 10th July 2012, when 40 women and men huddled over tea and biscuits in a cramped room to discuss collaborating on a concerted pro-choice effort. The short-lived Irish Choice Network was created, but it grew so quickly and gained so much momentum that it soon became clear that a proper island-wide movement was needed.[7]

In January 2013, they formally launched as the Abortion Rights Campaign (ARC) and called for a referendum on the Eighth Amendment. Consistently, ARC describe themselves as a volunteer-led, non-hierarchical, grassroots movement that carries the tagline of 'free, safe and legal abortion'. Anna Carnegie and Rachel Roth describe how an important part of their philosophy was always to break down abortion stigma, evident in the deliberate use of the word in their name.[8] Their website was launched in February 2013 and would become an important means of raising awareness and sharing information, as well as a platform for organising a range of events. Their early work focused on calling for action on the X case, including the #ARCaction 10 Days of Action for Choice campaign which was launched in March 2013. It aimed to deliver 30,000 'Greetings from Ireland – Legislate for X' postcards to TDs all around the country. This was one of hundreds of initiatives ARC would coordinate from 2013 to the present day, including karaokes for choice, a weekly MediaWatch, live streaming of film and theatre events, drop-in art workshops, clothes swaps and their popular SpeakOut events. Their biggest and most high-impact action was their Annual March for Choice. Anna and Rachel explain:

> The March for Choice that we organize each year around Safe Abortion Day in September has been called 'the first openly pro-choice activity' in Ireland. In 2012, 2,500 participants marched, and that number grew to a high of 40,000 in 2017. People wore jumpers and T-shirts emblazoned with the word REPEAL and ARC's slogan FREE SAFE LEGAL, creating visibility and fostering a sense of community among people who realized they were not alone.[9]

Another success was their role in supporting up to 32 locally based groups around the country. Rachel explained: 'In the few years before the referendum we put a lot of work into helping regional activists set up ARC groups and ended up with a regional or affiliated group in nearly every county.' ARC used a variety of fundraising initiatives including a successful relationship with the 'Workers Beer Company', a nonprofit organisation that provides volunteers for bar-work at music festivals. This not only raised important funds, it also helped raise the profile of ARC at major music events. By 2016, ARC was the largest and most high-profile organisation in the country and many people see their constant barrage of press releases, letters to politicians, public meetings and events as a significant catalyst in forcing the hand of reluctant politicians. In 2017, they launched their Abortion Rights Roadshow and travelled across Ireland holding information evenings, street stalls, pub quizzes, panel discussions and a whole host of actions organised by their members across the country.

The Abortion Rights Campaign was not the only group to come together in 2012 who would be central to the Irish repeal movement. That same year, a group of women, each of whom had independently travelled overseas to end a pregnancy because of foetal anomaly, accidentally met on an online parenting forum and then decided to meet in person. In April 2012, members of what would become TFMR met with 25 members of the Oireachtas who were at the time exploring how best to respond to the European Court of Human Rights Judgment in *A, B and C v Ireland* which is described in Chapter 4. Three of their members – Ruth Bowie, Jenny McDonald and Arnette Lyons – then appeared on the popular TV programme 'The Late Late Show'. This was a significant moment in the history of the Irish repeal movement. Nobody had previously talked openly about their own abortions. When people did, they usually remained anonymous for fear of a backlash from anti-choice organisations. In the summer of 2012 and now with a name, TFMR organised a formal support group which was attended by 30–40 people. 'Before TFMR there were no supports for women who were dealing with this situation,' their spokesperson told me, 'it was just whoever you happened to meet going to your own maternity hospital, and then wherever you were in touch with when you did travel, so there was no support.' TFMR has always been two organisations managed by the same people. There is TFMR which focuses on campaigning, and LMC bereavement support (formerly Leanbh mo Chroí – 'Baby of my Heart', in English) which offers peer support for anyone affected by fatal or serious foetal anomaly. Their spokesperson explained the bridge between the two organisations:

It is hard to describe how this affects you as a person, going through this experience … When people tell their stories, the journey home is always the most insightful thing. How do you bring your baby's body home? People were talking about getting the ferry so they could bring them back in the boot of their car, people having to wait for ashes to be couriered home to them. We couldn't do anything to change the fact that a baby that you were hoping to have wasn't going to survive, but we could do something about the extra layer of trauma from having to travel.

TFMR have built strong, at times effective, relationships with politicians. At one stage, they met with the Minister for Health James Reilly. Although their meeting appeared to go well, nothing substantive came from it and before long they realised that the Eighth Amendment needed to go. In 2015, they became part of the Coalition to Repeal the Eighth Amendment. Although there were times when TFMR were aware they were being somewhat pushed to the front of the referendum campaign, they believed they could help people 'go the journey', so to speak, in coming around to a wider pro-choice perspective. By hearing their stories, people could then be encouraged to engage with the circumstances of other people's stories who are also experiencing their pregnancy as a crisis. TFMR wanted people to stand in another person's shoes, just for a while, and imagine what they might be going through.

In 2014, Helen Guinane and Sinéad Redmond were part of a group who set up a Facebook page Parents for Choice (P4C) in response to a difficult, even hostile environment for pro-choice mothers and parents of young children. One particular trigger was a sharp and unexpected negative reaction to a photo posted on an online site dedicated to 'baby wearing' that showed a mother and her slinged-baby at that year's March for Choice. This backlash around the same time as the public found out about Ms Y (as discussed in Chapter 4) and the ongoing horror at the death of Savita Halappanavar, was palpable among many parents, especially those who had been through, or would soon be accessing, Ireland's maternity services. It was against these obstacles that P4C pointed out that many people who have abortions are parents. The organisers did not think that this was always made explicit and argued that the typical image conjured up of those opting for abortions was of someone young and single. They also worked to highlight how the Eighth Amendment greatly diminished the choices a person had over their maternity care, where legally they could not exercise full consent over their own body. The organisation's thought processes were always threefold: 1) referendum readiness, 2) challenging abortion stigma in a supportive setting, and 3) peer-to-peer support for people living in a country that held draconian and misogynistic laws. In 2015, a working group was set up, P4C joined the coalition, and they created a website to educate and recruit activists. Parents for Choice had a close working relationship with ARC, with some cross-over membership. They also worked closely with Alliance for Choice and Lawyers for Choice who were always on hand to answer questions.

Parents for Choice created online virtual learning spaces for those still unsure how they felt about access to free, safe, legal abortion – spaces where their volunteers facilitated safe conversations that were difficult to initiate on other parenting fora. They also worked to change the narrative on other parenting sites and to encourage people to take a look at the Parents for Choice website. This was emotionally draining work, but the discussions were worthwhile and strategically important. Their online presence also substituted for the near-impossibility of going to meetings that often weren't particularly parent friendly. Parents for Choice did a lot of grassroots work. Helen and Sinéad explain:

> The working group were part of and spoke at numerous protests, demos, actions and marches. In a week in May 2017 … we held coffee mornings countrywide, in venues including: Gorey, Ennis, Scariff, Meath, West Limerick, Finglas, Dunboyne, Dublin 6/6w Tramore, Dublin SW, Dublin 8 and 10, Wicklow and many more. These were held in people's homes or local child-friendly venues depending on what best suited the area and local host.

When they asked members how they felt about being involved, they recalled how P4C armed them with the self-assurance, information and language they needed, safe in the knowledge that P4C would support them. One member explained:

> P4C gave me the confidence to share my family's experiences with the Eighth Amendment during our three miscarriages and two high-risk pregnancies. It was a safe space to discuss the referendum and to educate and equip myself with the facts so I could properly advocate for a yes vote when talking to friends and family.

The group encouraged people not just to become pro-choice, but also to become abortion rights activists themselves. Another member clarified:

> I was a 'yes, but' when I joined P4C, with the information and respectful discussion in the group I turned to 'yes, no limits'. Not only did the group highlight my own prejudice, but also how much internalised misogyny I had. There's a lot of unpacking still to do, but P4C kick-started a new, more compassionate me.

The group also actively supported those seeking abortions, even though this was illegal and could have resulted in prison sentences. Helen and Sinéad explain:

> Another function of the group was the private support given to people experiencing crisis pregnancies. There were often threads

from these people – sometimes anonymously, sometimes not – and the then illegal option of using the abortion pill would be freely discussed and often other members would share their own experiences of using it. Members in the North even on occasion gave their addresses to members in the South in need. At one particular time, there was a complete customs clampdown, both North and South, with no pills from Women Help or Women on Web getting in. A group member born outside Ireland, whose retired mother had been a gynaecological nurse and was visiting soon, arranged with her mother and a very small number of other group members to have a number of prescriptions for the abortion pill filled in her mother's country of origin through her mother's old boss, which her mother then brought through the airport on her visit to her daughter. These pills were stored in a small number of member's houses around the country and distributed to people needing abortions.

Everything they did was family friendly and accessible. Children were always welcome at events, protests, or meetings and working-group members regularly gave presentations and talks with babies strapped on and toddlers at their feet. They organised a family-friendly bloc at every Annual March for Choice, post-march picnics in Merrion Square and booked venues in child-friendly pubs near the march finish. In 2017, and with children in slings, P4C presented at the Citizens' Assembly.

LOCAL GROUPS EMERGE ACROSS IRELAND

It is difficult to know just how many local groups emerged between 2012 and 2018. Some activists who started grassroots groups anonymously described their motivations to me. For example, 'There was no local group ... I have been harmed by this amendment and want it desperately repealed so I thought getting a group off the ground and door-knocking would be the way to go.' There are other instances too. 'There was no representation in Laois before I started Laois for Choice/Yes', one woman shared. In the South-East, we hear a similar story: 'two years ago, a friend with similar leanings approached me to start Rise & Repeal Waterford, and it went on from there.' Another example: 'I was involved with the student union in college, setting up an equality society. I found myself back living in my hometown, unemployed, and was seeing pro-repeal groups beginning to rise up, so I decided to start one in Westmeath.'

Some would go on to be part of the 32 regional groups that would form part of ARC and Kerry for Choice is one such example. In early 2016, the same year that Fine Gael's Programme for Partnership sought political agreement for the Citizens' Assembly, Paula Dennan organised a pro-choice meeting in a pub in Tralee, the largest town in the picturesque county of Kerry. This pub was to become the base for Kerry for Choice, a group that would meet regularly and provide a friendly space for women and men to come together and chat with other like-minded people. Together, they built a new community that became important for those involved. Almost immediately after forming, Kerry for Choice emailed ARC, the national pro-choice organisation they knew the most about, and asked for support. Kerry for Choice were glad to have the backing of a national organisation as they had tough work to do, both in terms of securing a referendum and then in canvassing for a yes vote. They knew they would be stronger with others, and ARC gave them a protective shield that made the more public-facing aspects a bit easier to handle. In other words, some of their members were worried about the hostile tactics of Kerry-based anti-repeal campaigners. Given the expanse of Kerry as a county, getting everyone in the same room was a tricky task. For this reason, Facebook became an important space for people to stay connected, even if they could not physically get to events. As membership grew, and people got to know each other, the Facebook site became a place of general solidarity and chat. However, its limitations were felt in terms of its capacity to stifle more visceral discussion, and its potential to exclude people who, for a variety of reasons, were not entirely comfortable with the online world. A few months after their inaugural meeting and with the support of ARC, Kerry for Choice held their first information stalls. At first, they focused on Tralee, Killarney and Dingle. As the group grew in numbers, they expanded to more towns and villages across the county. Initially, these stalls happened monthly, but as the campaign gained momentum and the prospect of a referendum increased, the stalls became twice-monthly and eventually weekly events.

From the beginning, Kerry for Choice knew that they needed to start as many conversations as possible about why the Eighth Amendment needed to be repealed, not just at their now-regular information stalls, but also via public meetings and letters to local newspapers. These combined tactics ensured politicians and the wider public saw that abortion rights could not be dismissed as a Dublin-only campaign. Their focus was squarely on the fact that at least one woman every week was leaving Kerry to have an abortion. When a referendum was called, Kerry for Choice knew the conversations they had been having over the previous few years would now switch to people's doorsteps. Once Together for Yes was launched, Kerry for Choice became Kerry Together for Yes and had multiple canvassing teams out every night. They also had daily information stalls, including some in towns and villages where they had not had a presence before, as new volunteers wanted increased visibility within the areas where they lived. This was most striking when, in April 2018, complete with a homemade banner, two women set up a stall for the first time in Cahersiveen, a town with a population of just over a thousand people.

Kerry for Choice is just one example of many groups that cropped up around the country, including Pro-Choice Galway, Rebels4Choice, Clare ARC, Pro-Choice Wexford, Tipp for Choice and Laois for Choice, to name just a few. These groups organised regular coffee mornings, public meetings, active online awareness-raising work, local demonstrations and high-impact stunts. In 2017, Tipp for Choice organised an #uncomfortableaboutthe8th campaign in response to a statement by the Tánaiste Simon Coveney that he was 'uncomfortable' about extending abortion rights. The Tipp for Choice campaign called on people to 'love bomb' Coveney with hand-embroidered cushions with messages calling on his government to repeal the Eighth. Other times, giant repeal banners were unfurled in prominent places such as the Spanish Arch in Galway (in March 2017) and the Rock of Cashel in Tipperary (October 2017). In early 2018, Anne Phelan of Phibsboro Dublin knitted a banner of repeal with Maser's iconic image which was displayed in a number of outdoor venues.

Many of these grassroots groups organised and participated in a range of direct actions that were wider than the singular issue of abortion. In 2017, there were demonstrations against church involvement in maternity services, which were organised in collaboration with the NWCI. There was also significant support for LGBTQI+ rights. In Carlow and in Dublin-West, there was a local campaign against the closure of respite beds for victims of gender-based violence. In the Mid-west, the Limerick Feminist Network which was a key organiser of pro-repeal activism, ran the 'Good Night Out in Limerick Campaign' in 2014. This was part of a wider global movement to end street harassment in pubs, clubs and city streets. In 2016, the same network organised the 'Morning After Pill' campaign which logged and published the best pharmacies from which someone could get emergency contraception.

A number of pro-repeal political activists from across independents and political parties, including Solidarity-People before Profit, the Green Party, Sinn Fein and Social Democrats, were each active in forming broad-based local groups in their local constituencies. This often began with a small open meeting amongst cross-party political activists and supporters from which a local coalition would be formed. These then commonly joined the Coalition. One of the largest groups was in Dublin Bay North, which had around 440 members and regular attendance at meetings of 40–60 people.[10] Another such group was Repeal the Eighth Dún Laoghaire, which began when Melisa Halpin, a Dún Laoghaire-Rathdown local councillor with People before Profit organised a public meeting in her constituency in 2015 on the theme of repealing the Eighth Amendment. Her impetus was the same year's successful Marriage Equality campaign. Reflective of a time when a pro-choice agenda was less talked about, attendance was small. Those who did show up were unperturbed and agreed to stay in touch to support that year's March for Choice. One year later, in September 2016, they held another public meeting and established themselves as Repeal the Eighth Dún Laoghaire. They joined the Coalition to Repeal the Eighth and organised a fundraiser to buy their own banner. A small group proudly walked behind the banner at the next March for Choice. In September 2017, more than a hundred people turned up for another public meeting, with a range of campaigners and speakers, including Ailbhe Smyth, the executive Director of Amnesty Ireland Colm O'Gorman, a speaker from the Union of Students in Ireland (USI), a representative from Trade Unionists for Choice, and Philomena Canning, a well-known home-birth activist and chair of Midwives for Choice. Local politicians from People Before Profit, the Labour Party, the Green Party and the Social Democrats all attended.

The larger group that emerged from this meeting continued campaigning. They handed out fliers for that year's March for Choice at a Sunday Farmers' Market, on commuter trains and at shopping centres across the constituency. At that stage, they had twenty or so regular activists, many of whom were campaigning for the first time. They also held a hugely successful Culture Night for Repeal which raised nearly €1,000. In late 2017, the group agreed to regularise their meetings for the first Saturday of each month, and to start canvassing in anticipation of a referendum. Their first canvass in January had just eight people. By May, and now re-branded Dún Laoghaire Together for Yes, this number had swelled to 30–40 people on each canvass with upwards of 80 people turning up at high-visibility events. Once again, Facebook played a major role, keeping them in touch with other groups and with Together for Yes's head office and helping them extend their reach laterally and link with groups outside of the Dublin area. Despite having campaigned on many social justice issues over the last two decades, Melisa believes the movement around campaigning for choice was the most phenomenal grassroots movement she has ever seen as, week after week in the first months of 2018, hundreds of mostly women became politically active, with many taking up leadership roles.

PRO-REPEAL AND ANTI-CAPITALIST – THE CREATION OF ROSA AND MERJ

In the spring of 2013 and on International Women's Day, ROSA (for Reproductive Rights against Oppression, Sexism and Austerity) was launched by a group within the Socialist Party. This was largely in response to the shift in public mood in 2012, including the reaction to the death of Savita Halappanavar. The group was not trying to replace the movement for repeal that was gathering pace, a movement of which they saw themselves as very much a part. But they did want to inject a political dimension into the national debate. Although they greatly admired the long-standing work of many feminists who had flown the flag for abortion rights for decades, they wanted to build a movement that was pro-choice and feminist, but also consciously anti-capitalist. These socialists had no faith in the Irish political system or, as co-founder Laura Fitzgerald puts it 'the conservatism of the establishment and the rubbish X-legislation they brought in, it was completely out of step with the change that people desired from below.' ROSA wanted to look concretely at how they could put pressure on the government to advance a much more radical repeal agenda and they didn't accept the narrative that many people needed convincing or needed to be managed delicately. Laura explains:

> It was our view that actually there was a big radicalisation amongst young people, of young women and young LGBTQ+ people in particular. And that there was a real openness to a left-wing, anti-capitalist, feminist analysis and an openness to a socialist feminism because it was a time of extreme economic crisis for capitalism, leading to huge austerity, massive inequality and injustice. The proliferation of absolutely obscene wealth and equality, etc. We wanted to bring that into the broader movement if you like.

ROSA's plan was to fully support a referendum on the Eighth but to also inject some political debate because they believed 'that on the actual issue of abortion itself, some of the long-standing campaigners were also kind of conservative.' For them, the focus on X-case legislation was a tactical error which fuelled the right-to-life/right-to-choose binary and was devoid of political analysis. ROSA were confident that the government would concede on a referendum but didn't trust them to bring in proper legislation to make abortion truly accessible. ROSA wanted to argue on women's health and women's lives more broadly. As working-class women, they were the ones that suffered the most from the reality of the Catholic Church's influences on public services. ROSA were building for a yes, but they wanted a left-wing yes. As Laura puts it:

> We are in a changing Ireland and we are interested in making it a progressive, equal place. And this movement has to seamlessly go on to fight against homelessness, poverty, inequality and for public housing, we are very firm on our excoriation of the political establishment, of conservativism. We want to build a movement on gender violence, we want to explicitly build an anti-capitalist and socialist-feminist movement. ROSA was organised on that basis. We are building a movement built on struggle not on lobbying. This is what made us different to other single-issue groups.

Where much national debate was about the need to travel overseas, ROSA focused on the abortion pill. Abortion was already happening in Ireland, and they wanted to bust myths and misogynistic tropes about late abortions. They reached out to Rebecca Gomperts of Women on Web, an international charity that organises contraception and safe abortion in countries where these are denied. Laura tells me:

> And Rebecca immediately understood and saw the power of this, she wanted to do it because she said it would increase awareness about the pills, etc. on the island of Ireland … But also she said, she saw that Ireland was a place where a breakthrough could be made, she shared our goal that if we campaign and we fight and we struggle we can win a victory that could provoke and encourage struggles in other countries.

Since their creation, ROSA have adopted very particular tactics, such as a high-profile street presence using street stalls, mostly in Dublin city centre, and media-grabbing events. In 2014, they recreated the 1971 'contraception train' taking 'the abortion train' to collect pills from Northern Ireland. Just like their predecessors, activists were greeted by the media and other coalition partners when they arrived back in Dublin's Connolly Station. In full view of the cameras, some activists theatrically ingested pills once they disembarked, a stunt that caught the attention of the US Senator Bernie Sanders who shared the images on his Facebook page. In 2015, their much-publicised Abortion Pill Bus with Women on Web travelled to Galway, Limerick and Cork, offering private consultations and breaking the law by giving out medication. Laura sets the scene:

> And they came onto the bus. People often in really desperate situations. This bus coming to their city or their town was for them a lifeline. And we openly broke the law. And yet we got absolutely no state intervention whatsoever. We often laughed and joked about the fact that the first time we did the abortion pill bus, the Gardaí were there and they actually got us to move. And it was really awkward, because from a traffic-calming point of view, we couldn't park in Eyre Square at the time, stupid idea, I don't know what we were thinking. They moved us on to park somewhere else outside a

church. And we were like 'oh god that looks terrible, we don't want to insult anyone's religion we were sitting outside a Catholic church, asking people to come onboard to see if they want to access abortion pills.'

ROSA was stronger in Dublin, but it did (and still does) have branches in Cork, Galway, Limerick and Belfast. It has many members who don't identify as socialist but who are interested in exploring anti-capitalist ideas and radical alternatives to the way things are.

Another expressly anti-capitalist group that formed part of the Coalition to Repeal the Eighth Amendment were Migrants and Ethnic Minorities for Reproductive Justice (MERJ). Their co-founder Emily Wazak explains:

MERJ came about because we were basically tired of always being the only two people of colour in the room. At any meeting, and being talked over the whole time or being told that we don't understand ... I gave years of my life to it thinking like, okay, you know, maybe someday, like the intersectionality, that they claim will happen. Then I thought, you know, what, like, actually, I'm tired of always being silent, and my skills or my value or whatever questioned, and my politics questioned for this sort of informal power, that was just reproducing itself.

MERJ is an anti-racist, abolition-focused, grassroots collective that works on a range of issues in response to reproductive injustices in Ireland. It was founded in 2017 by a group of women who were also migrants and who, as the quote above reveals, were not satisfied with the repeal movement's singular focus. They wanted to advocate a clear and conscious reproductive justice framework and create a paradigm shift similar to that which had happened in the US. Its founders had been active in the repeal movement before 2017 and had worked hard to infuse a reproductive justice approach. Emily explains:

That was one of the main criticisms I had of ARC and the other main groups. It was a single-issue group. To be honest, people didn't really use the term 'reproductive justice', it was more about reproductive rights. I almost never heard anyone use the term 'reproductive justice'. I did suggest that Anti-racism Network start using that framework and through that MERJ evolved. I've always been from a reproductive justice background. So that's why I was a little surprised that people pushed back against it when I brought it up originally. There were strategic reasons cited, which is fine.

Ultimately it made more sense tactically to be a smaller voice on the outside so that MERJ members could work in a way that was more meaningful to them. They were tired of people doing things *for* the migrant community. Migrant rights groups are capable of exercising autonomy and political sophistication in their own right. They also believed that the binary 'pro-choice' versus 'pro-life' paradigm was more damaging for many migrants, women of colour, people with disabilities and other groups who were being left out of the debate.

As Sarah Bodelsson puts it 'MERJ collaborated with organisations and groups in the reproductive rights movement to ensure migrants and ethnic minorities were heard and seen on panels, in Coalition meetings, and during public debates.'[11] However, being part of the coalition wasn't always positive. One of their co-founders explained their regular meetings:

> These were just a waste of time. We decided that our job was too big. We could not waste our time fighting for these things when they were not listening to us. Every single meeting was a battle, and it was a racist battle. It was literally us, as the only people of colour in the room, as the only migrants, in the room having to fight for every little fucking thing, like, you know, like language on the website or to use Savita. Basically, we said that if you want to use Savita then you have to be talking about migrants.

MERJ ran inclusivity training for other pro-choice groups. They also ensured representation for Irish Travellers and the activist (and now Senator) Eileen Ní Fhloinn shared a platform at one of their pre-referendum workshops. Ní Fhloinn spoke first-hand of how hard it can be for Traveller women to be openly pro-choice for fear of a backlash in an environment where the Catholic Church is held in high esteem: 'Abortion is seen as dirty in my community, it doesn't happen, we don't talk about sex, periods, women are very put down in my community, we are oppressed more because of our cultural barriers ... So within the Traveller community we have never really spoken about abortion.' Ní Fhloinn also illuminated significant barriers Traveller women face, including low levels of trust in the medical profession, care commitments and no money to travel. Historically, these conditions have forced many Traveller women to carry unwanted pregnancies to term. MERJ believed Traveller women also were being left out of the referendum campaign. As Ní Fhloinn puts it:

> What we are looking for is a legislation that will benefit all women, but I am afraid when we pass the referendum on the 25th, women from ethnic minority groups won't have the same access to abortion as women from middle-class areas ... Who is going to support us? Is it going to be free for everybody? Is everybody going to have the same access ... And at the moment I've learned a lot about history ... and I'm looking and thinking 'Where is the history of the women from ethnic minorities, we're not even in the history books.'[12]

THE CREATIVITY OF REPEAL

Those platformed in this chapter, and the work that they do, are just a sample of a nationwide grassroots movement that emerged at a time when local women's groups that had grown from second-wave feminism were no longer a politicising force. Many artists and journalists also played a leading role in making sure that the Irish public were constantly reminded of the continuous flow of people travelling to the UK or Europe, or buying pills online. To give some examples, in 2014 during a glitzy charity event in London, the direct-action feminist performance group Speaking of IMELDA[13] 'knicker-bombed' Enda Kenny, the then Taoiseach. Somehow, they managed to get a pair of knickers with the words 'Repeal the 8th' onto Kenny's plate. Their #knickersforchoice campaign then invited other people to write pro-repeal slogans on their own undergarments and hang these pants in prominent places. The following year, Cecily Brennan, Alice Maher, Eithne Jordan and Paula Meehan set up the Artists' Campaign to Repeal the Eighth Amendment. They appealed to fellow artists, writers, musicians and actors to sign a statement calling for repeal and encouraged artistic expression as a means to bring about change.

There were multiple high-impact interventions that created a constant flow of highly visible street art, poetry, photography, banners and street theatre. A full survey of the contributions of the arts is beyond the scope of this book. In 2018, Una Mullally curated just some of the art, literature, design, poetry, stories and journalistic writings in a crowdfunded edited publication *Repeal the 8th*. In its introduction, she writes:

> The acts of expression related to our restrictive abortion laws at this time take many forms. They are murals on walls and ideas for poems; they are essays and personal stories; they are screenplays and short stories; they are textile designs and photography; they are graphic design and things that we need to get off our chest. The collection of work is free-flowing, and purposefully chooses a thematic narrative of a linear one. The movement itself is both personal and collective, political and social, and we discuss it with humour and with tears, anger and mediation. It is both abstract and concrete.[14]

There was also an educational dimension to the repeal movement. From the outset ARC organised participatory, consciousness-raising education for its members and supporters. In an interview for the 2021 podcast *How the Yes was Won* (written and directed by Deirdre Kelly and Aisling Dolan) Sarah Monaghan describes the work:

> We travelled around Ireland, and we used a model that was from the International Pregnancy Advisory Service as well as an American Organisation called Catholics for Choice. We adapted this values-clarification training, and it was essentially about examining your own values, examining your own biases and examining your own stigma and the whole idea of it was, as activists to get you in a room and to be honest about the things that make you uncomfortable about abortion.[15]

In 2014, ARC began work on education programmes that were designed to widen conversations beyond the converted. ARC consulted with a range of groups more peripheral to the movement including the Pavee Point Traveller and Roma Centre, student groups and local women's groups. The hope was to partner with these organisations in creating safe, politicising, non-judgemental spaces that would counter abstract moral arguments and re-position reproductive health within the context of structural inequality.[16] These weren't the only such programmes on the island – similar work was done by the Alliance for Choice in Northern Ireland. Emma Campbell described these 6-week courses:

> These were delivered through women's community education centres. We didn't just go straight in and talk about abortion; rather we started from the birth of the women's movement and really the whole course was about feminism and rights. And we shared these materials with other pro-choice groups.

There were local examples too. Galway Pro-Choice facilitated education relating to self-managed abortions and abortion pill training. One member even travelled to Alabama in the US to discuss what the attendee described to me as 'the parallels between our struggles for repro justice'. With support from allies in the US and UK, Galway Pro-Choice members taught themselves how to be clinic escorts and abortion doulas and they also ran workshops on de-stigmatising and de-mystifying abortion. Limerick Feminist Network also undertook consciousness-raising work and open dialogue that created inclusive safe spaces for feminists to express themselves, share experiences and explore what feminism and equality means to them. Members of Parents for Choice also reported positives from the education workshops they took part in. One member told me:

> This group educated me and helped me to articulate my thoughts but more importantly it showed me that ordinary people with busy lives were out there trying to change the world and that I could be part of that too. This energised me to join my local Together for Yes group and to start conversations with those around me and even to wear the badges and merch. This group made me brave.

There were other high-impact interventions too. In 2014, Janet Ní Shuilleabháin used her time as curator of the twitter handle @Ireland to share her own story of travelling for an abortion. Across 107 tweets, she detailed how she had no option but to lie about her reasons for going; a trip that was her first time on an aeroplane. She talked about spotting and then bonding with other women journeying for the same reason, about recovering far from home, and about her work as an activist since.[17] In 2015, the comedian and writer Tara Flynn publicly told her story of abortion as part of Amnesty International's 'My Body, My Rights' event. The *Irish Times* journalist Roisin Ingle also shared her story. Both women helped challenge stigma about a decision neither woman regretted nor were ashamed of. In 2016, ARC linked their annual March for Choice to national centenary celebrations of the Easter Rising by theming it 'Rise and Repeal'. They organised a week of events that brought people together in art workshops and writing spaces and used an old press to replicate a 1916 newspaper containing opinion pieces, poetry and art. That same year, the 'Sydney Rose', Brianna Parkins, a competitor in Ireland's outdated televised Rose of Tralee beauty pageant surprised the host when, live on air, she publicly called for a referendum on repeal and received rapturous applause. There were constant commentary pieces in newspapers including by Kitty Holland, Una Mullally, Shona Murray, Fintan O'Toole, Colette Browne, Justine McCarthy and others too many to mention. Historical slogans such as 'Get your rosaries off my ovaries' and 'My body – my choice' were supplemented with direct calls to the Fine Gael government to call a referendum to abolish the Eighth.

When the referendum was eventually called, this was the flexible, adaptable, alternative system that joined forces in 2018. Groups did not lose their identity – in fact, many continued to run parallel campaigns and organise high-visibility stunts. But they did rebrand and undertook to use literature designed by a Together for Yes communications team. By handing over this control, these groups exercised significant trust around decisions on who would speak for the campaign, what the posters would say and what the general strategy would be. The next chapter focuses on this aspect of the union, with a particular emphasis on the messaging of Together for Yes and how this connected, or not, with the flamboyance of what came before it.

Where do I begin? Weak media campaign, weak poster campaign the leaflets were all terrible, with the exception of the third one. it was okay. Spokespersons are not hard enough. This campaign is not nice – we are constantly on the defence having awful arguments put to us and we have to sit there and be respectful and defend. I am very concerned we will lose. I am not happy at the TfY approach and I hope it does not cost us dearly.

Canvasser (2018)

6

The Together for Yes Campaign

This chapter draws from findings from an online anonymous question-naire circulated in the ten-day period before the referendum. It also at times draws from some one-to-one interviews carried out in the after-math. These findings will be signposted as such.

By the spring of 2018, there was no escaping the ubiquity of Together for Yes (TfY). Most towns and cities had some sort of local gathering and the national campaign was in full swing. There were high-profile endorsements from superstars such as Saoirse Ronan, Hozier, Cillian Murphy and Sinéad Cusack. There was even an international dimension to the campaign with famous faces such as P!nk, Emma Thompson, Russell Crowe, Mark Hamill and Courtney Cox all appealing to the Irish public to vote for repeal. By mid-May, every lamppost was plastered with campaign merchandise and just about every car seemed to be decorated with mostly 'Together for Yes' bumper stickers, but also 'Love Both' logos.

All manner of assemblages mushroomed as Ireland moved closer to the referendum date. Estimates suggest there were nearly a hundred professional or identity groups including the long-standing and influential Doctors Together for Yes, originally Doctors for Choice, which had been convened by Julie Kay in 2001 who was working with the Irish Family Planning Association (IFPA) at the time,[1] and Lawyers Together for Yes, originally Lawyers for Choice, whose members include Mairead Enright, Fiona De Londras, Ruth Fletcher and Vicky Conway. By 2018, there were Farmers Together for Yes, Catholics Together for Yes and even Dogs Together for Yes! The once sought-after black-and-white REPEAL sweater designed by Anna Cosgrave was now being mass produced in a range of colours and was worn by repealers young and old. Together for Yes had their own attire too, as did ARC. The topic dominated the country's radio, television and social media outlets. It was everywhere.

Estimates suggest there was anything up to 20,000 people dressed in yellow high-viz vests emblazoned with the Together for Yes logo, who were knocking on people's doors the length and breadth of Ireland. Based on my own research, two-thirds had been active for some time, the rest signed up when TfY was created. One Leitrim woman captured the mood when she wrote, 'I think the Eighth will be repealed, but as a canvasser, I feel even if it isn't we are changing the landscape one house at a time, abolishing shame.' As pro-repeal activists pounded the pavement night after night, it cannot be overstated just how significant the movement was in people's lives. To illustrate, this young canvasser told me 'It has been life changing, focussing my rage, distress and anxiety into positive, effective action. This is the beginning of something great for me and for the country.' Another said, 'I've loved it, loved the people I've met and the experiences good and bad have added to my life experience as a young woman in Ireland but if we had to start all this again in the morning, I don't think I could mentally and physically! Jesus, I hope it's repealed.'

Pro-repeal supporters were not the only people canvassing. There were also activists from Save the 8th who wore red, and Love Both who donned luminous pink fatigues. They too had their own branding. Their leaflets and posters promoted a central message that abortion stops a beating heart and is morally wrong regardless of the circumstances. For many Together for Yes activists, it was hard to ignore a misalignment with their own views on abortion and the content and tone of the fliers they were pushing through people's doors that almost exclusively focused on an individual, very private decision, made with the support of a trusting doctor. There was another problem too. The feminists who had led repeal and who consistently asserted the movement's grassroots nature were, by April 2018, almost invisible on the national stage. Instead, it was politicians and doctors addressing the general public. Some of these allies meant well, but they were not always able to tackle nuanced debates put forward by those against repeal and they often didn't hold even a basic social analysis.

Chapter 1 explained how 95 per cent agreed that uniting as Together for Yes was the right decision, while as many as 77 per cent strongly agreed. The most common reason given was that uniting led to the creation of a singular voice. A perfect example comes from this Midwives for Choice activist who described it as a 'genius idea, as we are all on the side for repeal, the issue is much bigger than any of us or any political agenda.' This did not mean people agreed with each constituent part of the campaign, but they understood the rationale of a collective approach; for instance, one participant remarked, 'Pragmatic decision, not aligned with all of my own personal values but nevertheless near enough to allow certain personal tenets to be parked while campaigning.' This sort of comment was echoed many times.

One of the most important elements for some activists was the capacity to keep their own name and identity whilst at the same time be part of something bigger. Together for Yes never sought to stifle this. As Ailbhe Smyth confirms:

> Together for Yes did actually function as one organisation. And we worked hard to make that very clear in what we were doing. What we didn't try to do was to stop or prevent what we couldn't stop or prevent. I mean, why would we prevent people from putting up posters ... People worried that they were going to lose their identities and it took a lot of persuading of people that you are not going to lose your identity whether you are the National Women's Council or a political party.

Central to the Coalition, which was now effectively Together for Yes, was a desire for groups to row in behind the campaign strategy of the three Cs of Care, Compassion and Change. Chapter 4 explored how this message and tone was decided upon, following focus groups that were facilitated by the advertising agency Language. This research had determined that the scars of previous referenda remained and as a result, Irish people did not talk much about abortions. When they did, many believed there should be limits put on access to abortion, preferring an approach that was 'caring and humane' and that involved doctors. People were okay to acknowledge a growing foetus, but they also held onto some myths, for instance, that there might be a rush on abortions if women no longer had to travel.[2] Research undertaken by Red C on behalf of Amnesty in 2016 also concluded that the most trusted sources of information were healthcare professionals and women who have had abortions.

The ultimate decision to run with this medicalised message and branding was made quickly and without the usual levels of consultation characteristic of the movement. This was in part because of a very real time constraint, as the period between the government calling a referendum and polling day itself was just four months. When I surveyed canvassers in the ten-day run up to the referendum, some activists were unhappy that there had not been more consultation before Coalition leaders unveiled the research findings along with the branding of TfY. This was at a meeting in the Teachers Club in Parnell Square, Dublin. A few activists talked about this meeting, with one person describing it as 'tense'. Others were unhappy that, as this person puts it 'the decision was made behind closed doors.' After the referendum, others shared memories of the event. One trade unionist believed that there was too much focus on research data and 'a refusal to take much heed of the experiences of those of us who were on the street, canvassing style, campaigning and therefore had a great sense of how ordinary people felt about abortion.' She continued:

> Despite the opinion polls for [the] marriage referendum being so good, the Yes campaign ran focus groups which, for me, indicated some conservatism and doubts people had. Leaders of the Yes campaign thought these [conservative ideas] were reflected in the actual result of that referendum, i.e., a lower majority than some of the polls. I think the exact opposite. Lessons should have been learned and the refusal of the Yes campaign to tackle some of the most outrageous claims and implications of the No campaign undercut their potential support.

One of the most efficient ways the campaign message was disseminated to the grassroots was through canvass training, which 53 per cent of activists attended. Some people hadn't the time (26 per cent), some didn't know about canvass training (14 per cent). The rest (7 per cent) didn't feel they needed it; for example, one person said, 'I am not sure about the value of the long training session, pairing experienced and non-experienced people together plus real on-the-door situations is the best training. Trust people.' Training was mostly one-off participatory workshops held in pubs, community centres, or anywhere else willing to offer space. ARC, Parents for Choice and some local repeal groups such as Galway Pro-Choice were already delivering canvass training, as were some political parties. Sometimes these rebranded as TfY, other times groups kept their own identity. For example, this Monaghan activist shared, 'we organised for ROSA to come and deliver a canvass workshop which not only provided us with brilliant training but effectively gave people the chance to sign up to volunteer and become more heavily involved in the local campaign.' Most people hugely appreciated the opportunity to role-play difficult conversations and to share their anxieties about canvassing. One woman describes a session in the upstairs of a Dublin pub as something that 'really helped to shake off the apprehension I had about the idea of going door to door'.

Geographically, the central hub of TfY was on Upper Mount Street, Dublin 2. This premises became known as 'HQ' and acted as the focal point for much decision making. But for canvassers, the heart of the movement was not HQ but their own local community. Usually (though not always), each electoral area had one TfY group made up of an array of political parties, pro-choice groups and the thousands of people who joined for the first time.[3] Typically, each constituency appointed a regional coordinator and a group of canvass organisers. One-quarter of the activists in this study were local organisers, 7 per cent were regional organisers and there was one national organiser. The majority (70 per cent) did not hold a leadership role.

Numbers varied across the country. A first-time canvasser in Dublin who is a member of the Social Democrats described the most challenging aspect of canvassing as 'too many canvassers on canvasses!' Compare this to rural Wicklow where this ARC member described the most challenging aspect as 'the lack of people being able to get out and support ... we heavily rely on the same people to canvass vast areas in our rural towns and outskirts.' In Monaghan, 'Not enough volunteers, we literally had three regular canvassers to cover a very, very large area.' And in Wexford, 'Being in a very conservative area means people were afraid to come forward to volunteer.' These and other rural-based canvassers also described a long-established culture where people not only did not volunteer but were less inclined to talk about how they would vote. One Galway activist noted, 'I feel people were afraid to show if they were supporting yes in a conservative area.' In Mayo, 'Canvassing in a conservative county is hard, people are unwilling to tell you how they'll vote, very narrow-minded thinkers, very religious.' These concerns were echoed by others and did not exist in a vacuum. Historically, there was a pattern of more conservative voting in rural Ireland, such as in two divorce referendums (1986 and 1996), and in the referendum that inserted the Eighth Amendment (1983). This pattern was disrupted in the Yes Equality campaign. Nevertheless, people were worried that the pendulum could swing back on an issue some believed was more contentious than same-sex marriage. Newspapers were also reporting division along an urban/rural divide. In May 2018, the British *Guardian* newspaper ran with a headline 'Abortion question divides rural Ireland as referendum looms', which claimed the balance of power resided in rural areas where people were unwilling to disclose their voting intentions.[4]

Some canvassers outside of cities and large towns definitely had their work cut out for them. One Offaly-based canvasser who describes their community as 'No-side heart land' reported that TfY posters were frequently removed from lampposts. She also talked about 'intimidation by local No campaigners'. Another rural-based canvasser reported 'bad encounters with irate people on the doors' and, from someone else, the challenges of 'maintaining a positive frame of mind when confronted with fundamentalist Catholic individuals on the doorstep'. Many people found it frustrating and disheartening that a lot of people didn't answer their doors. There were challenges in cities too, and it is important to remember things were different before May 2018. Even in the months before the vote, a lot of people did not talk about abortion. It was difficult to get venues for public meetings or when vendors did agree, they often cancelled once events were advertised because of complaints from anti-repeal activists.

Overall though, a much greater number of canvassers reported a more positive experience, so much so that some activists questioned if there was in fact a sizable majority to sway to the repeal side. Many (21 per cent) felt the high level of support from the general public was the most rewarding aspect of being involved. To give some examples, this Kildare activist wrote 'people door-to-door are every bit as passionate about removing the 8th as we are.' In Dublin, 'The amazing responses we get ... people answering their doors saying, "don't waste your time, we're voting yes all the way, go talk to those who need convincing."' This final response from a canvasser in Leitrim is the last of many I could have chosen:

It is actually always amazing, totally rewarding ... feels like we are doing a civic duty calling to people, talking to them, allowing some women to speak about things they have gone through and have kept silent, who look like they want to hug us, the love we get, it feels like such vital important work.

When members of the public had not quite grasped the reasons why a Yes vote made sense, many canvassers found that it was easy enough to, as this activist puts it 'turn a soft No into a Yes'. In fact, 22 per cent of activists said, 'swaying a YES vote' was the most rewarding part of canvassing.

The high intensity of the pre-repeal period was demanding, and many people prioritised it over pretty much everything else to the detriment of their personal relationships and their health. 'It's been an absolute priority; other things have suffered rather than my involvement', this Labour Party member explains. Another said, 'I have neglected work, studies, children and pets.' There were many comments that revealed a similar impact on their lives. Moreover, many people struggled to process what was going on around them: For example, 'I am crying all the time – at video testimonies, after the canvass, at posts on social media. I don't know if I'll have tears left, come the day of the results. I feel emotionally exhausted, and emotionally replenished, all at once.'

People had thoughts about what was working well in the campaign and also things that could have been better. When I asked 'What aspects of Together for Yes are working well?', the following themes emerged.

Table 6.1 What aspects of Together for Yes are working well – results 2018 (response rate 94%).

The grassroots/community-based nature of the campaign	56%
That there was one central message	26%
The national media strategy	18%
Uniting the different groups including political parties	15%
The canvassing itself	12%
Central organisation and support from HQ	6%
Using women's stories as part of the campaign	4%
Using healthcare professionals to endorse the campaign	3%
Crowdfunding	3%
Everything about the campaign	1%

Many canvassers complimented how things were organised locally. In Dublin, we hear 'local organisers are excellent in Dún Laoghaire. There is great support for those of us new to canvassing and there is a clear appreciation for anyone who is taking the time to participate.' In Kildare, we hear that 'spontaneous, self-organisation at a local level has been something to behold', with the activist continuing 'we don't have the party political/civil society infrastructure of the No side to draw upon, however how quickly people have managed to coalesce into a cohesive group in my own locality is inspirational.' The buzz and creativity described in Chapter 5 continued, and lots of actions were organised at the grassroots. Take the decision by Donegal Together for Yes to do a photoshoot in Malin Head, the most northerly point in Ireland, or 7 a.m. pickets on the road into Roscommon Town. There were music performances branded with TfY on Bray's seafront, flash mob performances on the Dublin Luas by the Resistance Choir, leaf-letting outside Ed Sheeran's concerts in Phoenix Park and a music and poetry gig in Maynooth, Co. Kildare. And all of this on top of door knocking morning, afternoon, and evening. There were other ways the creative juices of the repeal movement continued to flow. In early 2018, Erin Darcy conceived of the arts project 'In Her Shoes', a Facebook initiative that invited people to anonymously write their story of abortion then post this with a simple photograph of the shoes they were wearing. The invitation to readers was to put themselves in these women's shoes.[5]

There were also some problems at a local level, such as an overlap across constituencies, plans changing without notice and complaints that not everyone was kept up to date. This activist shared: 'Some of the canvasses have been badly organised; leaders not realising areas have already been done; leaders overstretched and losing canvassers … and didn't give us clear instructions on where to go next.' Others alleged there were too many first-time canvassers and worried that this might jeopardise the result. Quite a few people talked about tensions between the different political parties that put a strain on local cooperation. As one man put it, 'Some of the political parties are not working together but are canvassing separately for their own benefit.' Others complained that the smaller parties were left doing the grunt work: 'The parties could be doing more; the larger parties could get canvassers out every evening if they wished but seem not to want to.'

Some groups were quite hierarchical and it was not unusual for elected councillors to take on a lead role. This made sense in terms of local knowledge of the electoral system and some councillors had been active on repeal for quite a while. But this did not always work well, and there were times when elected councillors who were new to the cause took leadership roles over people with longer histories in the movement. Where these were men, it broke from an established objective of ensuring women would lead where possible. In my own constituency, the coordinator and three canvass leaders (all councillors) were men. In the district beside me, the constituency coordinator was also male. This canvasser commented, 'Selection of leadership in key areas needs more than just a local elected person who volunteers.' Sometime after the referendum, I heard about particular problems in one area, so I called up the local canvass organiser. 'It was so disappointing to me that some of the men involved in repeal insisted on being front and centre in our local repeal group', she told me. These men were experienced activists with backgrounds in trade unionism, left-wing politics, community activism and the anti-water charge movement. She explained, 'At the beginning, I thought it was great that they were involved, but after a while, it became very frustrating.' She continued:

> They talked over us, argued with us, dismissed us. It was infuriating. We were trying to fight against patriarchal oppression, and here were our supposed 'allies' patronising us and treating us like idiots. They just wanted to do things their way and any time we suggested a different way of doing things, they emphasised their experience and expertise and basically said 'You don't get it, we know best.'

She was 'very close to leaving until another woman reached out to me' and, with others, they implemented change: 'We agreed we were fighting a feminist battle in the most non-feminist way possible and decided to challenge it.' So:

> We pointed out every time they interrupted or talked over a woman. We insisted on taking a vote on everything rather than letting them

decide. We insisted that women take on any leadership roles that came up. It was a painful few weeks and then they just stopped coming to our meetings and we found out they had decamped to a Repeal group in a different town. I think, to them, it was just one more campaign in a long list of campaigns and there was no need to do things differently. Whereas we felt that if the campaign wasn't feminist, then how could the result be?

She believed this mostly impacted less politically experienced, younger women who 'had so much passion and commitment … it was the perfect time for experienced male activists to step back and let them take the lead and just support them, but they didn't … they talked the talk, but they didn't walk the walk.'

There are a number of reasons why it is important for men to be involved in repeal and other campaigns to improve reproductive rights. Many have been directly affected by the Eighth Amendment. Men have grieved the loss of unsustainable pregnancies, shared in decision making, travelled overseas with partners, bought pills illegally and supported people in any number of other ways. Some trans men were also directly affected and many men do not want to stay silent on an issue they feel just as passionate about. If men are not involved, it also reinforces the belief that 'not getting pregnant' is a woman's concern. However, when men take charge, the unspoken message is that society's big decisions are best left to them. Throughout the history of the repeal movement, there have been situations where feminists have had to argue the toss on the importance of female leadership,[6] and where men have been publicly instructed not to put themselves forward unless they are certain there isn't a woman interested in the role.[7]

Most people in Ireland likely weren't aware of any tensions within these last stages of what was ultimately a sucessful repeal movement. When you ask people on the inside of a movement to reflect on what isn't working, this will inevitably generate complex and sometimes contradictory experiences of the same event. When I asked 'What aspects of Together for Yes are not working well?', the following emerged.

Table 6.2   What aspects of Together for Yes are not working well, results 2018 (response rate 88%).

The message and tone of the campaign	42%
Delays in getting posters and leaflets out	18%
Too much focus on Dublin	17%
The national campaign and its spokespeople	10%
Aspects of local organisation	10%
No complaints with the campaign	8%
Central office (HQ) ignored or dismissed us	6%
Some volunteers were inexperienced	6%

The single biggest reason canvassers supported uniting as TfY was so that everyone could sing from the same hymn sheet. But one of the more significant findings to emerge from this research is that many people were not happy with the song they were being asked to sing. As many as 42 per cent expressed disapproval about the message and tone of the campaign and often with much emotion, though I never asked people about this or hinted at any concern I might have had. People also brought it up when I asked 'What was the biggest challenge of being involved?', 'What changes would you suggest?' and 'What else would you like to say?'

Some people did like the message. One woman wrote 'The videos are fantastic, the message is great, I'm happy with the leaflets.' Another believed that overall 'The messaging is great. Positivity and optimism of message. Focus on the woman and health care and focus on facts, positivity, care for others.' This last chosen contribution, by a canvasser in Roscommon, captures more support for the messaging:

> I think their message and campaign signs, etc. are very positive, and the plan of action seems good … It is good to have leaflets/t-shirts/ badges, etc. that match this national movement. It's been good to have posters to put up here. Also, I think the messaging is very good and stronger because it is less in your face than things like 'My body, my choice'.

However, many more were not happy with the content and tone of the campaign and made sure to raise this as often as they could. The most consistent and repeated criticism was that overall, the campaign watered down a rights-based approach. People didn't see any trace of this in the campaign's official slogans, which included: 'Sometimes a private matter needs public support', 'Every pregnancy is different; each decision is personal', or simply 'Together for Yes'. People thought the message was 'vague', 'too abstract' and 'doesn't really say anything'. This comment succinctly encapsulates the mood: 'I think Together for Yes have sanitised the entire campaign in an attempt to not offend anyone and appeal to "middle Ireland" and this has resulted in them not really saying anything in any of the campaign material, such as [the] posters.' Some people were not happy about being told what to say. As a case in point, this Dublin canvasser who has been active since 1983 wrote, 'I felt some of the language that has historically been used e.g., choice, were not used frequently enough on the literature.' In another example, again from someone involved for many years:

As with all major grassroots campaigns which are centralised there has been a feeling of the campaign almost being taken from us and we are now being told what to say and do, although as I said I do see the value in a coherent message. I think taking away the language that the grassroots movement was built on such as choice and bodily autonomy is in some way diluting the grassroots message in order to make it more palatable for the masses.

Lots of people loathed the posters. When answering the question 'What isn't working well?', one canvasser simply wrote 'Our posters!' Many coalition members used their own materials. ROSA produced thousands of posters and leaflets designed to deconstruct misconceptions about the numbers of women travelling and to highlight socio-economic contexts. One of their posters simply read 'Stop policing my body'. Termination for Medical Reasons also produced their own posters and leaflets, and the Green Party hung posters with the slogan 'Your sister, your friend, your daughter'. The Social Democrats ran with 'Yes for Dignity, Yes for Compassion, Yes for Health', whilst the Labour Party emphasised health through poster slogans like 'For Compassion in a Crisis YES'. People Before Profit hung multiple posters with the slogan 'Trust Women: our bodies our Choice' and the Workers Party ran with 'No enforced travel' and 'Protect women's lives'. Activists in Meath and Kildare also fundraised for their own leaflets and posters. Some canvassers praised each of these initiatives.

For example, 'I felt that the TFMR posters about the 8th taking their dignity were also very powerful but sadly not as widespread. We could have done with a few more of those.' Another is critical of the party in government: 'It's a GLARING message to the public that there are no Fine Gael posters out.'

Although people were clearly unhappy with the medicalised tone of a campaign based on the three Cs of Care, Compassion and Change, the alternative they pushed for was a focus that would highlight bodily autonomy. Some complained that the issue of obstetric coercion was dropped, despite it being an important part of the work of the Association for Improvement in Maternity Services (AIMS) and Parents for Choice, but there was no clear analysis of the absence of migrant voices, disability, or specific reference to the need to emphasise socio-economic circumstances. After the referendum, I spoke to Emily Wazak of MERJ about their experience of the Together for Yes campaign. I wanted to hear about their express ambition to centralise marginal voices. Emily reported tensions between MERJ and TfY. In particular, she described a stand-out movement when she lost faith in MERJ's capacity to singlehandedly influence the campaign without the support of larger allies. The incident centred around a press release in April 2018 that was designed to encourage young people to register and vote. MERJ were asked to send a member for the photo-shoot but wanted to have a more direct impact on the initiative also. So, Emily suggested that this was the ideal opportunity to extend the call to include naturalised migrants who had not yet registered to vote. This would have respected their Irish identities and could have illuminated the very specific situations some face when seeking to exercise their reproductive rights. As far as Emily was concerned, this proposal was accepted. However, this was not the case. She explained:

The next day was the launch, so they asked us to send a brown face of course, for protocol. And there is no mention of migrants at all. And when I pressed them, when I asked her about it, she said, I couldn't find a source to back up for your statistic on naturalised citizens. This despite how I literally could quote five different reliable sources for this data on the spot, including the Department of Justice ... for me, the Together for Yes experience was just one big gaslighting of migrants, and ethnic minorities and trans people ... .

Some canvassers were unhappy about delays in the distribution of posters, which were funded through a very public, highly successful crowdfunding initiative that was launched in April. In just four days, it surpassed its target of €50, 000 and raised over €500, 000. Many people saw this as an early sign of victory. With money in the bank, leaders had pledged to 'put posters across the country' and to fund 'additional advertising and promotional materials in other key outlets'.[8] But they struggled to deliver this in a timely manner and many people conflated delays with posters with a sense of neglect from HQ. One Tipperary-based canvasser believed 'Dismissing the pleas of rural campaigners for more [posters] was hurtful.' She continued:

> We were repeatedly contacted by people who had donated to pay for posters who couldn't understand why there was no poster in their small town or village, and we could not give them posters to erect till two weeks out from the vote. It was too little too late. It meant in many areas the Yes campaign appeared to be non-existent.

People working within HQ knew this was a problem. When I spoke to Ailbhe Smyth in 2021, she acknowledged 'the big mistake we did make was to do with logistics' and continued:

> Our posters were not ready early enough. And the point was the other side had their posters ready, very early, and put them up. On one level you might think that didn't matter, but it did. But the reason why we had planned to have our posters coming out by the end of March was because we didn't have any money, and our posters were going to have to stay there, we thought, the whole way through, if they didn't get torn down. So, we were still having to think very small at that time, we hadn't fundraised. But not having the posters up upset people on the ground and it disturbed them. It didn't inspire them with confidence. We were very conscious of trying to work subsequently with groups to say look, that was a mistake, but we've caught up.

For some activists, this disappointment spilled into a broader sense of detachment from the workings of HQ, which was often strongly expressed:

The posters were not evenly distributed e.g., Connemara initially got 19 posters. The roadshow plan was to hit major towns and cities and hold meeting in hotels that was preaching to the converted. They should have stopped in smaller towns and villages, particularly in rural Ireland. I emailed them several times about this and only through representation to my own political party got an answer and a result. I have a lot of issues with TfY.

People genuinely believed their neighbourhood would vote No and were worried that this was not being taken seriously. In Leitrim, this activist described 'regional groups' as 'really the poor relatives', whilst activists in Louth, Monaghan, Meath, Tipperary, Limerick, Wexford, Mayo and Kildare all reported feeling excluded from the campaign. For example:

> They are completely Dublin-centric and dismissive of anyone outside their bubble. We have used lots of our own money to fund our campaign, we had to get posters from anywhere we could and put them up ourselves because the TfY ones were late and when they did arrive only a few and quite small. The leaflet is wishy-washy and not one thing has been done to combat the lies and misinformation. We have organised ourselves into an amazing machine and if it is a Yes in Meath it is down solely to us in Meath and not to HQ at all. We are now fixing our own hard-hitting leaflet because they once again have not delivered nor listened to those who are on the doors and what we need to convince the undecideds.

The plight of those who felt less connected to the heartbeat of the movement was not lost on some urban canvassers and several people responded to what this Galway activist described as an 'over-concentration of people in certain areas which could have been managed by mobilising groups to rural areas'. She noted that 'people were crying out for canvassers in rural areas whilst we had mountains of people in urban areas.' Sometimes, HQ organised help by urban canvassers in less supported areas; other times groups organised this themselves. This activist explains, 'It was up to us to figure out that certain areas needed help and try to figure out how to deal with that ourselves.' People from the Alliance for Choice travelled from Northern Ireland to the border counties of Donegal, Monaghan, Cavan and Louth and some Dublin groups took it upon themselves to travel also. For example, Repeal the Eighth Dún Laoghaire canvassed in Dundalk, Co. Louth and in Co. Roscommon.

WHO ARE THESE PEOPLE? THE PUBLIC FACE OF REPEAL

In his review of the TfY campaign, Michael Barron describes central communications as the 'air offensive' to canvassers' 'ground offensive', and explains a strategy that was grounded in the focus-group findings that women and doctors were the most palatable spokespeople.[9] But this didn't always go to plan and one of the stand-out moments of the campaign was when RTÉ's last televised debate began with an apology by the presenter Miriam O'Callaghan that the debate would be between two male politicians. Minister for Health Simon Harris would argue the case for repeal. Peadar Tóibín, who had been expelled from Sinn Féin for his anti-abortion views, was against. Harris uncomfortably stated the obvious when he remarked 'We're standing here with the luxury of being two men who will never experience a crisis pregnancy', repeatedly and earnestly imploring the electorate to 'trust women'. Whilst the two men boisterously fought it out, stories broke off-air about furious behind-the-scenes rows where anti-repeal advocates had withdrawn their female speaker at the last minute because of growing rifts in their campaign. RTÉ's response was to also drop the obstetrician Mary Higgins (rather than drop Simon Harris) who sat in the audience instead. Twitter reacted. Elaine Byrne, the *Sunday Business Post* columnist and barrister tweeted 'the women are sitting down, contributing from the audience. The men are standing up debating with one another. Who in #rtept signed off on these optics? On a debate on abortion?' (@elaineByrne). Historian Mary McAuliffe tweeted: 'Simon Harris to debate Peadar Tóibín on #rtept about women's choices, agency and bodies and who gets to control them! I'm sure Harris will be good, but honestly, two men debating this issue on the final programme of the campaign 😕 '(@MaryMcAuliffe4). Eidin Ní She also got her spoke in, tweeting 'Two men on #rtept debating what women can do with their bodies- Ireland 2018' (@EidinNiShe). Some were more conciliatory such as 'Shame to see no women at the podiums given the subject matter, but no fault of either Harris or Tóibín. Let the debate commence #rtept #8thref' (@maccytothedee).[10]

This wasn't the only time RTÉ side-lined speakers that were chosen by Together for Yes in favour of politicians new to the cause. In fact, there were other occasions when people travelled to the broadcast studios in Donnybrook under the impression they would be contributing, only to find themselves sitting silently in the audience. This pattern didn't stop once the results were counted. In Dublin Castle, Grainne Griffin describes how she was ignored by a journalist in favour of a less central junior politician. She wrote:

> In the aftermath of the landslide referendum victory result, delivered by the most astonishing movement for women's reproductive rights ever seen in Ireland, he [journalist] had chosen to go to a male Senator, who wasn't centrally involved, for comment, rather than a female co-leader of the referendum campaign.[11]

When politicians put themselves forward to speak for the movement, this touched a particular nerve. One voice described it as a 'major mistake to push government politicians and Micheál Martin [opposition leader at the time] to the forefront of the campaign', continuing 'political activists who have a consistent record of campaigning on abortion rights have almost been silenced. The error of this should be especially obvious in light of the cervical smear test scandal.' This was not the only time the Cervical Check scandal (discussed in Chapter 2) was raised. This activist complained about 'associating with government spokespersons especially in light of Cervical Check scandal; overemphasis on authority (doctors and politicians) and underemphasis on experience (women, activists)'. One activist commented: 'It was really poor that the Minister for Health at the time was kind of lauded by elements of the feminist movement because he spoke well in a debate or two or whatever on the specific issue of abortion. This is somebody that was Minister during the cervical cancer scandal.'

More broadly, another said, 'Too many prominent, high-profile, privileged, right-wing, pro-capitalist members whose very presence in Together for Yes undermines the struggle women face in this country.' In an interview after the referendum, Emma Hendrick of People Before Profit who had kickstarted a pro-choice group in her own constituency criticised what she remembers as a near-adulation of senior politicians, not from HQ but at the grassroots: 'People were like "Oh isn't Simon [Harris] great"', continuing 'I mean Cervical Check happened at the same time and you weren't allowed to say anything about that'. Instead, the dominant message she heard was to get repeal through at all costs. She elaborated:

> I felt really, really disheartened because I went to a protest outside the Dáil for Cervical Check and there wasn't that many people there. And it was very disheartening because there was so many people out on canvasses, and so many people online. And I suppose it was a bit of a reality check, for me, kind of saying, these aren't all my people, you know, these are people who were here for the single issue, but they're never going to be radical, they're not going to be anti-capitalist, and they see this as you know, the last thing that Ireland has to shake off is its conservative abortion laws. And the minute we get a more liberal abortion law, you know, we'll all be free.

Together for Yes never endorsed any political party, but rather said they would work with anyone who was pro-repeal. But they did draft in a number of doctors as spokespeople who were trained up by the communications team. Doctors, especially Doctors for Choice, have always been a central and important part of the repeal campaign. Mary Favier, Peadar O'Grady, Julie Kay, Marian Dyer, Peter Boylan and others were prodigious activists over many years and continue to highlight shortfalls in Irish law.

Some canvassers liked that healthcare workers were centre-stage. For instance, this canvasser complimented 'plac[ing] doctors/medical opinion at the forefront of the debate'. Another thought more could have been done to bring obstetricians to the forefront. But there is no getting away from the fact that, in the later stages of the campaign, some traditionalists were given a platform that did not sit well with some canvassers and a much greater number of activists complained about turning on their televisions or radios and being bombarded with a message that, as this Dublin woman puts it, 'pushes healthcare narrative too much to the detriment of replying to concerns about abortion in other cases – soft messaging relying too much on doctors and experts rather than the lived experiences of those effected'. Quite a few people used the expression 'VIPs' in a derogatory way. As a case in point, 'doctors being VIPs and real women's stories not getting out unless on social media. Too much dependency on Foetal Fatal Anomaly'. A handful of people named what they believed was Dr Peter Boylan's tendency to over-exaggerate the dangers of abortion pills.[12] In April 2018, he and Simon Harris issued a statement warning people not to take abortion pills without medical supervision because of the risk of catastrophic side-effects, including a ruptured uterus. He repeated these claims at a ROSA event in Dublin and predicted that it was only a matter of time before someone would die. He was publicly challenged by Rebecca Gomperts, who is also a medical doctor, and who has been providing reproductive telemedicine since 2006 with Women on Web. She reframed prescriptive control as yet another marker of patriarchal paternalism within obstetrics. In reality the abortion pill is a safe medication that has been extensively used worldwide for over twenty years. Complications are rare, and most are easily managed with other medications or treatment. Uterine rupture is extremely uncommon and both ARC and ROSA have worked hard to bust the very myths Boylan was disseminating. Although medical supervision is generally advised, in some countries you can walk in off the street and buy misoprostol then take it at home.[13]

As it turned out, there was no real geographical divide on how the electorate voted. Writing in *The Kerryman* newspaper, Simon Brouder noted how rural voters confounded the predictions of liberal commentators and were 'far from the bastion of right-wing orthodoxy that many have claimed'.[14] One activist believes there was a pattern of 'performative morality' where people 'didn't want their neighbours to see or hear them saying "yes" to the "abortion people", but privately it's a very different story.' Her overall experience of canvassing in Monaghan had been 'disheartening' and as a canvass leader she had worked hard to lift morale. She explains:

> I used to say 'Look, the only thing that you have to remember is people in this town will have had an abortion. Somebody will have had to mind their kids; somebody will have found them money. And we have to remember that that's what people will be voting on.' And then it turns out that that the very place that we campaigned in and had a really resigned to a 'No' turn out to be 66 per cent.

Together for Yes are not to blame for the dynamics of local leadership. They also did their best to keep track of communications coming into a busy office where most people worked voluntarily. It is also recognised within social movement theory that there can be negative reactions and even mistrust towards centralised leadership especially where this wavers from what people see as the shared values of a movement.[15] Chapter 7 will document what transpired after repeal, when control was taken away from the repeal movement as normal business was resumed, through broken promises from government and a continued over-indulgence of medical opinion.

I think the government has only delivered bare bones legislation to say they've done it and kick the can further down the road. The way it was rolled out was awful, they didn't consult GPs beforehand or get them on side when people in more rural areas may have had legitimate concerns about protests against them. There are still areas without any services available to them and people still need abortions beyond 12 weeks.

Former canvasser (2020)

7

The Battle Continues

Written with help from ARC, TFMR, Sligo Action for Reproductive Rights Access (SARRA), Abortion Access Campaign West (AACW), the Alliance for Choice, MERJ, Southern Taskgroup on Abortion & Reproductive Topics (START), and with survey findings from 405 former canvassers gathered in 2020.

And then it was over. 'Repeal' became 'Repealed' and boisterous celebrations took place the length and breadth of Ireland. Activists relished in the success of a demanding campaign. Everyone seemed to be celebrating, not just canvassers but the many thousands of people who had talked openly with family and friends in a way that had never happened before. There were poignant vigils too, such as at a mural of Savita Halappanavar which was created by the street artist Aches. People flocked to Dublin's city centre to adorn it with flowers and messages, not only to memorialise Savita's avoidable death, but to acknowledge how this had propelled the movement forward.

However, the post-repeal period would leave many people feeling that, despite a comprehensive victory, the battle for meaningful access was just beginning. Three interconnected sites of resistance stand out both in the Republic of Ireland and also in Northern Ireland where things would also change. The first space was within Parliament where anti-abortion TDs and Assembly members would work hard to make it as difficult as possible to procure an abortion. The second site of resistance was within the medical profession, and the third would be the ongoing activities of anti-abortion organisations and their supporters. Each of these forces exerted powerful, and at times effective, opposition to the smooth roll-out of services.

ANTI-ABORTION POLITICIANS FIGHT BACK

The decision to back repeal worked favourably for Fine Gael, which in a remarkably short period of time became pro-choice and proud. Despite not being the ones who orchestrated a referendum that the public clearly wanted, they would be the ones to shape what was signed into law. In many respects, the die was cast before anyone voted, as an advance bill had already been agreed following the work of a specially convened Oireachtas cross-party Committee on the Eighth Amendment, which sat from April to December 2017, and was chaired by Catherine Noone of Fine Gael. Their job was to discuss the findings from the Citizens' Assembly (see Chapter 4), and then make proposals to government. It was clear from the start that some politicians would resist the Assembly's full recommendations. When the draft agenda of the first committee meeting was circulated, it focused on foetal fatality and a medical approach. Much less time was to be allocated for two of the Assembly's most important recommendations, namely 12-weeks on demand and for socio-economic reasons.[1] Ruth Coppinger (who shared her time on the committee with Brid Smith) objected to this initial order of business and asked for time to be set aside for women's voices and advocacy groups to share their expertise alongside the legal and medical experts who had already been lined up to address the committee. ROSA and ARC also contacted committee members and asked them to give each Assembly recommendation equal consideration. In the end, TFMR and the Rape Crisis Centre were amongst those to address the committee.

Following extensive deliberations, the committee rejected abortion for foetal abnormality by majority vote. Section 2.35 of the Report of the Joint Committee on the Eighth Amendment of the Consititution explains 'The Committee, while noting the burden placed on the woman and the family in such situations, does not accept that these are sufficient grounds for termination.' They also rejected abortion for 'socio-economic reasons', even though 72 per cent of Assembly members had supported this. Just five members voted in favour of abortion for socio-economic reasons up to 22-weeks, Clare Daly (Independent), Catherine Murphy (Social Democrats), Kate O'Connell (Fine Gael), Brid Smith (People Before Profit) and Senator Lyn Ruane (Independent). Eleven were against (including Sinn Fein and

Labour Party members) and there were five abstentions.[2] Sections 2.38 and 2.39 of the Committee's final report states:

> What became clear during evidence is that the majority of terminations are for socio-economic reasons that are unrelated to foetal abnormality or to rape. In addition, the Committee is mindful of that group of women who, for financial, domestic reasons or immigration status cannot travel or procure abortion pills over the internet. Notwithstanding the difficult and varied circumstances in which pregnant women may find themselves, the Committee is of the opinion that termination of pregnancy after 12 weeks for socio-economic reasons should not be provided for and considers that the distinction drawn by the Citizens' Assembly as regards gestational limits is therefore unnecessary.

On 26 March 2018, the Tánaiste Simon Coveney wrote an impassioned article in the *Irish Independent* explaining that he could only support 12-weeks since a person's last period (which typically equates to 10 weeks' gestation) and further stated 'I believe a pause period is appropriate at this juncture and expect Cabinet to consider between 48–72 hours, to ensure a fully considered decision.'[3] The next day, the General Scheme of a Bill to Regulate Termination of a Pregnancy (general scheme of a bill) was published. It endorsed abortion on demand up to 12 weeks 'in accordance with the medical principle that pregnancy is dated from the first day of a woman's last menstrual period' rather than and from 12 weeks' gestation, as the Committee on the Eighth Amendment had recommended. It sanctioned abortion for fatal foetal anomaly once two doctors certifiably agreed on this diagnosis. It would also take two doctors to agree if there was risk to life or serious harm to the woman. Anyone who breaks these rules would be prosecuted and could face up to 14 years in jail. Reflecting Coveney's outlook, the general scheme of a bill also recommended a 72-hour (3-day) mandatory wait period. This had been debated at committee stage and a number of experts had given their opinion on it, but it was never voted on. Before legislation was passed, Ruth Coppinger used time in the Dáil to put it on the record that there had not been a vote on the 3-day wait.[4] There was some debate on its timing when the law was debated in the Seanad, but nothing about deleting it outright.

Together for Yes accepted the General Scheme of Bill to Regulate Termination of a Pregnancy (2018) describing its contents as 'workable and reasonable proposals to allow women and girls to access the abortion services which they need, in a safe and regulated medical environment within the Irish health system'.[5] Although this may seem curious in retrospect, the timing of the general scheme of a bill is important in context. The referendum had been called two months earlier and the campaign was well under way. Ailbhe Smyth explains:

> It was really important that the general scheme of the bill would be published. Although actually, that was not really the business of the campaign. The referendum campaign was specifically to repeal the Eighth Amendment. Now of course, we obviously tracked it, because we had to do so strategically … From my point of view, it was much more about recognising that we now had a general scheme. There were a lot of problems with the general scheme but we had to carry on with what we were doing, pragmatically. And in fact, one of the biggest problems that the campaign had in those early weeks in March and into April, was the general hue and cry that 'the 12 weeks are too much.'

Activists were also given the impression that, if the public did indeed vote to repeal the Eighth Amendment, there would be opportunities to contribute to the contents of the final law after 25 May. However, this didn't transpire in any meaningful way. In July 2018, the Department of Health published an updated General Scheme of the Health (Regulation of Termination of Pregnancy Bill) 2018. People were invited to comment on this second iteration and many professional associations and civil society organisations including the Coalition, ARC, Amnesty Ireland and the NWCI all made detailed submissions. These mostly recommended parity with WHO guidelines, therefore removing criminalisation, extending gestational limits, allowing abortion for foetal anomaly, giving prescriptive authority to specialist nurses, and lifting the 3-day wait.[6] The submissions were acknowledged, but not substantively engaged with. In part this was likely because many of the same changes were suggested amidst a total of 180 revisions that were proposed and debated in the Dáil's cross-party Health Committee in November 2018. All TDs could attend and only members could vote.

The vast majority of amendments were tabled by pro-choice politicians, including Louise O'Reilly, Brid Smith, Joan Collins, Ruth Coppinger, Catherine Murphy and Kate O'Connell, who sought to reverse limits laid out in the advance bill. To give some examples, there were debates on rewording 'to end the life of a foetus' to 'an induced abortion to end a pregnancy using a medical or surgical procedure'. And on including the word 'abortion' rather than 'termination of pregnancy'. There was also an amendment to delete 'means a female person of any age' and substitute 'means a person of any age who can become pregnant'.[7] This would have made no difference to the mostly cis women who access abortion services, but its absence effectively ignored the needs of trans men, stigmatised non-binary people and reinforced an essentialist interpretation of womanhood that does not fit everyone. All of these suggestions were repeatedly rejected by the Minister for Health in favour of 'what the people voted for', by which he meant the general scheme of a bill despite probably knowing that most people who voted Yes were unlikely to have studied its contents in depth. Harris also cited legal advice he had received that prevented certain changes which Brid Smith asked him to make available to all committee members.

At the same time, anti-choice politicians including Mattie McGrath, Peadar Tóibín, Peter Fitzpatrick Carol Nolan, Mary Butler, Michael Fitzmaurice and Noel Grealish worked hard to stymie the smooth introduction of legislation. Their method was to seek what are sometimes called Targeted Regulation of Abortion Providers laws, or TRAP laws. This is a common tactic in the US, where politicians who openly oppose abortion impose as many barriers as possible whilst fawning concern for women's health. The TRAP proposals put forward were at times abhorrent. Take for example a suggestion to prosecute a person for failing to ensure the 'dignified disposal' of foetal remains. The pregnant person would have to opt for burial or cremation. This copied a bill signed into law by former US Vice President Mike Pence when he was governor of Indiana. Another TRAP proposal was a mandatory ultrasound to record the foetal heartrate which the person would then have to confirm they were invited to listen to. When commenting on equally repugnant amendments about collecting and storing data, this abridged contribution from Fine Gael TD Kate O'Connell gives you a flavour for the proceedings:

As usual, amendments nos. 43, 43a and 43b are being presented as a good thing, when, in fact, they are more about shame and the surveillance of women. The crux of their genesis was revealed in some of the recent contributions which indicate that alarm bells should go off once a woman has had two or three abortions … Where would those alarm bells go off? Would there be a red light in a convent or local church? Is this some sort of policing of promiscuity? Is it about policing pregnancy? … The amendments hark back to views held in the past … these amendments are about power, control over women, shame and surveillance. Those who have put their names to the amendments should be ashamed in front of the women in their lives.[8]

The conveyor belt of potential modifications and long-drawn-out debates resulted in repeated delays, with some journalists speculating that legislation might not be passed before the end of the year. Then, just before midnight on 7 December 2018, TDs voted 90 votes to 15 (with 12 abstentions) to introduce the Health (Regulation of Termination of Pregnancy) Bill (2018). Simon Harris hailed its creation 'a new era for Irish women' who could access the care they needed on domestic soil. On 20 December, the new Act was signed into law by President Michael D. Higgins. On 1 January 2019, abortion service began. That same week, the Health Services Executive (HSE) launched its website myoptions.ie which ensures a confidential smooth pathway into services. Just two weeks later, the first sign of problems surfaced when Brid Smith and Ruth Coppinger brought a case to the Dáil about a young pregnant woman who was carrying a foetus with a severe and likely life-ending abnormality. She had presumed she could have an abortion in Ireland but was advised by a doctor to travel because they could not certifiably guarantee the baby would die within 28 days, even though this was the most likely scenario.

In February 2020, a general election returned a very different government with notable pro-repeal absentees including Ruth Coppinger and Kate O'Connell, who each lost their seat in tightly contested constituencies. Clare Daly was gone too, as she was elected to the European Parliament in July 2019. The Health (Regulation of Termination of Pregnancy) Act was debated again in March 2020 when several emergency amendments were tabled in response to the Covid19 pandemic.

These were to remove the 3-day wait, to give prescriptive authority to specialist nurses and midwives, and to introduce telemedicine. Predictably, there were objections from anti-abortion politicians and only telemedicine was approved and only for the duration of the Covid pandemic. Inadvertently, this brought early abortion services more in harmony with what many of those who canvassed for repeal had imagined and removed a significant barrier for people who struggle to make two GP visits.

It took a while for a new government to be formed. When it was, there were some high-profile promotions of known anti-abortion politicians. Jack Chambers of Fianna Fáil became the government chief whip and his party colleague Norma Foley became minister for education in her first successful bid for the Oireachtas. In June 2020, Foley was praised by the Iona Institute for telling a newspaper columnist she was open to making a case for greater restrictions.[9] Neither appear to have joined an all-party 'Oireachtas Life and Dignity' group which launched its first report in December 2020. The government they are part of – a tripartite of Fianna Fáil, Fine Gael and the Green Party – launched their programme for government in the summer of 2020 with ambitious commitments. It repeated promises on safe exclusion zones and vowed to take a closer look at women's experiences when accessing all health care. There would be a dedicated women's health action plan and increased supports to maternity services. The National Maternity Strategy would be fully implemented, as would the recommendations of the Scally Report into Cervical Check. They promised much needed regulation and funding for fertility treatment, an extension of BreastCheck and again, free contraception. At the time of writing, none of these recommendations have been fully advanced, or for many even partly advanced.

Although removing the Eighth Amendment only applied to the Republic of Ireland, there were also post-repeal changes in Northern Ireland as momentum immediately built for all-Island access. The process was greatly assisted by a June 2018 UK Supreme Court ruling that it would not intervene in a case brought by the Northern Ireland Human Rights Commission (NIHRC) on behalf of a young woman called Sarah Ewart. Five years earlier, Ewart had become the face of the NI movement when she was denied an abortion despite a fatal foetal anomaly. Most judges agreed that current laws breached Ewart's human rights, but they ruled that the best course of action was for an individual, and not the NIHRC, to take a case. The headlines this story generated, coming so soon after Ireland's public vote, kickstarted political debate.

Since 1999, Northern Ireland has been mostly governed by a devolved structure called the Northern Ireland Assembly (or Stormont). In the summer of 2018, Stormont was in crisis having collapsed the previous year on a separate matter, meaning Northern Ireland was being governed by the UK parliament in Westminster. Almost immediately then-Prime Minister Theresa May stated that she supported the extension of laws on abortion to Northern Ireland, even though she relied on the staunchly anti-choice Democratic Unionist Party (DUP) for a government majority. The DUP immediately objected but were quickly drowned out by support across the chamber from the UK Labour Party and the Liberal Democrats. The task of designing a new law, and at the same time a law on same-sex marriage, was then given to the Northern Ireland Office. By the mid-2019, the process had stalled until, with cross-party support, Labour MP Stella Creasy tabled a fresh amendment compelling MPs to exercise their human rights obligations and extend abortion services to Northern Ireland. Overall, this process resulted in the UK Parliament's Northern Ireland (Executive Formation etc.) Act 2019, which passed through the House of Lords in the summer of 2019 and was immediately suspended until October, creating a stopwatch for Stormont to re-convene. This did not happen and, at midnight on 21 October 2019, celebrations began as abortion and same-sex marriage were both decriminalised.

When Stormont did resume in January 2020, one of its first tasks was to establish guidelines for what was, on paper, the most liberal abortion laws on the Island of Ireland. A person can end a pregnancy on request up to 12 weeks and with a doctor's consent up to 24 weeks, if there is a health risk (physical or mental) to the woman. There are no gestational limits where there is a risk to life or grave injury to the woman. However, anti-abortion politicians have repeatedly sabotaged its implementation, with many people suspicious of the actions of Ulster Unionist Party member and Minister for Health Robin Swann. By late 2021, the Department of Health had yet to commission services, meaning no dedicated funding had been allocated. Some Health Trusts do provide early medical abortions (EMAs) via their community-based sexual health clinics, but surgical abortions are more difficult without dedicated funding for staff, meaning that people continue to travel after 10 weeks, even though the law allows EMAs up to 12 weeks. Often, the cheapest option is to go to Britain, as abortion is costly in the Republic of Ireland when a person doesn't have a social security number. There has been no public awareness campaign and no self-referral pathway like myoptions.ie. Instead, the charity First Contact have taken on to be the first point of contact for people seeking information. Emma Campbell, co-convener of the Alliance for Choice, explained: 'It is so ludicrous that we have the brilliant law, and so many problems accessing it … it is really frustrating for us. We get women phoning us all the time saying, "I thought it was completely legal now, why is it so difficult, why is it so hard to find out?"'

In 2021, the NIHRC launched legal action against the UK government, the Northern Ireland Executive and the Department of Health for their collective failure to commission services. In March 2021, the Alliance for Choice sent an open letter to Swann, calling for the immediate introduction of services which was signed by 25 Northern Ireland groups including women's groups and LGBTQI+ support organisations. There is no sign that the DUP will back down, and some party members remain active in a UK cross-party parliamentary group linked to Right to Life UK. In March 2021, Paul Givan of the DUP brought forward a private member's bill to ban abortion in cases of non-fatal anomaly. Sinn Féin were widely criticised by pro-choice groups and journalists alike for speaking out of both sides of their mouth when they abstained on the vote. In July 2021, the UK government directed Northern Ireland authorities to ensure abortion services were available by March 2022. First Minister Paul Givan responded by vowing to resist Westminster's attempts to force the hand of Stormont.

RESISTANCE FROM WITHIN THE MEDICAL PROFESSION

Every circumstance where a person legally seeks an abortion needs to be sanctioned by at least one doctor. The clinician(s), and not the pregnant person, determines if legal criteria are met, making doctors powerful gatekeepers where their attitudes can have a direct impact on a person's ability to access abortion. It didn't take long for anti-abortion doctors to cause a stir and, again, this started before legislation was finalised. In 2018, an extraordinary general meeting of the Irish College of General Practitioners descended into chaos when anti-abortion GPs staged a walkout to awaiting journalists. One GP described 'an air of menace in the room [as] a group of 40–50 pro-lifers were clearly squaring up for a fight'.[10] Soon after legislation was passed, the group Doctors for Life released a press statement vowing to change the law.[11] Healthcare workers do have a right to refuse to be involved on moral grounds as outlined in section 22 of Ireland's Health (Regulation of Termination of Pregnancy) Act. This allows for conscientious objection (CO), which is common in other parts of the world. However, balancing a person's right to access a procedure that they are legally entitled to, and the mechanics of making space for reasonable objection is tricky. Sweden, Finland and Iceland don't allow CO; public employees must put aside their personal ethics in favour of professional ethics. As Bitzer puts it, they must accept that their 'duties towards the woman override all others, because without her body there would be no new life and without her support there would be no good life.'[12]

Some activists are convinced that CO is a big part of the reason why only around 10 per cent of GPs have registered with myoptions.ie, leaving large parts of the country with no services, especially in rural areas. There are reports of certain doctors exerting significant power locally. For instance, one activist complained 'Entire towns and communities are deprived of the services because of their beliefs.' Another wrote, 'There are whole areas near me where women cannot obtain an abortion because no GPs have signed up. Nobody should be surprised by this; it was a bad idea from the start putting it in the hands of GPs.' Some tensions about the urban/rural divisions resurfaced:

> Here in rural Wexford, we still have no doctors who have signed up to the plan … It can be very difficult to see these books come out and people (usually, I'm afraid, in Dublin) saying that the abortion issue is mostly sorted when for those of us in rural areas we are still denied access to local help.

Even if there *was* better GP coverage, there is still a problem with secondary care. In fact, just 10 out of 19 hospital-based maternity services in Ireland offer full abortion services.[13] In June 2019, four obstetricians in St Luke's Hospital, Co. Kilkenny, including Trevor Hayes of Doctors for Life, wrote to GPs advising them that abortion would not be available at the hospital's maternity service. The link between services and CO seems clear in this instance, but we cannot discount its impact at other sites either or underplay its effect in the day-to-day. One midwife and activist reported ongoing negative attitudes in her place of work. She stated, 'Conscientious objection is a big issue amongst nursing staff', continuing 'attitudes amongst some staff members need to change. There is a lot of prejudice. I have witnessed nursing staff treat patients presenting for surgical termination with less kindness than other patients.' Research by ARC released in 2021 also found attitudinal problems not just with healthcare workers but amongst ancillary staff too:

> I visited my GP first, assuming she could prescribe the necessary medication, she refused treatment. I had to call MyOptions to find GPs in my area that perform abortions, I rang three different practices and two of the receptionists were very rude on the phone to me. One hung up on me before I even had a chance to say thank you or goodbye. It was very distressing. At this point I had to call MyOptions for a second time, I was extremely upset because I wanted to have the abortion ASAP. She gave me numbers for doctors outside of my county.[14]

For doctors who do provide abortions, a voluntary network of obstetricians and GPs called START (Southern Taskgroup on Abortion & Reproductive Topics) has formed. I spoke to one GP provider and member of START who explained, 'In the wake of the overwhelming referendum result we felt a burden of responsibility, as we were acutely aware of the lack of clinical knowledge and experience amongst doctors in Ireland (ourselves included!) with regard to abortion care.' In response, START provides education to their colleagues, highlights deficiencies in care and advocates for service users. The presence of START is a hugely positive development and one that ARC are keen to support. Helen Stonehouse and JoAnne Neary (ARC conveners) make the point:

> We have some amazing, committed providers, most publicly the START group, but there are many areas without community based

services. Refusal of care (so-called 'conscientious objection') and the lack of safe access zones makes it easy for doctors to step back from providing abortion care, and the persistence of the paternalistic, controlling culture that developed under the 8th can make it hard for doctors to step up. It will take a long time to undo the impact of 35 years under the 8th Amendment.

THE 'PRO-LIFE' CRUSADE CONTINUES

Another persistent battleground has been the actions of self-titled 'Pro-Life' groups who were never going to simply accept defeat. As this activist puts it, 'The No side will campaign for ever against us. We may have won the battle, on the 8th. However, the No side view this as a war.' Within days of the vote, Niamh Ui Bhriain, the spokesperson for the Life Institute, publicly blamed both media and government for misleading voters, claiming that the victory was actually a 'reluctant yes'.[15] The Irish 'Pro-Life' Movement have maintained a strong online presence and hold annual conferences and marches. But perhaps their most successful intervention has been persistent vigil-style protests outside GP clinics and maternity hospitals. It took just two days for these to begin. On 3 January, 2019, a Galway GP was picketed. In a radio interview that day, Ailbhe Smyth described the protests as 'public harassment ... deliberately seeking to deter women from accessing an entirely lawful health service'.[16] These anti-choice vigils were not inevitable – in fact, many groups warned that this would happen and expressly asked that Irish law would include safe access zones (SAZs). Simon Harris seemed to concur but, so as not to delay access, he promised to consider the issue separately. However, despite publicly condemning protesters on a number of occasions, Harris repeatedly dragged his heels. In May 2019, Louise O'Reilly, TD for Sinn Féin, questioned him in the Dáil about the delay and he assured her he would make good on his promise that summer and ordered a scoping inquiry into international best practice.[17] He could have just asked Lawyers for Choice or the Irish Council for Civil Liberties (ICCL), saving everyone time and money. Instead, the report that was produced recommended even more research into constitutional and human rights implications (Reddy, 2019, p. 14). Everyone agrees that there are challenges when creating SAZs that centre around a person's right to protest. But it can be done, and the ICCL have provided examples where a balance has been struck in Australia, Canada and in parts of the UK and the US.[18]

In September 2019, the Garda commissioner Drew Harris rowed into the debate when he wrote to Simon Harris to assure him that public offence laws were sufficient. Drew Harris recounted 'no incidence of criminality has been reported or observed' and that there was 'no evidence to suggest that there is threatening, abusive or insulting behaviour directed towards persons utilising such services'.[19] One wonders if he asked anyone at the receiving end of this abuse how they saw things, or if he considered how these protesters often work hard to stay on the right side of public order laws on harassment by staying silent and seemingly polite. I doubt he pondered how protests designed to shame and humiliate women do not happen in a vacuum, but within a global culture where women are often seen as fair game in terms of other people's right to approach and deride them at will. Most women will tell you they are already on high alert in public spaces. Several local councils have passed bye-laws to prevent anti-abortion protestors observing, stalking, threatening, or obstructing anyone entering a healthcare facility, but these have mostly stalled over legal technicalities about the powers of local councils to implement such measures. In an attempt to kickstart some sort of action from government, Holly Cairns, Social Democrat TD, questioned Minister for Health Stephen Donnelly in March 2021 on his plans for implementing SAZs. He responded, '... there has been a limited number of reports of protests or other actions relating to termination of pregnancy' describing this as 'an extremely positive development'. He further stated:

> Where problems do arise with protests outside healthcare services, there is existing public order legislation in place to protect people accessing services, employees working in the service and local residents ... The Department of Health has previously liaised with An Garda Síochána around safe access to termination of pregnancy services, and the Garda National Protective Services Bureau issued a notice to all Garda Stations raising awareness about the issue. The notice directed that any protests be monitored, and breaches of existing law dealt with.[20]

These laws are not working. In 2021, a study by University College Dublin and Doctors for Choice found one in six doctors have experienced a 'verbal threat or attack' since services were introduced.[21] The Limerick Feminist Network have tracked daily, sometimes twice-daily protests outside University Hospital Limerick and regular protests outside Limerick Family Planning Clinic. There are also reports of demonstrations in Donegal, Galway, Kerry, Roscommon, Tipperary, Louth and Dublin. In the spring of 2021, Limerick Feminist Network launched the national Together for Safety campaign, which focuses on the urgent need for SAZs.

When I asked former canvassers about their thoughts on Irish laws, the absence of SAZs was the issue that generated the most upset. One activist said they were 'disappointed that laws to create safe zones seems to be deprioritised'; another shared 'exclusion zones needed. Vigilance needed so public opinion doesn't turn back such as what is happening in UK/US.' And again, 'not having the exclusion zones in place yet is frustrating as this was a core component to ensure that women and healthcare providers wouldn't get harassed.' Table 7.1 below lists other concerns also.

Table 7.1   What are your thoughts on the way things have panned out in terms of access to abortion and reproductive rights more broadly – results 2020 (response rate 96%).

No Safe Access Zones	45%
No local GPs providing a service	37%
An unnecessary 3-day wait	19%
Conscientious objection	9%
12-week gestational limit	6%
No provision for foetal anomaly	3%

On paper, there are several reasons why GP provision makes sense and thousands have availed of this service. It is the most discreet and convenient way to procure an abortion and it normalises treatment amidst general primary care. But it only works if there are sufficient numbers of GPs prepared to prescribe abortion pills or to refer people to secondary care. According to this Sligo activist, a county with no GPs registered with myoptions.ie, some doctors 'are too concerned about intimidation from anti-choice groups and lack of training to put their name on the HSE register at this point'. Three years on, Sligo

Action for Reproductive Rights Access (SARRA) is one of a number of pro-repeal groups who are still fighting for local services. Abortion Action Campaign West (AACW) are equally concerned about services, or lack thereof, in the West of Ireland. According to AACW, people do not always understand the diverse landscape of the West, where finding a GP can be difficult simply because your broadband is terrible or because there is no public transport servicing your area. AACW have produced a booklet that explains the law in English, Irish, Portuguese, Polish, French, Arabic and Italian, and have distributed this to community and youth groups, migrant support groups, trade unions, libraries and student unions across the West of Ireland.

Overall, activists believe inequality of access is compounded by our demeaning 3-day wait which rarely results in someone changing their mind. Instead, these delays can push a person outside of the timeframe for early abortion, especially someone with an irregular menstrual cycle.[22] The anger of activists was at times palpable; for example, one said 'the waiting period and several Dr's visits NEED TO GO.' Activists know these sorts of barriers mostly impact people without time and money, in a coercive relationship, with a disability, or with too many care commitments, where taking two trips, three days apart and miles from home is simply impossible. A number of activists talked about migrants living in Direct Provision who are especially impacted, given that many Reception Centres are outside of cities and large towns. Others referred to 'marginalised women' or 'the most vulnerable'.

WE'RE EXHAUSTED! BURNOUT AND THE TOLL OF REPEAL

It is clear from these testimonies that people understand just how much more work there is to be done. But a less talked about side of their efforts is just how hard it can be to stay the course. Undoubtedly there are rewards. The camaraderie and sense of solidarity which repeal canvassers talked about at length is proof of this. Nevertheless, one of the strongest themes to emerge two years post-referendum was how activists were simply shattered and burnout was the single biggest reason why one-third of activists had disengaged from reproductive rights activism. A former canvasser explains, 'I am not as available as I would like due mainly to burnout. The time personally committed means I also need to rebalance the scale in favour of my family! ...

I need to take some timeout to regroup and wait till my children are older to return.' Another long-time activist shares, 'To be honest, as much as I loved working on the campaign, the experience drained me by the end.' They continue: 'The abuse I faced with the opposition and the physical exhaustion from being on the go 24/7 while studying law. So, I have decided to take a step back to focus on that for now, but I do intend to get involved again as soon as I feel ready.' Someone else makes the point:

> I have tried to get involved in two things but found I was still very burnt out from repeal activism … things would trigger me in the new activism circles because they brought back memories of repeal. Things that during repeal I felt I just 'put up' with. So, I've decided not to get involved in anything just yet.

Burnout was also a dominant theme amongst the two-thirds of people who were still active. In fact, when I asked people to think back on the referendum period from March–May 2018, just 37 per cent remembered this positively and 15 per cent shared mixed feelings. For instance:

> It was a mostly positive experience but for the last month or so it was all encompassing. I remember it taking over every free moment. My relationships took a hit and I didn't sleep for the last ten days of the campaign. There was a major crash after, I felt I needed to withdraw and found it very hard to engage with anything related to gender equality for a while after.

When activists were asked 'When you think back on the period before the referendum vote – when you were out canvassing, leafletting, setting up stalls, moderating websites and social media accounts etc. – how do you remember it now?', nearly a third (32 per cent) of all activists only talked about the campaign negatively. Specifically, people reported the sheer toll it took on their mental and physical health. They were exhausted, even traumatised, by the hectic pace of the pre-referendum period and of a campaign that sometimes took over their lives. This ARC member wrote:

It was exhausting physically and emotionally – we had so much ground to cover. You didn't know what was going to answer the door – was someone going to abuse you? Or were they going to tell you a traumatic family secret? That definitely took its toll. To be honest, I don't think I'm right from it yet.

Others were worried about the impact on those around them. As a case in point: 'It was a difficult time for many of my young comrades and I spent a lot of it looking after others that were struggling.' The person also had to deal with their own challenges at the same time. They continue: 'I was newly out as trans and had limited energy for canvassing but glad I did my bit. But it was a difficult process to debate one's bodily autonomy with strangers.' In 2018, 32 per cent cited malevolent encounters with anti-choice activists and their supporters as the most difficult aspect of being involved. These scars remain in 2020. One woman wrote, 'I was visibly pregnant, so I was very conscious of how it looked for me to be canvassing. I received a lot more verbal aggression/insults than my canvassing peers.' Another canvasser, based in Leitrim, simply described it as 'hard work, a lot of abuse, been called a baby killer and getting holy water thrown at us'.

For many people the personal strain was magnified by the topic. Everyone, but especially women, have a reproductive story and it can be hard to talk openly and publicly about abortion and bodily autonomy without this being triggered. This activist shares 'repeal definitely took its toll on me … for a while I was just exhausted but even after that I felt like I had a lot to do in terms of dealing with my own abortion and I had probably used the referendum to avoid dealing with that personal situation.'

In her research on activist burnout more broadly, Emma Craddock highlights a gendered dimension that makes women more susceptible.[23] This isn't because women are more fragile but because the image of 'the ideal activist' is a person who is able to prioritise 'the cause' over everything else. This can particularly impact many women who in today's world are supposed to hold down a job, give quality time to kids, be fully in control of their reproductive health and pick up the slack in terms of elder-care and domestic responsibilities. All the while, she must be well-groomed and sexually desirable. Add being an activist to the mix, and it is easy to see how this creates challenges. As a case in point, this woman explained:

> Trying to repeal the 8th consumed my life, when it came time to canvass I all but abandoned my kids, leaving the older teens to look after the younger ones so I could go out every night. It was a hectic time, fraught with worry for us that we wouldn't win. We had huge opposition in Donegal, and they were scary in their attacks of us, even had a few show up to our launch to yell at us all. I remember it as a fraught and tense time.

Some pro-repeal activists believe there were unhealthy expectations on what a person was expected to do with an unspoken culture that you needed to be on the go the whole time. Research by Doris Murphy, the cofounder of Pro-Choice Wexford, equally captured this point. One activist in her study shared:

> I also felt very much that in TFY [Together for Yes] (and in ARC [Abortion Rights Campaign], to a lesser extent), there was a culture of busy-ness and egoic burnout – as in, if you were tired and stressed and overworked, that meant you were an amazing activist and deserved praise for it. I think it is a dangerous territory to give someone praise for working themselves to the ground … It's a delicate subject matter because in one way, of course people deserve support and praise for all the hard work they've put in, but in another way, if we praise and value people working themselves to the bone, aren't we just continuing to propagate a patriarchal, capitalist culture, where 'more work = better' and 'taking time for reflection and care = weakness'?[24]

In my own study, the topic of care is described as 'a controversial area' by one activist who continued, 'Attempts were made by some to address this but were not supported and many activists have suffered as a consequence.' She goes on to say 'This has further silenced activists because they have nothing left to give and no one to guide them through the experience. It's something that should be addressed as many are still not recovered from the intensity of the campaign.'

The issue of burnout, and a sense of a collective failure to sufficiently address this, also emerged when I spoke to key people within organisations. TFMR described member fatigue as a 'major issue', continuing 'some people were re-traumatised telling their story over and over again, just the exhaustion … people didn't have anything to help them to process what they had been through. There was nothing, so that was a bit of a failing I guess after the referendum.' Kerry for Choice told me 'burnout among our activists is still a big issue. We've been on hiatus since mid-2019 when our most active volunteers – including our convening team – stepped back. With the legislative review due we are slowly finding our way back to local pro-choice activism.' In North Wicklow Together for Choice and Equality 'There's definitely still an element of fatigue after repeal. People put their body and soul into that campaign.' Much the same came from within ARC which has been active in attempts to collectively support the well-being of its members since 2018. Their co-conveners JoAnne Neary and Helen Stonehouse are very tuned into the impact of burnout and the particular demands of the referendum campaign. They explain:

> So many of our members gave so much of their time and energy, as canvassers and regional coordinators as well as within the structure of Together for Yes. It was a time of emotional intensity, the impact of which we're still dealing with. There was a significant amount of burnout across the campaign, particularly as we moved straight into campaigning for improvements to the draft legislation (which was wholly ignored by the government). Many of our members took a much-needed break from pro-choice organising.

As early as September 2018, they published a blogpost called 'It's okay to feel Shite: Self-care after the referendum'. Three years on, they still organise collective spaces for healing and well-being. This builds on a wider culture where there is an ongoing concern for member well-being. For example, ARC meetings, whatever the topic, typically begin with time and space to share how people are. ARC also works to a model where people choose what they wish to work on and can step out of spaces whenever they need to. Nobody is allowed to assign a task to another person.

When Stephen Donnelly announced to Cabinet in March 2021 that the scheduled review into Ireland's abortion legislation was to begin, activists had already started recovering and regrouping and were clear on what their demands would be. But immediately there were more broken promises. Simon Harris had assured activists in 2018 that any review would be 'external and independent' and that 'it will not be an in-house job, if I may call it that. We would commission someone external and independent to carry out detailed research, which would then be published.'[25] However, three years on, his successor Donnelly described a three-strand approach: that would focus on service users, and on providers, and that would include a process of public consultation. Donnelly did explain there would be 'research to inform the service user and service provider strands [that] will be commissioned and carried out independently'; however, the Department of Health would itself manage public consultation separately. He then described a process where civil servants would analyse the results of these strands, write a report, and submit this to the Minister for Health for consideration.[26] Immediately, pro-choice groups complained that this fell short of what was promised. They pooled resources and collaboratively submitted letters of concern seeking clarification on the terms of reference. These concerns were repeated by the National Women's Council of Ireland (NWCI) when they launched the research paper 'Accessing Abortion in Ireland: Meeting the Needs of Every Woman'. 'Accessing Abortion in Ireland' calls for a review of the 12-week limit, abolition of the 3-day wait, removal of the 28-day limit, an end to criminalisation and nationwide access.[27]

In June 2021, Minister Donnelly met with representatives from a number of groups including the NWCI, ARC, the Irish Family Planning Association (IFPA) and TFMR. Donnelly agreed that an independent chair was the optimum approach and assured those present that there would be high levels of consultation. Regardless of its outcome, the capacity of the Irish reproductive rights movement to reunite and mobilise so quickly is testament to its ongoing strength. Might this movement learn from the past so as to ensure future actions seek justice not only in abortion access but the wider reproductive oppressions that are inflicted on people every day? This question will be taken up in my final chapter which asks: where to next for reproductive rights activism in Ireland? Can our movement be more deliberately framed by a reproductive justice outlook?

Mid-pandemic, visualising any kind of future is hard, but it's safe to say that ARC is going to be around for a while. We are a long way from comprehensive abortion access – and that is only part of the fight for reproductive justice. Abortion, contraception, maternity, fertility, sexual health – we should have freedom of choice in all of these areas. We are committed to protecting our rights and continuing to fight for better care. We believe that grassroots feminist organising can create real change in our society – we already have.

ARC Co-conveners, 2021

8

In the Struggle for Reproductive Rights, Where to Next?

It was the autumn of 2020, and Emma was in hospital for her 20-week scan. Because of Covid-19 restrictions, Richard had to wait in the carpark. They didn't mind too much; their plan was that she'd call him when the time was right so he could listen to the heartbeat. But the phone call he got was not what they imagined. He was summoned inside to meet two doctors who were poring over Emma's scan. 'Unfortunately, there is a quite significant issue with the brain', one doctor nervously told them, before ordering further tests. Alobar Holoprosencephaly was the diagnosis, meaning that the foetus would not develop normally and would either spontaneously abort before term, or die soon after birth. At best, the life expectancy would be a year. Much to their surprise, the couple were then told they'd have to travel to England. At first, they didn't quite believe what they were hearing. That was the old Ireland, they thought, things were different now weren't they? It took three weeks to get an appointment. Then, in the middle of a global pandemic, they flew to London and Emma was admitted for a difficult induction and birth. When Richard shared their story with the Irish press, he described a ticking clock in the background getting louder and louder as they fought against time to organise their son's cremation, then make their return flights home. When they did get back, things didn't settle down right away. Emma was admitted to hospital twice, once as an emergency after they rang an ambulance. 'Most people I have spoken to still believed Ireland's laws protected people in our situation', Richard wrote in 2021 'people at the lowest and most vulnerable, but they don't. This needs to change, Ireland needs to support its people going through this.'[1]

Since 2012, Termination for Medical Reasons (TFMR) have supported people who have no option but to travel overseas at their own personal expense for the health care they need. It seems fair to speculate they did not imagine they would still be doing this in 2021, especially given that their plight was at the front and centre of the 2018 campaign. But TFMR are still needed; not just for support through their LMC bereavement group but to emphasise that these are some of the people who continue to get on planes for abortions.

Securing a referendum was a significant victory for the repeal movement and one that was built on decades of civil disobedience and grassroots activism that forced the hand of a once-hostile government. Although Fine Gael continue to claim they were progressive players they, and their government partners Fianna Fáil, are the ones who are still behind the curve. Despite a truly comprehensive vote for change, Irish laws still abjectly fail to provide respectful, affordable, local reproductive health care not just for foetal fatal anomaly, but for many people left behind by extremely restrictive laws. None of this is a surprise. The concerns raised by activists and shared within this book were also raised with the health minister in 2018. No opposition amendments were accepted and submissions by reproductive rights groups, healthcare organisations and representative groups were ignored.

This book also asks some critical questions about the Together for Yes campaign. Many activists struggled with its message, not with the benefit of hindsight, but in real time. Certainly, those who led the final stages faced an unenviable bind. The only way abortion could be legislated for was if the Eighth was repealed. The only ones with the power to call a referendum, were members of a distinctly neoliberal government. The Committee on the Eighth Amendment had already removed provision for abortion for socio-economic reasons and for foetal anomaly, and there was nothing the campaign could do about this. There were internal factors also such as a strong liberal element within the movement, the heavy burden of previous defeats, and in some quarters, a mistrust in the electorate's capacity to vote Yes, despite opinion polls stating the opposite. Combined, these factors created a dynamic where people (including me) were afraid to push voters they saw as conservative to endorse more radical views. Fiona de Londras describes this as 'an uncomfortable tension between what we believed in and what we thought we needed to do or say to win the referendum'.[2] The atmosphere created in many branches of the movement was to stay on message and get over the line at all costs. Everything else could be dealt with afterwards.

In its defence, the message did shift the national conversation out of the realm of morality in a way that had never happened before. There is no turning back from this. For the first time ever, abortion became health care. This is an important alteration in the Irish psyche that should not be underestimated. As Ailbhe Smyth explains:

> The messaging has been criticised I know, but one of the most effective shifts we made was to move the debate right out of the arena of morality, i.e., abortion, 'evil or good', 'good or evil', and move it onto another terrain, which was to say, actually, it's not about morality, it's not about good or evil. It's about need. It's about what is it that a woman needs. So, it then becomes about health and health care and so on, which a lot of people may not have liked, but which was extremely effective in dis-embedding the abortion debate from the morass of bitterness and controversy it had been embroiled in for so long, where you couldn't move without there being 'yes', 'no', 'yes', 'no' oppositions.

The campaign message's focus on privacy also normalised abortion on demand without any explanation other than not wanting to be pregnant. Many activists (again including me) didn't think this possible just a few years earlier and its fixed nature within the repeal campaign was undoubtedly influenced by the central role of the Abortion Rights Campaign (ARC). It would be wrong of me to paper over other important positives also. Firstly, creating a united voice was strategically beneficial and the alternative would have played into the hands of the anti-abortion movement and could easily have led to defeat. The Coalition to Repeal the Eighth (the Coalition) held a singular focus to repeal, and throughout its history it never sought to change the way its membership held a range of competing perspectives. Secondly, the repeal movement showcased the successful synthesis of a small group of left-wing TDs, particularly from Solidarity-People Before Profit but also independents across the Dáil and Seanad, and a grassroots movement that it helped create. This synergy helped secure a tremendous win and the impacts for those activists involved was often life-changing. Several people joined left-wing political parties, feminist networks, environmental groups, reproductive rights groups and local community campaigns. Many grassroots groups that have emerged have injected new life into feminist politics in Ireland and continue to be to the fore of consciousness-raising education, street protest, campaigns against gender-based violence and obstetric violence, Church involvement in maternity care, contraception, image-based violence and much more. Local activism cannot take all the credit for this politicisation and it is important not to discount the role of the arts and journalism.

However, there is no getting away from the fact that some grassroots activists thought Together for Yes were somewhat out of step with the public mood and that there is nothing concrete to suggest that the electorate would not have responded to a more diverse, inclusive approach that could have centralised those most impacted by the Eighth Amendment when it was in situ. Concessions were made or, as one activist puts it, 'There was a complete failure to generalise to other issues.' Although there was a nod to LGBTQI+ inclusivity, this wasn't sufficiently reflected in the message, leaving little room to manoeuvre in addressing the need for trans-inclusive language in legislation. Although the history of patriarchal injustice and female incarceration weighs more heavily on the working class, their stories were sidelined in favour of more palatable middle-class representatives. Despite images of migrant women of colour being appropriated and their mistreatment used as a wrench to force a referendum in the first place, we pretended that race didn't matter and glossed over the day-to-day discrimination endured by many of these same women. We left behind our Mincéir citizens and compounded Ireland's history of prejudice against Irish Travellers. We walked away from these conversations when arguably they mattered the most.

Some believe that a consequence of the referendum campaign's short-term thinking was to increase the burden of work for some grassroots groups. Emily Wazak of MERJ explains:

> I mean, to be honest, I know that the white feminists don't understand the impact of their messaging exclusion because people who are the most vulnerable are still having to help each other illegally to get pills, not only illegally but under the nose of Direct Provision managers or immigration authorities and things like that,

you know trying to help each other get visas, trying to talk people through immigration, all of the things. The people who decided that migrants weren't important, they are not the people that migrants are going to. So, it is making more work for us, it makes it harder for us to take care of our own communities.

For MERJ, the erasure of migrants from the campaign, but also the failure to acknowledge this shortcoming, stung. Cristina Florescu told me 'We've had a lot of people reach out to us privately to condemn the actions of their peers, which is great', but continued:

But the damage done was done publicly. Migrants and ethnic minorities were excluded from public platforms. Our members continue to be attacked by people who are supposed to be allies, publicly. Their emotional labour in dealing with a Twitter fight or negative comment is public and although it might seem trivial, for people who are fighting against a capitalist, white supremacist system, this is yet another added weight to carry on a daily basis.

In the autumn of 2019, MERJ held a well-attended conference called 'Challenging White Feminism, Moving beyond the Politics of the Together for Yes Campaign', and appealed for public accountability for the campaign's failure to engage with the complex barriers facing many migrants. In the podcast 'Disturbing the Peace' created by Rachel O'Neill (and broadcast in November, 2019), MERJ members Paolo Rivetti and Sonia Balaglopalan again called for public accountability and called out a post-repeal self-congratulatory tone that still marginalises migrants and minorities, people with disabilities and trans people.

In 2021, Alannah Murray, formerly of Disabled Women Ireland, criticised Irish social justice activism, describing a 'toxic' culture where, as a young woman with a disability, she was pushed forward to speak for the cause when this suited, but with little regard for her own personal well-being; both financial and emotional.[3] Murray describes surface-level concerns where people sometimes advised her to slow down, but then their contradictory actions where she was simultaneously 'consumed by the constant cacophony of favours', with few accommodations to ensure equality of participation. She too describes a culture where everyone needed to be 'on message' and described 'a hierarchical structure of deities that us lowly campaigners were expected to aspire to, to listen to, and never question' for fear of being labelled difficult or of jeopardising the campaign. She was disillusioned by a power dynamic that supported the status quo and 'a campaign run by white, Irish, settled people. Women who made me feel comfortable because they looked and sounded like me.' She continued, 'I will never forgive myself for letting them in my ear, and they let me sacrifice my ethics for the sake of victory, which allowed me to celebrate while trans women, non-binary people, and migrants were deemed unpalatable. While the North, as always, fought for itself.'

Rather than pretend that criticisms don't exist, the strength of a movement is its capacity to evaluate past performances and learn lessons that can influence future work. As Cristina Florescu from MERJ explained:

> The reason why we're so critical … is not because of personal beef or because we as a group feel hurt, but because we believe that this replicates other oppressive discourses … We believe that social justice movements need to include everyone, and they need to reflect the fabric of the society affected by a certain issue to make sure that no one gets left behind.

Her hope for the repeal movement going forward is to

> Be uncomfortable with it [criticisms] and be genuinely open to actions that will help all parties move forward. Without being performative, without being defensive, without being scared of being uncomfortable. We understand that it's hard to criticise or accept criticism of a movement you've poured your heart and soul into, but otherwise, we will create a glorifying narrative of white feminism and replicate racist, exclusionary power imbalances in social justice movements.

This genuine openness and capacity to reflect on an imperfect, but nonetheless successful referendum campaign should be a feature of Ireland's reproductive rights movement that, by the spring of 2021, was building again. Many people who had stepped back re-engaged and numbers swelled in ARC which is still the largest volunteer-led reproductive rights organisation in Ireland. Their co-conveners Helen Stonehouse and JoAnne Neary explained their priority as continuing to seek free, safe, legal and local abortion across the Island of Ireland. They explain how 'our legislation leaves far too many people behind and places far too many barriers in front of those seeking to control their own reproductive journey. Naturally, the impact of those barriers is most strongly felt by those already marginalised in society.' Helen and JoAnne continue:

> These may be minor inconveniences for many, but for undocumented migrants, disabled people, those in precarious employment, or those living with domestic violence, these quickly become insurmountable barriers. The current legislation is not fit for purpose and we're eager to change that ... rights are meaningless without access.

There are also many other active groups across the country: the aforementioned Abortion Action Campaign West (AACW), Sligo Action Reproductive Rights Access (SARRA), Tipp for Choice, Pro-Choice Galway, Carlow Choice and Equality network, Dundalk for Change, Rebels4choice, Inishowen Together (Donegal), Kerry for Choice, Fingal Feminist Network (formally Fingal ARC), ARC Offaly, Clare ARC, Leitrim ARC, Dún Laoghaire Together for Choice and Equality, North Wicklow Together for Choice and Equality, and Limerick Feminist Network, which is leading the Together for Safety campaign.[4] ROSA has also grown and there are active groups in Belfast, Limerick, Cork and Dublin. Other groups maintain Facebook pages and may reform in the future. Emma Hendrick of Dublin South-West Together for Choice and Equality explains, 'We are here but we are dormant, I think people were burnt out from repeal ... but we will re-ignite.' Further details of active groups are included at the end of this book.

The annual March for Choice has continued. In 2018, there was a celebratory feel to the event when the focus was on services for Northern Ireland. In 2019, the theme was 'No One Left Behind', and in 2020 (and moved online) 'Care at Home' shone a light on the fifty or so early abortions that fail each year. In 2021, the focus was Breaking Barriers. ARC have also researched the effectiveness of Irish services and continue to broaden their scope beyond the singular issue of abortion. JoAnne and Helen explain:

> Since Repeal, we've written submissions on sex work legislation, on improving the RSE (relationships and sexuality education) curriculum, on ending Direct Provision, on equality for Travellers, on gender equality and racial discrimination. We've also worked to raise awareness of wider issues through blog posts and social media campaigns on issues such as obstetric violence, period poverty, trans health care, free contraception. We've also recently hosted a panel on the intersections between trans health care, bodily autonomy and reproductive rights – we hope to expand on this work in the future.

ARC also work closely with the Northern Ireland Alliance for Choice (the Alliance) who have launched online workshops on self-administering abortion and have delivered 6-week programmes for doulas. The Alliance is not the only group active in Northern Ireland. The Ulster University pro-choice society has 40–50 active members and much of their work is about de-stigmatising abortion. Derry Alliance for Choice also remain active on a range of reproductive rights issues.

An Abortion Working Group (AWG), composed of 25 civil society organisations and healthcare providers was convened in 2019 and chaired by the NWCI[5] to provide a space for pro-choice groups to collectively advocate for safe access to abortion. Orla O'Connor, Director of the NWCI explains 'the Working Group is dedicated and collaborative space that the NWC convenes to provide a platform for national and local organisations working to improve abortion care in Ireland. It is just one aspect of their much broader work in the area of reproductive rights.'

Put these activisms together and it is clear that Ireland has a vibrant, vigilant creative reproductive rights movement who can work together, use creative expression and put pressure on reluctant politicians. This movement must take strength in the landslide referendum result in 2018 and be ambitious in its demands. This ARC member sets out her own advice to all of us when she notes:

There was a tendency in the referendum campaign, as there was earlier in the campaign for marriage equality, to focus on persuading a particular type of voter – older, middle-class, settled, white, Irish-born, socially conservative – who is both unrepresentative of both society and the electorate and is unlikely to be particularly persuadable. The fact that we've done that twice now and got away with it doesn't mean it was a good strategy and I hope we won't make the same mistake next time.

The need to keep active is essential. In May 2021, eleven TDs from the cross-party Life and Dignity Group launched the Foetal Pain Relief Bill which is a re-hash of a TRAP law attempted in 2018. Again, this directly mirrors patterns in the US, where the anti-abortion movement has successfully carved away at many reproductive rights. For example, in May 2021, the Texas 'heartbeat law' was signed, banning abortion as early as six weeks with no exceptions. These are just some of a raft of restrictions people increasingly face and many Americans must now travel miles for an abortion. Although some controls have been struck down in lower courts, in September 2021, the Texas 'Heartbeat law' (or Senate Bill 8) was upheld by the US Supreme Court – conservatively weighted since the appointment of Amy Coney-Barrett who is a former member of the US group Right to Life. Senate Bill 8 clearly violates the 1973 Row v. Wade Supreme Court ruling that constitutionality protects a women's right to abortion. A similar tactic worked in Poland when, in 2020, a Constitutional Tribunal Ruling banned abortion for foetal anomaly. Abortion is now only allowed where a woman's life is at risk or where a pregnancy is as a result of rape.[6] Poland is not the only European country with tight restrictions. Some other countries also insist on wait-periods or counselling. Three (Andorra, Malta and San Marino) prohibit abortion and two (Monaco and Liechtenstein) allow it only where there is risk to a woman's life or health, or in cases of rape or foetal anomaly. But there is hope. In December 2020, abortion was legalised in Argentina, also a Catholic country and again because of a 'green-wave' grassroots feminist resistance movement. Activists are confident that this landmark decision will permeate throughout other countries in Latin America, including Brazil where there is an active, radical feminist movement. In June 2021, people in Gibraltar also voted by 62 per cent to ease tough abortion restrictions.

THE WIDER DEMANDS OF REPEAL

One of the strengths of a reproductive justice approach is how it continually draws our eye to much broader concerns and away from the limiting binaries of a singular legalistic and morally focused discussion on abortion. Every stage of the process that repealed the Eighth had wider demands, including the need for progressive, affordable, culturally appropriate reproductive health care and education services. The 2017 Citizens' Assembly made four ancillary recommendations:

1. Improvements should be made in sexual health and relationship education, including the areas of contraception and consent, in primary and post-primary schools, colleges, youth clubs and other organisations involved in education and interactions with young people.

2. Improved access to reproductive healthcare services should be available to all women – to include family planning services, contraception, perinatal hospice care and termination of pregnancy if required.

3. All women should have access to the same standard of obstetrical care, including early scanning and testing. Services should be available to all women throughout the country irrespective of geographic location or socio-economic circumstances.

4. Improvements should be made to counselling and support facilities for pregnant women both during pregnancy and, if necessary, following a termination of pregnancy, throughout the country.

These were endorsed by the Committee on the Eighth Amendment who instructed the Dáil to introduce a scheme of free contraception, a thorough review of RSE, and equal and better access to obstetric care for all women irrespective of where they live or their socio-economic status. Some progress has been made. In April 2019, A Working Group on Access to Contraception was established and invited open submissions. The Irish Family Planning Association (IFPA) made a lengthy submission as did other pro-choice groups who had worked hard on repeal. When the working group reported on their scoping enquiry in October 2019, it identified significant gaps in local access, a lack of knowledge on contraception options, and, for many people, an insurmountable cost barrier which can run to hundreds of euros for certain procedures. Upon receiving its report, Simon Harris announced that the first-phase rollout of free contraception for those aged 18–25 would begin in 2021. He blamed budget restraints for the lag. Covid-19 brought further delays and at the time of writing, no clear pathway has been identified to advance this policy. As Ailbhe Smyth puts it:

> I keep reminding people we're still looking for free contraception, which was promised but has not been delivered. That's so obvious. If you really want sex to become a lot safer for people who can become pregnant, you make contraception freely available, and give people all of the information that they need about it.

The Iona Institute have objected to this scheme on the basis that contraception increases abortions, despite no evidence to support this.[7]

There have been other reproductive health-care related delays as a result of the government response to the Coronavirus. Some sexual health services were suspended, including the insertion and removal of coils, and sterilisations. There have also been pauses in cancer-screening programmes. Between March 2020 and March 2021, BreastCheck was only operational for three months. By the end of 2020, there were widespread reports of over 99,000 Cervical Check delays.

Maternity rights also became an explosive issue in 2020–21, when many people were denied their right to have a birth partner attend outside of a short window during labour and immediately post-birth. Reports surfaced of women receiving bad news alone and of increased levels of medical intervention from the sheer stress of it all. Emma Carroll and Ciara McGuine were both affected, so they decided to set up a Facebook page called 'In Their Shoes', allowing others to anonymously share their stories. They explained their motivation to me:

> Our initiative had a simple aim – to give a voice to the voiceless being affected by the restrictions across maternity care in Ireland since March 2020. We were both familiar with Erin Darcy's work from the time of Repeal and saw just how effective it was. The premise of her work was simple, telling the stories of those who had been

so devastatingly affected by Ireland's archaic stance on reproductive health, but it was so very effective. We could provide the facts and figures on why, in the case of Covid, maternity care restrictions are entirely unjustified, but we realised it would just not resonate with people in the same way as the stories of those affected, in their own words, would.

Some of these sanctions may have been avoidable if our public health-care system had not been so disastrously hollowed out by decades of neglect by the state. In February 2020, a HIQA (Health Information and Quality Authority) safety inspection of maternity hospitals reported understaffing and physical environments that were well below international standards.[8] Whilst these old-fashioned, cramped conditions were commonly cited as the reason for Covid-19 restrictions, this midwife who posted anonymously on 'in their shoes' has another take on what is going on:

> Pregnant people need their partner's support. It boggles the mind of the ordinary person that they can't get it. But for those of us in the system it doesn't. It's just one more way to control women. Repealing the 8th took power from the patriarchy, but here's a chance for them to grab it back. No evidence, just power, like much in the maternity system … Episiotomies, CTG [foetal monitoring], no evidence for either, but it gives them, not the pregnant person, a sense of power. It's horrific. It needs to end. I'm fed up.[9]

In May 2021, the Association for Improvements in Maternity Services (AIMS) Ireland began protesting outside maternity hospitals across the country. There was also pressure from other advocacy organisations, some TDs and journalists, including Zara King. All pointed out how restrictions were denying a person's right to have a birth-partner (often the child's parent) present from admission to discharge as was typically the case before the pandemic. It was late August 2021 before restrictions began to be relaxed but only in some hospitals. This was some time after public health guidelines allowed pubs and restaurants to resume indoor dining.

There has also been renewed concern about the State's ongoing failure to separate maternity care from the Catholic Church. The Church-State collusion described in Chapter 3 isn't just historical. In

2017, a Fine Gael government chose to build a new National Maternity Hospital on land worth €200 million that is owned by the religious order the Sisters of Charity. The NWCI and other reproductive rights organisations including AIMS, ROSA and ARC protested, and some high-profile obstetricians, in particular Peter Boylan, vehemently objected. Many repeal activists I spoke with also complained. There were demands that the 'National maternity hospital NOT [be] Connected IN ANY WAY to church' or, from someone else, 'I think religious influence in Ireland, in particular the Catholic Church is a huge issue for women's reproductive rights.' In 2021, it became clear that the Sisters of Charity have reneged on their 2017 promise to gift the land that the hospital is scheduled to be built on to the people of Ireland. Instead, €800 million of public money will build a maternity hospital on land owned by this religious order to be managed by a private subsidiary company called St Vincent's Holdings. This company, and not the government, will appoint the board of directors. Although St Vincent's Holdings have repeatedly promised all legal procedures will be performed in this hospital, can we really trust their word when we know that abortions are never carried out on land owned by the Catholic Church, the world's largest and most organised anti-choice lobbyists? The Campaign Against Church Ownership of Women's Healthcare chaired by Jo Tully re-energised its campaign and initiated a letter-writing drive asking members of the public to raise the issue with their local TD. Activists from the campaign were joined by many repeal activists when they marked the third anniversary of repeal by protesting outside the Dáil dressed in the red-and-white attire of Margaret Atwood's Handmaids and calling for our national hospital to be public and secular. Hundreds of activists also protested outside the Dáil in a second demonstration organised by the Campaign Against Church Ownership of Women's Health in June 2021, many donning repeal merchandise. Many of the speakers were familiar faces from the repeal movement. Collectively they called on the government to either compulsorily purchase the land or pull out of the deal altogether.

In terms of relationships and sexuality education (RSE), there has been some movement, some of which was as a result of grassroots local protest. In May 2019, parents at Castleknock Educate Together Primary School in Dublin mounted a picket outside the school because the board of management had hired the Catholic marriage agency

Accord to deliver RSE. This forced the school to climb down from its decision and is also thought to have influenced a directive from the national patron body of Educate Together (ET) that all RSE should be delivered in a way that is consistent with a multidenominational ethos. In October 2019, a report from the Oireachtas Education Committee deemed current practices outdated. At the same time, the National Council for Curriculum Assessment (NCCA) reviewed the curriculum and recommended a rights-based, holistic approach that would focus on identity and self-esteem, consent, LGBTQI+ matters, positive sexual expression, and contraception. ARC broadly supported these recommendations and alerted the NCCA to the need to include abortion laws and services. Predictably, anti-choice activists objected to what the Iona Institute describe as 'morally neutral education'. In the Dáil, Peadar Tóibín of the political party Aontú argued a national approach would breach parental rights.[10] This argument thinly veils these objector's real motivation where, without anything to back it up, sex education is thought to result in more sex and therefore more unwanted pregnancies. The government's current timeline for a revised RSE programme is 2022–23. In the meantime, by spring 2021, just half of Irish schools were meeting the current minimum state requirement.[11]

FROM REPRODUCTIVE RIGHTS TO REPRODUCTIVE JUSTICE

'The Reproductive Justice Movement has an enormous agenda,' write Loretta Ross and Rickie Sollinger, 'it aims to build a world in which all children are wanted and cared for, in which supports exist for families of all sizes and conditions and in which societies give priority to creating the conditions for people to be healthy and thrive.' It is an expansive philosophy that centres around three core rights. To recap, these are

1) the right *not* to have children through the use of contraception, abortion, or abstention;
2) the right *to* have children under conditions of our choosing, and
3) the right to parent in a safe, healthy environments.

A reproductive justice framework also seeks the right to gender freedom and freedom of sexual expression and moves beyond a reproductive healthcare model which although crucial in establishing vital services, can be time-consuming, limited in its capacity to address access issues and does little to tackle the root causes of health inequalities. Reproductive justice advocates also challenge a reproductive rights model that obscures the limits within which 'choice' is exercised and that ultimately trusts in the political system to deliver change. Tactically, rights-based activism can over-rely on strategies that assume people have access to elected officials, be this through an email or a ballot box. This under-appreciates the fact that many people who are marginalised are locked out of electoral politics, or may have little faith in a system that is not representative of their lives and that has done nothing to change their material circumstances. Reproductive justice is therefore about opening uncomfortable conversations about how capitalism organises our world, conversations that although fundamental to a person's reproductive well-being, are frequently sidestepped. This includes reckoning with racism and the exploitation of the working class, taking a stance on the right to housing, decent work and the need for publicly funded care supports, and engaging with the brutality of borders. Some local groups have embodied this approach. By way of example, Fingal ARC have rebranded as Fingal Feminist Network and describes itself as 'a grassroots intersectional feminist group organising to advance equality, human rights, and collective social rights'. One of their co-founders, Laren Folen, explains, 'Our grassroots ethic recognises the necessity in organising autonomously from below as a means of push back against patriarchal, capitalist and racialised systems.' They have actively responded to a rise in far-right activism and racist attacks in the Fingal area (an expansive area in North Dublin with a population of around 300,000) and have mobilised campaigns to end Direct Provision and address racism.

A reproductive justice framework can attract support from a wide audience. When I asked activists about the biggest issue for the women's movement in Ireland today, 26 per cent said childcare and 20 per cent said housing. It is obvious that affordable childcare directly impacts a person's capacity to have a child. Ireland has one of the most expensive childcare systems in Europe[12] and many people feel uncomfortable about the industry's reliance on exploitative labour. Housing and homelessness are also a major issue. Over 100,000 families are on the State's housing waiting list and women are more likely to be homeless that their European counterparts, more likely to hide their situation because services are geared towards men, and more likely to head homeless lone-parent families.[13] This Parents for Choice member wrote 'The government needs to build social housing and stop paying huge sums to hotels and hubs, etc.' Another argued, 'We need a complete overhaul of housing policy towards public housing, rent controls and protections against evictions.' And again, 'The right to housing and social inequality are fundamentally feminist issues.' Twenty-two per cent believe the gender pay gap is the biggest issue for the women's movement to address and 23 per cent want more to be done about health care more broadly. Some canvassers think the repeal movement failed to harness the energy at the grassroots to tackle these issues. As one person puts it: 'Imagine if the Together for Yes group, or even 5 per cent of it had been mobilised to fight seriously on housing or health care.' From someone else: 'I see it as the most active and engaged time for a feminist movement and politics, unfortunately much of energy seems unchanneled afterwards.'

As many as 19% per cent believe that part of the problem in today's world is an absence of female politicians. But does it really matter if a woman is elected to Dáil Eireann when the neoliberal policies they implement compound inequality? Four women have served as Tánaiste in Ireland,[14] including Joan Burton, former leader of the Labour Party. Like her counterparts, she implemented neoliberal policies including harsh austerity cuts to local elder-care services, health care and disability services, thereby greatly increasing the care burden for many women. She also cut fuel allowances, school uniform and footwear allowances, rent supplements and school transport.[15] As the socialist Deirdre Cronin put it at the time:

> Women have become the main targets of the war on welfare instigated by … Joan Burton, in a disgraceful attempt to deflect blame away from those really responsible – the banks, the developers, the capitalist class and system as a whole – and focus people's minds on the necessity of slashing public spending.[16]

In a more recent example of the futility of voting for women based on gender rather than policy, Mairead McGuinness, Maria Walsh and Frances Fitzgerald were three of four MEPs who in 2019 voted against increasing search-and-rescue missions in the Mediterranean. The vote was lost by two. Nearly 1,500 migrants that we know of drowned in the Mediterranean the following year.[17]

One of the biggest problems with much social justice activism today is its mistrust, even hostility, towards groups that are expressly anti-capitalist. This was a feature of aspects of the repeal campaign where the actions of socialist-leaning groups were at times frowned upon. In 2020, one non-ROSA activist told me about events in her local group where she heard 'disparaging comments that were made about ROSA implying they were too extreme and thus damaging the campaign'. She explained:

> I believed this narrative until I canvassed an area that had previously been canvassed by ROSA and people on the doors spoke highly of them. After the vote there was a lot of Twitter drama to the same effect of ROSA being too extreme. I felt like this was not an accurate representation of how ordinary voters felt about ROSA and reflected poorly on those who made the comments. I hate to think of in-fighting between people who believe in choice.

A People Before Profit activist talked about knowing 'what was said about us behind closed doors' and maintains there was a strong anti-working-class bias within her local Together for Yes group. She explains:

> I remember having to argue within my group, who claim to be progressive, to canvass working-class areas. They didn't think there was any point. That is the community that came out the strongest in Yes Equality, and that is the community that is most affected by repealing the Eighth. They are the women who can't afford to travel, they are the marginalised, they are the people of colour but yet the [middle-class] people who were in my Together for Yes group didn't feel there was a need to canvass those areas. That is just outrageous.

Others felt that, on the national stage, pro-repeal leaders turned their heads to the political right and not the political left. This was certainly the behaviour of the mainstream media and I was struck by the words of one prominent left-wing, working-class activist who told me 'From

March [to] May 2018 my phone never rung as little.' And while there has been much rhetoric on the need for the Irish reproductive rights movement to be more inclusive moving forward, left-leaning groups such as MERJ and ROSA remain outside of the NWCI-convened working group on Abortion. When I asked one ROSA activist about this exclusion she responded, 'they'd never let socialists around that table.'

Differences between reformist, liberal visions of feminism and more radical interpretations are not new. As liberals seek to unite women against the tyranny of sexism within existing structures of society, a more radical and anti-capitalist model seeks to change the system itself. While some liberal feminists are not interested in changing the status quo, many are committed to equality. These same people often take up jobs in state-funded feminist and social justice organisations in the hope that their work might align with their politics. I know first-hand that working in nonprofit groups can feel great and there are times when you make a real difference in a person's life. In an attempt to advance reforms, many civil society groups have adopted the vernacular of reproductive justice. As they rush to 'diversify', people of colour and people with disabilities are asked to join committees and working groups, sometimes even to retrospectively legitimize work that has already been done. Minority groups are listed as 'allies' and mission statements are carefully re-crafted to 'acknowledge' and even 'understand' intersectionality. This all-important and often well-meaning image change is topped off with websites, leaflets and posters that reflect a range of 'abilities' and 'ethnicities'. In no time at all, an intersectional, self-aware group is outwardly presented to the world. The reality of these freshly transformed environments is that the experiences for people who are structurally oppressed is often worse. They are always in demand for photo-shoots and representation on committees, often without pay. When they do get a seat at the table, they are expected to speak respectfully and on behalf of the homogenised group they are supposedly representing. To quote Emily Wazak:

It was really important that we weren't just seen as being there to bring our experience ... we are not just sad stories; we bring our own analysis. You might get a brown face on a panel, but who owns the platform? Who decided on the platform and who doesn't? Right now it's still being decided by whiteness or proximity to capitalism, there is the listening and then the doing after that, that is the main thing.

A reproductive justice framework resists virtue signalling, where empty gestures uphold a whole set of paternalistic and decontextualized assumptions about reproductive decision making and critically evaluates the capacity of state-funded cohorts to initiate change. We simply have to look at their history to see how their modus operandi is largely rooted in power and privilege, where the white middle-classes give time and money to 'the deserving poor'. As Sarah Jaffe puts it, 'Nonprofits are not, despite their supposedly not in service of the profit motive, exceptions to the capitalist system but embedded in it, necessary for its continued existence.'[18] Their outreach model is also centred on the belief that some people are unable or unwilling to engage in approaches that others have decided are best for them. This perspective is captured by the ROSA activist Emma Quinn who shared the following story when she describes an experience at a Coalition to Repeal the Eighth Amendment meeting in 2014:

> There were hundreds of people there and I was quite new to politics but there was something very specific about that meeting that I will always remember. I decided to stand up and say something ... I basically made the point that working-class women have a key role to play because they're the ones most impacted in lots of different ways. When the meeting ended, one of the Coalition leaders came down to me and said, 'I was wondering, is there any way that you would do outreach to working-class communities?' The idea that just because I had a working-class accent, it hadn't mattered what I had said, nothing about me politically had resonated, my opinion didn't matter, just that I had 'the voice to do outreach'. Even the idea of outreach 'like working-class people are some special group' I just found it so offensive ... working-class women had already been a key part of society, the idea that you need a special outreach group for 'those people' offended me; we are not some niche category of people, we are the ones dealing with the consequences of these laws every day.

In her manifesto for conceptualising reproductive justice theory, Loretta Ross is clear that a reproductive justice approach includes 'the need to challenge conceptual practices of the pro-choice movement that not only understates issues of intersectionality and white supremacy but also offers no radical alternatives to neoliberal capitalism and its emphasis on rights and choices.[19] The Irish reproductive rights movement can push forward to defend and improve a substandard reproductive healthcare system, but should it also turn away from electoral politics as the panacea for a better world? There is no reform pathway that can challenge carceral feminism, institutional racism, precarious employment, or that 41 per cent – or 700 million – women of reproductive age live under restrictive abortion laws with as many as 23,000 dying from unsafe abortions every year.[20] The Irish reproductive rights movement has proven that change only happens from struggle. A reproductive justice model can extend this struggle beyond singular issues and guide us in creating a better, kinder, more sustainable world for ourselves and for future generations.

Independent/Non-Funded Groups
Active in 2021

Abortion Rights Campaign (ARC)
Principal aim: To maintain and improve abortion access but we do focus on other issues also.
Active membership: >50 people.
Activities: Regular meetings, leader on campaigns on reproductive rights, support the campaigns of others, deliver workshops, write to TDs, raise questions in the Dáil.
Funding: Merchandising and local fundraising.
Why are you still together: The work still isn't done. Winning the referendum was so important, but it was only the first step in achieving free, safe, legal and local abortion care. And abortion care is only one part of reproductive justice. We're going to be here until no one has to travel for abortion, until abortion is treated as an everyday part of sexual and reproductive health, until people have real, meaningful choice – that means the choice to continue a pregnancy as well as to end one, regardless of your circumstances. We're a long way from that – but we've come *so* far.

Alliance for Choice (Northern Ireland)
Principal aim: We are a grass-roots, non-hierarchical feminist collective comprised of women and pregnant people who are activists, that have been refused abortions, have been forced to travel for abortions, or have barriers to access. We believe in abortion access and reproductive justice for all who need it.
Active membership: c. 11–20 people.
Activities: Regular meetings, leader on campaigns on reproductive rights, support the campaigns of others, delivered self-managed abortion pill workshops, activist training, abortion doula training, abortion and faith training, abortion and disability, difficult questions

about abortion and self-care workshops, sought to raise questions in the NI Assembly.

Funding: Merchandising and other local fundraisers.

Why are you still together: The NI executive has failed to commission abortion services in the North despite the decriminalisation of abortion in 2019. We provide a fundamental service to people in need across the North and will continue to do so until every person who requires access to abortion health care and reproductive rights receives it.

Association for Improvements in Maternity Services Ireland (AIMSI)

Principal aim: AIMS Ireland is run on a fully voluntary basis by women from all regions of Ireland, most with young families. AIMS Ireland committee members represent a wide range of birth choices and experiences, but come together under the common view of improving services.

Active membership: 8–10 attend core organisational meetings, manage social media accounts, or do some other form of work. More than 50 attend issue-related meetings and protests and contribute to social media discussions informing the work of organisations. We also have a support team that provides support to women relating to pregnancy, birth, and access to services.

Activities: Regular meetings, leader on campaigns on reproductive rights, support the campaigns of others, deliver workshops, write to TDs, raise questions in the Dáil. We provide evidence-informed information on our website on a variety of pregnancy, birth and post-partum related issues including access to services and current issues as they emerge.

Funding: Merchandising and local fundraising.

Why are you still together: AIMS Ireland works for the improvement of reproductive and maternity services. This includes abortion service provision. Work across all these areas of reproductive rights continues. Ireland has a long road to reproductive rights for all people.

Lawyers for Choice

Principal aim: To maintain and improve abortion access in Ireland.

Active membership: c. 1–10 people.

Funding: None.

Activities: We have been involved in discussions with the NWCI group, ARC and TFMR re: the legislative review. We used to run workshops and might again but have been relatively dormant since 2019.

Why are you still together: Because people still ask us to explain/ analyse the law.

Migrants and Ethnic Minorities for Reproductive Justice (MERJ)

Principal aim: To create a space where migrant and ethnic minority people can come together, share politics and experiences, learn from each other and support one another in the struggle for a more just society.

Active membership: Varies from a small number to much more for specific mobilisations.

Activities: Consciousness-raising education that deliberately focuses on reproductive justice, street protests, events that seek to link capitalism, misogyny, transphobia, racism, and workers' exploitation to reproductive rights.

Fundraising: Donations.

ROSA (for Reproductive Rights against Oppression, Sexism and Austerity)

Principal aim: ROSA's guiding principle is that of socialist feminism. In order to change society, we can't rely on the elite adopting feminism. Progressive change comes from powerful public pressure from below. This was the case in Repeal when young women and non-binary people led canvasses, had challenging conversations, shared their stories on social media and participated in marches and protests – resulting in an overwhelming vote for bodily autonomy …

Active membership: >50 people. We are able to create a core of dedicated and collaborative activists and take bold initiatives sometimes aimed at raising awareness, other times aimed at winning progressive reforms and change.

Activities: Regular meetings, street protests, leader of campaigns that are broader than reproductive rights, raising questions in the Dáil. Regular political meetings that analyse the context in which we live and that link capitalism, misogyny, transphobia, racism, and workers' exploitation.

Fundraising: We fundraise through our membership and through public support.

Why are you still together: Because socialist feminism provides a unique perspective for addressing gender and racial oppression as well as exploitation, and we believe that as the crises of capitalism deepen, this will be a more popular idea amongst young women and non-binary people who are becoming politically active.

START (Southern Taskgroup on Abortion & Reproductive Topics)

Principal aim: To maintain and improve abortion access in Ireland.

Affiliation: Independent.

Active membership: >250 abortion care providers.

Activities: Regular meetings, written to the Minister for Health and Minister for Justice to inform them of the anticipated problems with provision during the Covid pandemic and to ask that remote provision of abortion care would be permitted during the Covid emergency. Partnership with Irish College of GPs delivering training for GPs.

Why are you still together: We provider peer support for abortion care providers and mentoring for new providers. We seek to include new providers in the abortion care community of healthcare providers in Ireland.

TFMR (Termination for Medical Reasons) Ireland and LMC Support

Principal aim: Access to abortion after diagnosis of foetal anomaly or in other medically indicated circumstances. Bereavement support, access to medical diagnostics and pre-natal screening and non-directive health care.

Active membership: We have lots of members whom we support, but our entire team running the charity and campaign group consists of four members plus a couple more who do ad hoc tasks, not day-to-day activities.

Activities: Regular meetings, leading campaigns on reproductive rights, pledging support to other campaigns, media work, letters to TDs and government ministers. Workshops on healing and recovery from grief after losing a baby through TFMR. This training is focused on running support groups and peer support rather than campaigning.

Funding: Merchandising and other local fundraisers.

LOCAL GROUPS

Abortion Access Campaign West

Principal aim: To maintain and improve abortion access, but we do focus on other issues also such as public ownership and control of the new NMH. Sexual health education, free contraceptives for all.
Affiliation: Independent.
Active membership: c. 1–10 people.
Funding: We receive a non-government grant that doesn't pay any wages, but covers some day-to-day costs.
Activities: Regular meetings, campaigning on reproductive rights, support for campaigns by others, preparing for the review of the legislation, supporting campaigns abroad, for example, Polish women's fight for abortion rights and highlighting issues on social media.
Why are you still together: Many gaps remain in the 'rollout' of services. Women still travel abroad. There seems to be no cohesive policy around TFMR and the chilling effect of fear of criminalisation still exists.

Alliance for Choice, Derry

Principal Aim: We fight for reproductive justice so have always sought better support for parents and children, as well as abortion rights.
Affiliation: ARC.
Active membership: >50
Activities: Regular meetings, street protests, campaigns relating to reproductive rights, educational workshops, letters to politicians. Educational workshops.
Funding: None.
Why are you still together: While abortion is legal, access is difficult; welfare reform means many families are forced to end a pregnancy they might want to continue if they could afford it.

ARC Offaly

Principal aim: To maintain and improve abortion access.
Active membership: c. 1–10 people.
Affiliation: ARC.
Activities: Campaigns for reproductive rights, letters to politicians.
Funding: None.

Why are you still together: Offaly has no abortion providers listed on MyOptions. We do know there are doctors who are providing, but only to their own patients. Rural access is very poor, and we have next to no public transport here in Offaly. We recently had Gianna Care set up in Offaly.

Carlow Choice and Equality Network

Principal aim: To maintain and improve abortion access, but we focus on other issues also.

Affiliation: Together for Choice and Equality Network.

Active membership: c. 10 active and >50 non-active members. We have elected representatives, policy advisors and lecturers who help us raise issues related to our campaigns (such as the campaign for a women's refuge in Carlow).

Activities: Street protests, leading campaigns over image-based sexual assault and the Mother and Baby Homes in Carlow. Workshops, campaigning for more safe accommodation at the Carlow Women's Refuge. We make people aware of how our elected representatives vote, particularly if it impacts key issues (such as the review of abortion legislation).

Funding: None.

Why are you still together: We still have work to do.

Dundalk for Change (Louth)

Principal aim: To maintain and improve abortion access, but we do focus on other issues also.

Active membership: 21–30 people.

Affiliation: Independent.

Activities: Regular meetings, lead new campaigns on reproductive rights, write to TDs and run workshops in response to specific needs.

Funding: Merchandising and other local fundraisers.

Why are you still together: Because the fight is not over.

Dún Laoghaire Together for Choice and Equality

Principal aim: To maintain and improve abortion access, but we do focus on other issues.

Active membership: c. 11–20 people.

Affiliation: Together for Choice and Equality Network.

Activities: Campaign about other issues, support for campaigns organised by other groups, we have written to politicians, and sought to raise a question in the Dáil.

Why are you still together: Many aspects of Irish society need addressing: Mother and Baby Homes, investigations into exclusion zones, smear debacles, exclusion zones for abortion providers, access for abortions across Ireland, National Maternity Hospital issues (no church influence), Direct Provision travesty, no shelters for abuse victims in our area.

Fingal Feminist Network (Formally Fingal ARC)

Principal Aim: We are a grassroots intersectional feminist group organising to advance equality, human rights, and collective social rights.

Affiliation: ARC.

Active membership: c. 1-10 people.

Activities: Regular meetings, street protests, campaigns relating to reproductive rights and wider local issues, educational workshops, letters to politicians. Organised anti-racism demonstration and have sought to counter far-right political activism in the Fingal area and have been involved in the creation of community organising against racism.

Funding: None.

Why are you still together: Because our grassroots ethic recognises the necessity in organising autonomously from below as a means of push back against patriarchal, capitalist and racialised system. There is work to be done in reproductive rights

Galway Pro Choice

Principal Aim: Mainly reproductive justice and gender-affirming care – full range of reproductive justice, including parental/maternity assistance.

Affiliation: Independent.

Active membership: We currently have about 10 members max that attend meetings and keep up with conversations, but if we were to hold a protest or event, we get higher numbers and we've been having new members engaging lately.

Activities: Regular meetings, street protests, campaigns relating to reproductive rights, educational workshops, letters to politicians. We held a trans/non-binary awareness week relating to abortion access. We have attended protests relating to anti-racism and as a counter-protest to a discriminating organisation. We had planned a very large feminist festival – 'This Legislation is Shite Fest' – just before Covid hit, which was unfortunately going to be a big event for us.

Funding: Merchandising and other local fundraisers.

Why are you still together: We consider ourselves to be consistently and unapologetically radical in that we believe everyone should be able to access abortion services as early as possible, as late as necessary. The current legislation and access in Ireland is extremely limited. Aside from abortion access, we are fighting for access to gender-affirming care and trans bodily autonomy. We also stand with impoverished parents who cannot afford necessities and whose parental rights become questioned simply due to poverty. We feel that our presence helps to keep de-stigmatising the subjects and we also need to keep reminding people not to sit down in the 25th mile of the marathon, because we are far from our goals of reproductive justice.

Inishowen Together (Donegal)

Principal aim: Broader than just abortion, other issues are just as important to us too.

Affiliation: ARC.

Active membership: c. 11–20 people.

Activities: Street protesting, campaigns on other issues, pledging support to other people's campaigns, writing to politicians.

Funding: None.

Why are you still together: There are many issues to work on. We enjoy working together.

Kerry for Choice

Principal aim: To maintain and improve abortion access.

Affiliation: ARC.

Active membership: c. 1–10 people.

Activities: Pledged support for the wider work of ARC.

Funding: None.

Why are you still together: There is still a divide in how accessible abortion services are in rural areas, which is why Kerry for Choice hasn't disbanded. Gianna Care [an anti-choice agency] also opened a branch in Tralee, so we feel there is a need for an active pro-choice group to push for the necessary and promised legislation that would regulate rogue crisis pregnancy agencies.

Leitrim Abortion Rights Campaign

Principal aim: We campaign for sexual health and reproductive rights in Ireland and globally. This includes the provision of free, safe, legal and accessible abortion, freely available contraception and objective sex education.

Affiliation: ARC.

Active membership: We have a small nucleus of active members (3–5) but a larger network of activists available at any given time.

Activities: Regular meetings, street protests, campaigning on reproductive rights and other issues, support to other people's campaigns, letters to politicians and raising questions in the Dáil.

Funding: Merchandising and other local fundraisers.

Why are you still together: Our objectives have not yet been achieved. We will continue to strive for full reproductive rights and to raise awareness of the issues surrounding our campaign.

North Wicklow Together for Choice and Equality

Principal aim: Much broader than just abortion. Big focus on the new National Maternity Hospital and diversity issues.

Affiliation: Together for Choice and Equality Network.

Active membership: We have a small core group but an active and engaged group of c. 60 people who will volunteer and help on events/ activities as they arise.

Activities: Supported campaigns organised by others, written to local politicians, have sought to raise a question in the Dáil.

Funding: None.

Why are you still together: To keep issues alive, to inform, to hold our TDs accountable, to question those seeking election and share their responses so people can make an educated decision on who to vote for. Many believe that repeal fixed abortion access, so right now education and awareness is very, very important.

Rebels4choice (Cork)

Principal aim: To maintain and improve abortion access and advocate for reproductive justice more broadly.

Active membership: 1–10 people.

Affiliation: ARC.

Activities: Regular meetings, leading campaigns on reproductive rights, letter-writing workshops, communications workshops.

Funding: Merchandising and other local fundraisers.

Why are you still together: To work for a good review of the legislation, so that people currently left behind are taken care of – but there will never not be a need for us. To improve access for all groups who were left behind by the abortion legislation. To ensure evidence-based and equitable provision of abortion services on the island of Ireland. To support international campaigns for reproductive justice.

ROSA Cork

Principal aim: To maintain and improve abortion access, but we do focus on other issues also.

Active membership: c. 11–20 people.

Affiliation: ROSA.

Activities: Street protests, new campaigns on other issues.

Funding: Merchandising and other local fundraisers.

Why are you still together: ROSA is a socialist feminist movement that focuses on the core of all issues in society, which is capitalism. Capitalism will never favour anything but itself and therefore must be challenged, especially when it comes to women's and LGBTQ+ issues.

ROSA NI (based in Antrim)

Principal aim: We are a socialist feminist organisation. We fight for abortion rights and access as well as against sexism, homophobia, transphobia and oppression and exploitation in all its forms. We see these struggles as connected to the fight against capitalism that relies on division, exploitation and oppression.

Active membership: c. 11–20 people.

Affiliation: ROSA.

Activities: Regular meetings and support for ROSA national events. We hold regular discussion groups. These can be reading groups, online public meetings and internal discussions. We organised a socially distanced stand-out against gender violence following the murder of Sarah Everard and the police response to this. With the recent attack on abortion rights in Stormont we have also launched a stickering campaign on the issue of abortion rights. Support for campaigns organised by others includes international solidarity campaigns and a campaign called Supporting Women Newry. ROSA regularly organises educational discussions – including about historical aspects of the revolutionary women's movement as well as discussions about the nature of capitalism.

Funding: Merchandising and other local fundraisers.

Why are you still together: ROSA adds a socialist feminist perspective, analysis and approach. With covid and its impact on working-class women and non-binary people in particular (eg job losses, shouldering the burden of the fight against covid as key workers, increased caring responsibilities including homeschooling, people leaving their jobs due to these pressures, the 'shadow pandemic' of gender violence) the need for a socialist feminist approach is more important than ever.

SARRA – Sligo Action Reproductive Rights Access

Principal aim: To advance women, girls and pregnant people's reproductive health and abortion rights, in particular through state provision of free, legal and easily accessible abortion services, in Co Sligo.

Affiliation: Independent.

Active membership: c. 1–10 people. Limited resources and volunteers, so we probably cannot focus on as many other issues as we would like to.

Activities: Regular meetings, lead campaigns on reproductive rights, write to local politicians and seek to raise questions in the Dáil. Active support for abortion rights in Northern Ireland.

Funding: None.

Why are you still together: We are still campaigning for GP and hospital abortion services in Sligo, both town and county, where there are still no services nearly three years after the referendum.

Tipp for Choice (Tipperary)

Principal aim: To maintain and improve abortion access, but we do focus on other issues also.

Affiliation: ARC.
Active membership: c. 1–10 people.
Funding: None.
Activities: Regular meetings, campaigns on reproductive rights, support for other campaigns.
Why are you still together: We reformed for the review. Tipperary needs a group to counter our TDs (3/4 anti-choice). We need to campaign for more doctors providing abortion and because no hospital in Tipperary provides surgical abortions.

Together for Safety (Limerick)
Principal aim: We are specifically lobbying for legislation for Safe Access Zones around health centres.
Affiliation: ARC.
Active membership: c. 11–20 people.
Activities: Regular meetings, we have written to politicians and sought to raise a question in the Dáil, presentations on the issue as in as many settings and to as many groups as possible.
Funding: None.
Why are you still together: There are daily protests outside the maternity hospital in Limerick and we want pregnant people and their families to be able to access health care in privacy and peace.

Ulster University Pro-Choice Society
Principal aim: To maintain and improve abortion access, but we do focus on other issues also, especially de-stigmatising abortion.
Affiliation: Independent.
Active membership: c. 40–50 people.
Funding: Fees from joining.
Activities: Regular meetings, support to other people's campaigns, educational workshops when there is a need, letters to politicians.
Why are you still together: Abortion is still not accessible for all those who need it and we are continually seeing our rights being threatened by anti-choice politicians and groups.

Notes

PROLOGUE

1. In McCafferty, 1985, p. xxiii.
2. Sweetman, 2020, p. 45.
3. Savita Halappanavar died from septicaemia in 2012. She was actively miscarrying and had requested an abortion, but this was refused. Her death, and its impact on Irish society is discussed at various points throughout this book, especially in Chapter 4.

1 INTRODUCING THE REAL HEROES

1. Speech by Leo Varadkar following the declaration on the Referendum on the Eight Amendment, www.taoiseach.gov.ie/ (retrieved 9 December 2018).
2. Wade, 2012.
3. www.thejournal.ie/fianna-fail-protect-rights-of-unborn-3646886-Oct2017/ (article 14 October 2017) (retrieved 16 November 2020).
4. Thirty-Fourth Amendment to the Constitution Bill, 2014. www.oireachtas.ie/en/debates/debate/dail/2014-09-25/21/ (retrieved 18 April 2021).
5. Speeches at: www.oireachtas.ie/en/debates/debate/dail/2018-05-29/15/#spk_178/ (retrieved 27 December 2019).
6. This was via two online anonymous questionnaires. Eligibility '*interacting with the general public by; knocking on doors as part of a team, distributing leaflets at static stalls (such as at shopping centres or train stations), and/or interacting with the public as a website moderator or social media organiser*' (emphasis added). In 2018, I disseminated to all groups affiliated to Together for Yes, and in 2020, to groups still together and circulated by ARC and the Coalition to Repeal the Eighth.
7. As testimonies were anonymous, I can't gauge duplication. There was similar geographical spread, mostly women (84 per cent); only 35 per cent got involved in 2018.
8. Thirty-six per cent of people in the 18–25 age range talked about negative encounters, dropping to 25 per cent of those aged 26–34 and 24 per cent of those aged 45yrs+.
9. See Healy, Sheehan, & Whelan, 2015, for an account of Yes Equality.
10. Griffin et al., 2019, p. 120.
11. Fitzgerald, 2021.

12. https://twitter.com/DeirdreDuffyDC/status/1220309325387878400/ (retrieved 11 April 2021).
13. Della Porta & Rucht 2013, p. 3.
14. Kennedy, 2021.
15. Lowe and Hayes, 2019.
16. www.gov.uk/government/statistics/abortion-statistics-for-england-and-wales-2020 (retrieved 29 June 2021).
17. Clarke, 2019.
18. www.abortionrightscampaign.ie/2020/09/25/care-at-home-after-failed-abortion/ (retrieved 5 April 2021).
19. www.oireachtas.ie/en/debates/question/2021-03-03/section/870/ (retrieved 6 April 2021).
20. In a UK study, 32 per cent were against abortion, dropping to 10 per cent believing it was wrong in all circumstances (Park et al., 2013, p. 19).
21. Research by Rocca et al., 2019, found just 5 per cent regret their decision to end a pregnancy.
22. Kissling, 2017, p. 1.
23. Jackson, 1992.
24. Ibid., pp. 1–2.
25. Thompson, 2017, p. 253.
26. Earner-Byrne, 2019.
27. Delay, 2019.
28. Sheldon & Wellings, 2020, p. 7.
29. Illich, 1976.
30. Macintyre, 1973, p. 132.
31. Jones, 2011, p. 285.
32. McBride Stetson, 2002, p. 137.
33. Kissling, 2017, p. 2.
34. Doan, 2016, pp. 71–72.
35. Schoen, 2015, p. 14.
36. Gutiérrez, 2004, p. 233.
37. Ross, 2017, p. 171.
38. https://forwardtogether.org/tools/a-new-vision/ (retrieved 21 March 2021).
39. Ross et al., 2017, p. 19.

2 REPRODUCTIVE OPPRESSIONS IN IRELAND

1. Fitzsimon et al., 2021.
2. In 2019, the combined wealth of 2,153 people was greater than the combined wealth of 4.6 billion people: Coffey et al., 2020.
3. Allen & O'Boyle, 2013, p. 4.
4. Sweeney, 2019.
5. Silliman et al., 2004.
6. Lynch, 2018, p. 142.

7. Cahill, 2001, p. 334.
8. Dundes, 1987.
9. UN, 2019, pp. 5–6.
10. World Health Organization, 2018, p. 8.
11. HSE, 2020a, p. 51.
12. Keating & Fleming, 2009, p. 519.
13. Burke, 2006.
14. Cited in Wade, 2017, p. 495.
15. Ibid., pp. 496–497.
16. Scally, 2018, p. 115.
17. www.thejournal.ie/vicky-phelan-221-5240838-Oct2020/ (retrieved 1 November 2020.
18. Costa, 2018.
19. Funge et al., 2020.
20. HSE, 2020a.
21. Ireland's *Confidential Maternity Death Enquiry* noted 'a five-fold difference in maternal mortality rates amongst women from Black Ethnic backgrounds and an almost two-fold difference amongst women from Asian Ethnic backgrounds compared with white women': CDE Ireland, 2019, p. 3.
22. Manning, 2014.
23. Naughton, 2013.
24. Lentin, 2013.
25. Fitzsimons et al., 2021.
26. For example, people who are deaf were discouraged from socialising together and were not taught sign language, in case they might marry and potentially increase the prevalence of deafness. See www.pbs.org/weta/throughdeafeyes/deaflife/women.html which provides information on this practice globally. My own neighbours, an elderly deaf couple, told me sign language was discouraged when they were young for this very reason.
27. Powell & Nickolson, 2019.
28. Its researchers include Prof. Eilionóir Flynn, Dr Jenny Dagg, Dr Áine Sperrin and Ms Maria Ní Fhlatharta. They understand disability broadly to include anyone who identifies as having a disability. This might be physical, intellectual, psycho-social, mental health, chronic illness, or another health diagnosis. It might be some of these together. Their project also recognises additional mediating factors such as gender, race and class. It includes the experiences of rural and urban inhabitants, institutionalised people, disabled migrants, and disabled people in the LGBTQI+ community.
29. These findings were presented at a webinar which can be found at: (49) Real Productive Justice Online Roadshow – YouTube.com watch?v= WKruLnt3ctw/ 10 May 2021.
30. Davis, 2003.

31. Ibid., p. 61.
32. www.iprt.ie/site/assets/files/6332/iprt_position_paper_on_women_in_the_criminal_justice_system.pdf/ (retrieved 24 March 2021).
33. Irish Penal Reform Trust, 2014.
34. Fenton, 2018, pp. 159–161.
35. Gilligan, 2019.
36. HSE, 2020b.
37. Moore, 2020.
38. Interview with Dr Vicky Conway on the Policed Podcast, broadcast 1 January 2021.
39. Black Pride Ireland (est. 2019) is an LGBTQIA+ organisation that describes itself as 'by Black queer people, for Black queer people in Ireland'. It is 'anti-capitalist, pro-choice, pro-sex worker' and as dedicated to 'the empowerment and uplifting of Black queer people here and everywhere': https://blackprideireland.ie/index.html#about/ (retrieved 9 March 2021).
40. Lally, 2021.
41. Woman's Aid, 2019, p. 9.

3 IRELAND'S DARK HISTORY OF INJUSTICES
AGAINST WOMEN

1. Government Publications, 1922.
2. Valiulis, 2011, p. 575.
3. Ferriter, 2009, pp. 299–300.
4. For a full history, see https://womenworkersunion.ie/history/ (retrieved 19 November 2020).
5. McAuliffe, 2011.
6. In Conrad, 2001.
7. Valiulis, 1992, p. 169.
8. Luddy, 2005.
9. Ibid., p. 194.
10. Valiulis, 1992, p. 43.
11. Leane & Kiely, 2004.
12. Ó Fátharta, 2015.
13. Mother and Baby Home Factsheet March 2017. Produced in partnership with the Adoption Coalition Worldwide. Thanks to the Coalition for supplying this.
14. Garrett, 2016.
15. Gallen & Gleeson, 2017, estimate a minimum of 14,607. Hogan, 2019, puts the figure as high as 30,000.
16. For an account of the role of the Gardaí, listen to 'The Policed Podcast' (episode 11).
17. Mac Cormaic, 2013.

18. Hogan, 2019, p. 65.
19. Ibid., p. 64.
20. Bray, 2021.
21. 'UN asked to intervene over Ireland's response to "systemic racism" in mother and baby homes', 16 April 2020 (retrieved 19 May 2021, from www.thejournal.ie/racism-mother-and-baby-homes-united-nations-5397125-Apr2021/).
22. Raftery & O'Sullivan, 1999.
23. Pembrook, 2019.
24. Inglis, 2003, pp. 140–141.
25. Sweetman, 2020, pp. 118–119.
26. Smyth, 1988, p. 335.
27. For full history, see https://onefamily.ie/about-us/our-history/ (retrieved 24 November 2020).
28. Coyne, 2018.
29. Connolly & O'Toole, 2005, p. 22.
30. Connolly & O'Toole, 2005, list members as Association of Women's Citizens of Ireland, Business and Professional Women's Clubs, Chartered Society of Physiotherapists, Cork Federation of Women's Organisations, Dublin University Women Graduates Association, the ICA, Irish Association of Dieticians, the IHA, National Association of Widows, National University Women Graduates Association, Soroptimists Clubs of Ireland, Women's International Zionist Organisation, Women's Liberation Movement, Women's Progressive Association.
31. Ibid., pp. 68–70.
32. Figure calculated from public data collected by the UK Department of Health Statistics and refers to women resident in Ireland who travelled to both England and Wales. It is widely accepted this is an underestimation as it excludes Scotland or other European countries and does not include people who do not disclose an Irish address, which according to the clinics such as the British Pregnancy Advisory Service (BPAS) was something people frequently did to protect confidentiality or avoid paying the mandatory overnight stay for non-resident women.
33. Kennedy, 2020.
34. O'Toole, 2014.
35. In Sanger, 2017, p. 5.
36. *McGee v. The Attorney General* [1974] IR 284. The McGee case led to limited legalisation of contraception although it would be six years before the Family Planning Bill (1979) which permitted married couples to access contraception with a prescription. It also allowed conscientious objection for doctors and pharmacists.
37. Barry, 1991, p. 113.
38. Cited in Ferriter, 2020.
39. Source: A 1982 leaflet from the Anti Amendment Campaign outlining their reasons for opposing the holding of a Referendum. The leaflet has

the founding statement of the Campaign as well as a list of public figures and groups that backed the campaign.

40. Gordan, 1984, p. 17.
41. Probably the most explicitly pro-choice statement made by the AAC was a letter sent by Lorraine Scully to the *Irish Times* on behalf of the steering committee. She writes: 'Over the past few months, correspondents have discussed the legal, medical, theological and philosophical aspects of the proposed amendment ... Although these arguments are fundamental to an informed and balanced opposition to the amendment, they do not relate to the practical problems of women living in present day Ireland': *Irish Times,* 15 July 1982. From this point onward, if you examine the press statements issues by AAC they all largely emphasise the politico-constitutional issues and ignore abortion itself.
42. Pauline Jackson, cited in Connolly 2003, p. 164.
43. SPUC was a radical anti-abortion group that operated on the frontlines of abortion campaigning in Ireland for many years. Many members were active in PLAC though not, it appears, at a leadership level.
44. Connolly 2003, p. 11.
45. McCann, 2016.
46. Ruane, cited in Ferriter, 2009.
47. See Cacciaguidi-Fahy, 2005.
48. Hug, 1999, p. 154.
49. Bacik, 2013, p. 22.
50. DeLondras & Enright, 2018, p. 3.
51. Ibid., p.2.
52. Sweetman, 2020, pp. 208–209.
53. Ibid.
54. Maguire, 2001.
55. McCafferty, 1985, p. 104.
56. Ibid., pp. 107–110.
57. Ibid., p. xxi.
58. Eileen Flynn, cited in 'The Stories That Time Forgot', *Irish Times*, 30 November 1999.
59. Carbery, 2008.
60. Duffy, 1995.
61. Carbery, 2008.
62. Smyth, 1988, pp. 340–341.
63. D'Alton et al, 2010., p. 79.
64. Government of Ireland, 2009, p. 41.
65. Meaghar, 2009.
66. www.nwci.ie/learn/newsflash-article/banulacht_closure (retrieved 9 December 2020).
67. Magrath & Fitzsimons, 2019.
68. Other left-wing activists including Mary Ryder, Mary Gordon and Eddie Conlon were also central to the AAC.

4 AFTER THE EIGHTH, THE SLOW MOVEMENT FOR REPEAL

1. On 26 June 1986 a referendum was held to remove the Constitutional ban on divorce. The proposal was overwhelming rejected with over 63 per cent voting no. Divorce remained illegal in Ireland until 1996 when a referendum to legalise narrowly passed with 50.28 per cent support.
2. Kennedy, 2020, pp. 110–118.
3. Cited in Hug 1999, p. 158.
4. Ibid., pp. 159–160.
5. Ibid., p. 160.
6. Abortion clinics are required to return abortion notification forms to the Chief Medical Officers in respect of abortions carried out in England and Wales. These figures cited above only refer to women who gave Irish addresses. Figures for the 1980s and 1990s are available via the British National Archives: https://webarchive.nationalarchives.gov. uk/20130123231223/http://www.dh.gov.uk/en/Publicationsandstatistics/ Statistics/StatisticalWorkAreas/Statisticalpublichealth/index.htm (retrieved 6 June 2021).
7. *Attorney General v. X*, [1992] IESC 1; [1992] 1 IR 1.
8. McDonagh, 1992, p. 89.
9. Kingston, 2001, p. 31.
10. Irish Family Planning Association, n.d.
11. For a detailed outline of the Women on Waves visit to Dublin, see www. womenonwaves.org/en/page/769/ireland-2001 (retrieved 6 June 2021). The organisation would also go on to set up Women on Web.
12. Muldowney, 2015, p. 139.
13. *P.P. v. Health Service Executive* [2014] IEHC H622.
14. *A, B and C v. Ireland*, No. 25579/05 Eur. Ct. H.R. (2010).
15. De Londras, 2012.
16. Doherty & Redmond, 2015, p. 273.
17. See Holland, 2013.
18. Holland, 2014.
19. www.merrionstreet.ie/MerrionStreet/en/ImageLibrary/Programme_for_ Partnership_Government.pdf (retrieved 6 June 2021).
20. The submissions the Citizens' Assembly received on the Eighth Amendment of the Constitution are listed here in chronological order: https://2016-2018.citizensassembly.ie/en/Submissions/Eighth-Amendment-of-the-Constitution/Submissions-Received/ (retrieved 6 June 2021).
21. The deliberations of the Citizens' Assembly is available at www. youtube.com/watch?v=1dD-NokfUz8&list=PL8jOxQOnEpsg-Xn8nzEkLdv5pwOFP5odt&index=18 (retrieved 6 June 2021).
22. Cited in Griffin et al., 2019.

23. This committee heard additional evidence from medical, legal and human rights experts and will be discussed in Chapter 7.
24. See Griffin et al., 2019.
25. For a detailed discussion around the Together for Yes name, see ibid., pp. 110–12.
26. See Barron, 2019.
27. See, for example, Red C poll commission by Amnesty International Ireland in 2016: www.amnesty.ie/amnesty-internationalred-c-poll-reveals-irish-public-want-expanded-access-abortion-political-priority-incoming-government/ (retrieved 6 June 2021).
28. Kearney, 1997, p. 189.
29. Mullally, 2018b.

5 NO QUIET REVOLUTION – THE GRASSROOTS GATHER

1. From research with community educators about the neoliberalisation of their work: Fitzsimons, 2017.
2. O'Rourke, 2018.
3. This was to pay for a controversial 2008 blanket guarantee given to Irish banks which resulted in Ireland entering into an IMF structural re-adjustment programme more typical of so-called developing countries.
4. *The Mahon Tribunal* cost c. €250 million and resulted in the resignation of Bertie Aherne and the imprisonment of some senior politicians and public servants.
5. Episode 5 'Legislate! How the Yes was Won' podcast, hosted by Deirdre Kelly and Aisling Dolan.
6. Shared in an interview within Episode 5 'Legislate!'.
7. www.abortionrightscampaign.ie/2013/02/21/welcome-to-the-abortion-rights-campaign-website/ (retrieved 19 April 2021).
8. Carnegie & Roth, 2019.
9. Ibid., p. 112.
10. Thanks to Marnie Holborow for this information.
11. Bodelsson, 2018, p. 9.
12. Ní Fhloinn, 2018, p. 108.
13. Their website explains IMELDA was a code for abortion by women who travelled to England in the 1980s and '90s.
14. Mullaly, 2018b, p. 2.
15. This extract is taken from Episode 7 'Repeal!'.
16. ARC, 2015, p. 14. I designed some of these workshops (Fitzsimons & Connolly, 2015).
17. Ní Shuilleabháin, 2015.

6 THE TOGETHER FOR YES CAMPAIGN

1. Interview with Niall Behan in Episode 5, Legislate, of the podcast 'How the Yes Was Won'.

2. Griffin et al., 2019.
3. Together for Yes's mobilisation team directed c. 2,500 people into local groups. Others signed up through Facebook or word of mouth.
4. Sherwood, 2018.
5. Erin has complied some of these stories into a beautifully illustrated book called *In Her Shoes, Women of the Eighth* published by New Island Press.
6. Taylor, 1998.
7. This was a policy in ARC when stewarding the Annual March for Choice.
8. Quotes taken from www.thejournal.ie/together-for-yes-crowdfunding-3957637-Apr2018/ (retrieved 1 January 2020).
9. Barron, 2019, p. 48.
10. Some tweets from www.buzz.ie/news/prime-time-eighth-referendum-debate-285998 (retrieved 20 January 2019).
11. Griffin et al., 2019, p. 197.
12. Usually mifepristone and misoprostol, which are ingested a few days apart.
13. Jelinska & Yanow, 2018.
14. Brouder, 2018.
15. Della Porta & Rucht, 2013, p. 223.

7 THE BATTLE CONTINUES

1. Although there was some debate, it was never clearly determined what qualified as a socio-economic reason.
2. The full voting patterns and a commentary are provided by Bardon, 2017.
3. Conveney, 2018.
4. www.oireachtas.ie/en/debates/debate/dail/2018-11-29/37/ (retrieved 14 December 2020).
5. www.togetherforyes.ie/12-weeks/ (article date 5 April 2018) (retrieved 27 September 2020).
6. There were some important differences. For example, ARC and the Coalition called for removal of the 3-day wait; the NWCI asked that this begin at the first point of contact.
7. www.oireachtas.ie/en/debates/debate/select_committee_on_health/2018-11-06/2/ (retrieved 21 April 2021).
8. www.oireachtas.ie/en/debates/debate/dail/2018-12-04/35/ (retrieved 31 December 2019).
9. https://ionainstitute.ie/news-roundup/education-minister-open-to-pro-life-amendments-to-abortion-law/ (article date 15 July 2020) (retrieved 1 December 2020).
10. Cullen, 2018.
11. www.irishdoctorsforlife.com/doctors-for-life-press-statement-christmas-2018/ (retrieved 6 June 2021).
12. Bitzer, 2016, p. 195.

13. Those not providing services are Kerry General Hospital Tralee, South Tipperary General Hospital, St Luke's General Hospital Kilkenny, Wexford General Hospital, Letterkenny General Hospital, Portiuncula Hospital Ballinasloe, Sligo General Hospital, Midland Regional Hospital Portlaoise.

14. www.abortionrightscampaign.ie/2021/06/29/over-six-thousand-people-were-able-to-access-abortion-care-within-ireland-in-2020/ (retrieved 30 June 2021).

15. Ui Bhriain, 2018.

16. www.irishexaminer.com/breakingnews/ireland/thats-deplorable--pro-choice-campaigners-hit-out-at-anti-abortion-protest-outside-gp-clinic-895575.html (article date 4 January 2019) (retrieved 29 December 2020).

17. This was carried out by the Oireachtas Library and Research Service.

18. www.iccl.ie/wp-content/uploads/2020/01/ICCL-Investigation-Abortion-Safe-Zones.pdf (retrieved 14 December 2020).

19. Bray, 2019.

20. www.oireachtas.ie/en/debates/question/2021-03-03/section/870/ (retrieved 6 April 2021).

21. Dempsey et al., 2021.

22. World Health Organization, 2012.

23. Craddock, 2019.

24. Murphy, 2020, p. 430.

25. www.oireachtas.ie/en/debates/debate/select_committee_on_health/2018-11-06/2/ (retrieved 21 April 2021).

26. This was shared in response to a question raised by Mick Barry TD with the Socialist Party.

27. NWCI, 2021.

8 IN THE STRUGGLE FOR REPRODUCTIVE RIGHTS, WHERE TO NEXT?

1. Stevenson, 2021.

2. De Londras, 2019.

3. Murray, 2021.

4. I circulated a final questionnaire in March/April 2021 and invited groups to identify themselves and tell me about the work they were doing under pre-determined headings.

5. Members: ARC, Abortion Support Network; Alliance for Choice; Amnesty Ireland; BelongTo; Cairde; Coalition to Repeal the Eighth Amendment; Disabled Women Ireland; Doctors for Choice; Dublin Well Woman Centre; Gynaecology & Obstetrics Women's Network (GOWN); Irish Council for Civil Liberties (ICCL); Inclusion Ireland; Irish Family Planning Association (IFPA); Lawyers for Choice; London Irish Abortion

Rights Campaign; National Collective of Community Based Women's Networks (NCCWN); National Traveller Women's Forum; National Women's Council of Ireland; Start Group; Transgender Equality Network Ireland (TENI); TFMR, Women's Aid; UCC School of Law; Union of Students in Ireland (USI).

6. This ruling originated from a year-long legal challenge against a 1993 law by the right-wing Nationalist Law and Justice Party. The majority of judges that voted on the issue were from the same party.

7. https://ionainstitute.ie/should-contraception-be-free/ (article 13 November 2019) (retrieved 17 April 2021).

8. HIQA, 2020, p. 10.

9. www.facebook.com/inourshoescovidpregnancy (retrieved 9 December 2020).

10. www.oireachtas.ie/en/debates/debate/dail/2019-09-26/42/ (retrieved 4 April 2021).

11. https://evoke.ie/2020/12/20/news/half-of-irish-schools-fail-to-provide-mandatory-sex-education-classes (retrieved 13 April 2021).

12. Eurydice, 2019.

13. Mayock & Bretherton, 2015.

14. Mary Harney of the Progressive Democrats, in coalition with Fianna Fáil, Mary Coughlan of Fianna Fáil, Francis Fitzgerald of Fine Gael and Joan Burton of the Labour Party.

15. This was when Burton was part of a coalition government with Fianna Fáil between 2012 and 2016.

16. Cronin, 2012, p. 31.

17. https://missingmigrants.iom.int/region/mediterranean (retrieved 17 April 2021). This is only the number that we know of and is widely thought to be an undercalculation.

18. Jaffe, 2021, p. 121.

19. Ross, 2017, p. 190.

20. https://maps.reproductiverights.org/worldabortionlaws (retrieved 22 July 2021).

Bibliography

Allen, A., & Lehrner, N. E. (2008). Social Change Movements and the Struggle over Meaning-Making: A Case Study of Domestic Violence Narratives. *American Journal of Community Psychology, 42*: 220–234.

Allen, K., & O'Boyle, B. (2013). *Austerity Ireland: the Failure of Irish Captialism*. New York: Pluto Press.

Amnesty International (2016). *What You Need to Know about Attitudes to Abortion in Ireland*. Amnesty International. Retrieved 25 June 2020, from www.amnesty.ie/poll/

ARC (2015). *Annual Report 2015*. Dublin: Abortion Rights Campaign.

Bacik, I. (2013). The Irish Constitution and Gender Politics: Developments in the Law on Abortion. *Irish Political Studies, 28*(3): 380–398.

Balakrishnan, R. (2002). *The Hidden Assembly Line; Gender Dynamics of Subcontracted Work in a Global Economy*. Bloomfield, CT: Kumarian Press.

Bardon, S. (2017). How the Eighth Amendment Committee Voted. *Irish Times*, 13 December. Retrieved 6 June 2021, from https://www.irishtimes.com/news/politics/how-the-eighth-amendment-committee-voted-1.3326580

Barron, M. (2019). *Learning from the 2018 Together for Yes Campaign*. Dublin: Together for Yes.

Barry, U. (1991). Movement, Change and Reaction. The Struggle over Reproductive Rights in Ireland. In A. Smyth, *The Abortion Papers Ireland, Volume 1*. Cork: Attic Press.

Bitzer, J. (2016). Conscientious Objection – To Be Or Not To Be. *European Journal of Contraception & Reproductive Health Care, 23*(3): 195–197.

Bodelsson, S. (2018). An Ignition of Hope for Reproductive Justice in Contentious Times. In C. Florescu, E. Balboa, J. Sassi, & P. Rivetti, *We've Come A Long Way: Reproductive Rights of Migrants and Ethnic Minorities in Ireland* (pp. 9–20). Dublin: MERJ.

Bray, J. (2019). Existing Laws Adequate to Deal with Abortion Protests Says Garda Commissioner. *Irish Times*, 26 September. Retrieved 6 June 2021, from www.irishtimes.com/news/health/existing-laws-adequate-to-deal-with-abortion-protests-says-garda-commissioner-1.4031727

Brouder, S. (2018). No Sign of Rural/Urban Split as Repeal Wins Out. *The Kerryman*. 2 June. Retrieved June 21, 2021, from www.independent.ie/regionals/kerryman/news/no-signs-of-ruralurban-split-as-repeal-wins-out-36959661.html

Burke, S. (2006). The Michael Neary Case: Arrogance, Power and the Catholic Ethos. *Magill*, 8 March. Retrieved 9 March 2021, from https://magill.ie/archive/michael-neary-case-arrogance-power-and-catholic-ethos

Cacciaguidi-Fahy, S. (2005). The Substantive Issue and the Rhetoric of the Abortion Debate in Ireland. In A. Wagner, T. Summerfield & S. Benavides Vanegas, *Contemporary Issues of the Semiotics of Law* (pp. 141–164). London: Hart.

Cahill, H. (2001). Male Appropriation and Medicalization of Childbirth: An Historical Analysis. *Journal of Advanced Nursing, 33*(3): 334–342.

Carbery, G. (2008). Eileen Flynn, Teacher Sacked in 1982, Dies. *Irish Times*, 11 September. Retrieved 25 June 2021, from www.irishtimes.com/news/eileen-flynn-teacher-sacked-in-1982-dies-1.937690

Carnegie, A., & Roth, R. (2019). From the Grassroots to the Oireachtas. Abortion Law Reform in the Republic of Ireland. *Health Human Rights, 21*(2): 109–120.

CDE Ireland (2019). *Confidential Maternal Death Enquiry Ireland. Data Brief no. 4.* Cork: MDE Ireland. Retrieved 26 November 2020, from www.ucc.ie/en/media/research/nationalperinatalepidemiologycentre/MDEDataBriefNo4December2019.pdf

Citizens' Assembly (2017). *First Report and Recommendations of the Citizens' Assembly.* The Citizens' Assembly. Retrieved 2 December 2020, from https://2016-2018.citizensassembly.ie/en/The-Eighth-Amendment-of-the-Constitution/Final-Report-on-the-Eighth-Amendment-of-the-Constitution/Final-Report-incl-Appendix-A-D.pdf

Clarke, M. (2019). Mara Clarke: The Law and Resulting Provision are Leaving Too Many People Behind. Retrieved 21 March 2020, from www.abortionrightscampaign.ie/2019/09/28/mara-clarke-the-law-and-resulting-provision-are-leaving-too-many-people-behind

Coffey, C., et al. (2020). *Time to Care, Unpaid and Underpaid Care Work and the Global Inequality Crisis.* Oxford: Oxfam.

Committee on the Eighth Amendment of the Consititution. (2017). *Report of the Joint Committee on the Eighth Amendment of the Consititution.* Dublin: House of the Oireachtas.

Connolly, L. (2003). *The Irish Women's Movement: From Revolution to Devolution.* Dublin: The Liliput Press.

Connolly, L., & O'Toole, T. (2005). *Documenting Irish Feminisms, The Second Wave.* Dublin : The Woodfield Press.

Conrad, K. (2001). Fetal Ireland: National Bodies and Political Agency, Eire. *Eire Ireland, 36*(34): 153–173.

Conveney, S. (2018). Here's How My Thinking Changed on the Eighth Amendment. *Irish Independent,* 26 March. Retrieved 6 June 2021, from www.independent.ie/irish-news/simon-coveney-heres-how-my-thinking-shifted-on-the-eighth-amendment-36743798.html

Costa, M. (2018). The Particularity of Migrants and Ethnic Minorities in Ireland. In M. A. Justice, *We've Come a Long Way*, 2nd edition (pp. 29–33). São Paulo: Editora Urutau.

Coyne, E. (2018). Cherish founder: I regret ever working with Catholic Church. *The Times*, 12 June. Retrieved June 21, 2021 from www.thetimes.co.uk/article/cherish-founder-i-regret-ever-working-with-catholic-church-shp87qckz

Craddock, E. (2019). Doing 'Enough' of the 'Right' Thing: The Gendered Dimension of the 'Ideal Activist' Identity and its Negative Emotional Consequences. *Social Movement Studies, 18*(2): 137–153.

Cronin, D. (2012). Women and Austerity. *Irish Marxist Review, 1*(1): 30–33.

Cullen, P. (2018). Conscientious Objection: GP Abortion Meeting 'Bitter, Chaotic, Uncivil'. *Irish Times*, 4 December. Retrieved June 21, 2021, from www.irishtimes.com/news/health/conscientious-objection-gp-abortion-meeting-bitter-chaotic-uncivil-1.3718864

D'Alton, E., Fenton, M., Maher, H., & O'Grady, M. (2010). Grounding Higher Education in the Community: The case of Waterford Women's Centre and Waterford Institute of Technology. *Policy and Practice: A Development Education Review, 10*: 78–88.

Davis, A. (2003). *Are Prisons Obsolete.* New York : Seven Stories Press.

de Londras, F. (2012). Past Time for Meaningful 'Action on X'. *Magill*, 22 February. Retrieved 5 June 2021, from https://magill.ie/society/past-time-meaningful-action-x

de Londras, F. (2020). Intersectionality, Repeal, and Reproductive Rights in Ireland. In S. Atrey & P. Dunne, *Intersectionality and Human Rights Law.* Oxford: Harte Publishing.

de Londras, F., & Enright, M. (2018). *Repealing the 8th, Reforming Irish Abortion Law.* Dublin: Polity Press.

Delay, C. (2019). Pills, Potions, and Purgatives: Women and Abortion Methods in Ireland, 1900–1950. *Women's History Review, 28*(3): 479–477.

Della Porta, D., & Rucht, D. (2013). *Meeting Democracy: Power and Deliberation in Global Justice Movements.* Cambridge: Cambridge University Press.

Dempsey, B., Favier, M., Mullally, A., & Higgins, M. F. (2021). Exploring Providers' Experience of Stigma Following the Introduction of More Liberal Abortion Care in the Republic of Ireland. *Contraception, 2*(36): 1–6.

Doan, A. E. (2016). *Opposition and Intimidation: The Abortion Wars and Strategies of Political Harassment.* Ann Arbor: University of Michigan Press.

Doherty, C., & Redmond, S. (2015). The Radicalisation of a New Generation of Abortion Activists. In C. Conlon, S. Kennedy, & A. Quiltey, *The Abortion Papers, Volume 2* (pp. 270–274). Cork: Cork University Press.

Duffy, R. (1995). Unacceptable Conduct. *Irish Times*, 14 October.

Dundes, L. (1987). The Evolution of Maternal Birthing Position. *Public Health Then and Now, 77*(5): 636–641.

Earner-Byrne, L. U. (2019). *The Irish Abortion Journey, 1920–2018.* London: Palgrave Macmillan.

Eurydice. (2019). *Key Data on Early Childhood Education and Care in Europe – 2019 Edition.* European Commission.

Fenton, S. (2018). On Northern Ireland. In U. Mullally, *Repeal the 8th* (pp. 153–168). London: Unbound.

Ferriter, D. (2009). *Occasions of Sin: Sex and Society in Modern Ireland.* London: Profile Books.

Ferriter, D. (2020). Marian Finucane a studio voice of profound searching. *Irish Times,* 4 June. Retrieved 6 June 2021, from www.irishtimes.com/opinion/diarmaid-ferriter-marian-finucane-a-studio-voice-of-profound-searching-1.4129723

Fitzgerald, L. (2021). Socialist Feminist Struggle Against Gender Violence. *Socialist Alternative, Spring*(12): 23–24.

Fitzsimons, C. (2017). *Community Education and Neoliberalism: Philosophies, Practices and Policies in Ireland.* Zurich: Palgrave-Macmillan.

Fitzsimons, C., & Connolly, B. (2015). Women's Reproduction and Rights. Retrieved 25 June 2021, from http://mural.maynoothuniversity.ie/9425/

Fitzsimons, C., Hassan, B., Nwanze, L., & Obasi, P. (2021). *Researching the Experiences of Muslim Women in Irish Maternity Settings.* Amal Women's Association and the Irish Human Rights and Equality Commission.

Funge, J. K., Mathilde, C. B., Johnsen, H., & Nørredam, M. (2020). 'No Papers. No Doctor': A Qualitative Study of Access to Maternity Care Services for Undocumented Immigrant Women in Denmark. *International Journal of Environmental Research and Public Health,* 2 September.

Gallen, J., & Gleeson, K. (2017). Unpaid Wages: The Experiences of Irish Magdalene Laundries and Indigenous Australians. *International Journal of Law in Context, 14*(1), 43–60.

Garrett, P. M. (2016). Unmarried Mothers in the Republic of Ireland. *Journal of Social Work, 16*(6): 708–725.

Gilligan, R. (2019). The Family Foster Care System in Ireland – Advances and Challenges. *Children and Youth Services Review, 100*(3): 221–228.

Gordan, M. (1984). Fighting for Control: The Ongoing Struggle for Reproductive Rights. *Irish Feminist Review, 84.*

Government of Ireland (2009). *Report of the Special Group on Public Service Numbers and Expenditure Programmes, Volume 2.* Dublin: Government Publications.

Government Publications (1922). *Constitution of the Irish Free State (Saorstát Eireann) Act, 1922.* Retrieved 2020, from www.irishstatutebook.ie/eli/1922/act/1/enacted/en/print.html

Griffin, G., O'Connell, O., Smyth, A., & O'Connell, A. (2019). *It's a Yes! How Together for Yes Repealed the Eighth and Transformed Irish Society.* Dublin: Orphen Press.

Gutiérrez, E. (2004). We Will No Longer be Silent or Invisible. In J. Silliman, M. Gerber Fried, L. Ross, & E. Gutiérrez, *Undivided Rights: Women of Colour Organise for Reproductive Justice.* Cambridge, MA: South End Press.

Healy, G., Sheehan, B., & Whelan, N. (2015). *Ireland says Yes: The Inside Story of How the Vote for Marriage Equality Was Won.* Dublin: Merrion Press.

HIQA (2020). *Overview Report of HIQA's Monitoring Programme Against the National Standards for Safer Better Maternity Services, With a Focus on Obstetric Emergencies.* Health Information and Quality Authority.

Retrieved 4 October 2020, from www.hiqa.ie/sites/default/files/2020-02/Maternity-Overview-Report.pdf

Hogan, C. (2019). *Republic of Shame*. UK: Penguin, Random House.

Holland, K. (2013). *Savita: A Tragedy that Shook a Nation*. Dublin: Transworld.

Holland, K. (2014). Timeline of Ms Y Case. *Irish Times*, 4 October. Retrieved 25 June 2021, from www.irishtimes.com/news/social-affairs/timeline-of-ms-y-case-1.1951699

hooks, b. (1982). *Ain't I a Woman: Black Women and Feminism*. London: Pluto Press.

HSE (2020a). *Perinatal Statistics Report 2017*. Healthcare Pricing Office. Retrieved 10 May 2021, from www.hpo.ie/latest_hipe_nprs_reports/NPRS_2017/Perinatal_Statistics_Report_2017.pdf

HSE (2020b). *Rapid Assessment and Community Response to Suicide and Suspected Suicide in Dublin South*. HSE. Retrieved 3 December 2020, from www.hse.ie/eng/services/list/4/mental-health-services/connecting-for-life/publications/rapid-assessment-report.pdf

Hug, C. (1999). *The Politics of Sexual Morality in Ireland*. London: MacMillan.

Illich, I. (1976). *Medical Nemesis; The Expropriation of Health*. New York: Pantheon Books.

Inglis, T. (2003). *Truth, Power and Lies: Irish Society and the Case of the Kerry Babies*. Dublin: UCD Press.

Irish Family Planning Association (n.d.). *Rogue Crisis Pregnancy Agencies in Ireland – Anti Choice and Anti Women*. Dublin: Irish Family Planning Association. Retrieved 22 November 2020, from www.ifpa.ie/sites/default/files/documents/media/publications/rogue_agency_factsheet.pdf

Irish Medical Council (2019). *Guide to Professional Conduct and Ethics for Registered Medical Practitioners (Amended). 8th Edition*. Dublin: Irish Medical Council.

Irish Penal Reform Trust (2014). *Travellers in the Irish Prison System. A Qualitative Study*. Dublin: Irish Penal Reform Trust.

Jackson, P. (1992). Abortion Trials and Tribulations. *Canadian Journal of Irish Studies, 18*(1): 112–120.

Jaffe, S. (2021). *Work Won't Love You Back*. London: Hurst and Company.

Jelinska, K., & Yanow, S. (2018). Putting Abortion Pills Into Women's Hands: Realizing the Full Potential of Medical Abortion. *Contraception, 97*(2): 86–89,

Jones, E. L. (2011). Attitudes to Abortion in the Era of Reform: Evidence from the Abortion Law Reform Association Correspondence. *Women's History Review, 20*(2): 283–298.

Kearney, R. (1997). *Postnationalist Ireland: Politics Culture Philosophy*. London: Routledge.

Keating, A., & Fleming, V. (2009). Midwives' Experiences of Facilitating Normal Birth in an Obstetric-led Unit: A Feminist Perspective. *Midwifery, 25*: 518–527.

Kennedy, S. (2020). The Right to Know: Gender, Power, Reproduction and Knowledge Regulation in Ireland. In M. Corcoran & P. Cullen, *Producing Knowledge, Reproducing Gender: Power, Production And Practice In Contemporary Ireland.* (pp. 110–129.). Dublin: UCD Press.

Kennedy, S. (2021). *Meeting the Needs of Every Woman.* Dublin: The National Women's Council of Ireland.

Kingston, J. (2001). *The Need for Abortion Law Reform in Ireland: The Case Against the Twenty-Fifth Amendment of the Constitution Bill.* Dublin: Irish Council for Civil Liberties.

Kissling, E. A. (2017). *From a Whisper to a Shout.* New York: Random House Inc.

Lally, C. (2021). Domestic Violence: 'Deep Concern' Over Cancellations of 999 calls to Garda. *Irish Times.* Retrieved 26 June 2021, from www. irishtimes.com/news/crime-and-law/domestic-violence-deep-concern-over-cancellations-of-999-calls-to-garda-1.4592369

Lawlor, S. (2005). Disgusted Subjects: The Making of Middle-class Identities. *Sociological Review, 53*(3): 429–446.

Leane, M., & Kiely, E. (2004). Female Domestic and Farm Workers in Munster, 1936–1960: Some Insights from Oral History. *Saothar, 29:* 57–65.

Lentin, R. (2013). A Woman Died: Abortion and the Politics of Birth in Ireland. *Feminist Review, 105*(1): 130–136.

Lowe, P., and Hayes, G. (2019). Anti-Abortion Clinic Activism, Civil Inattention and the Problem of Gendered Harassment. *Sociology, 53*(2): 330–346.

Luddy, M. (2005). A 'Sinister and Retrogressive' Proposal: Irish Women's Opposition To The I937 Draft Constitution. *Royal History Society (London, England), 15:* 175–195.

Lynch, K. (2018). The Culture of the Irish Maternity Service. In C. Florescu, E. Balboa, J. Sassi & P. Rivetti, *We've Come a Long Way: Reproductive Rights of Migrants and Ethnic Minorities in Ireland.* São Paulo, Brazil: Editora Urutau.

MacCormaic, R. (2013). UN Watchdog Criticises Magdalene Report for Lack of Independence. *Irish Times,* 3 June. Retrieved 6 June 2021, from www. irishtimes.com/news/un-watchdog-criticises-magdalene-report-for-lack-of-independence-1.1415043

Macintyre, S. (1973). The Medical Profession and the 1967 Abortion Act in Britian. *Social Science and Medicine, 7*(2): 121–134.

Magrath, C., & Fitzsimons, C. (2019). Funding Community Education in Ireland – Making the Case for a Needs-based Approach. *Journal of Social Science Education, 18*(4): 38–50.

Maguire, M. J. (2001). The Changing Face of Catholic Ireland, Conservatism and liberalism in the Ann Lovett and Kerry Babies Scandals. *Feminist Studies, Social Science Premium Collection, 27*(2): 335–358.

Manning, E. (2014). *Establishing a Maternal Death Enquiry in a Low Maternal Mortality Context.* World Health Organisation. Retrieved 25

June 2021, from www.who.int/maternal_child_adolescent/epidemiology/maternal-death-surveillance/case-studies/ireland/en/

Mayock, P., & Bretherton, J. (2015). *Women's Homelessness in Europe.* Switzerland: Springer.

McAuliffe, M. (2011). The Irish Woman Worker and the Conditions of Employment Act, 1936 Responses from the Irish Free State Women Senators. *Saothar, 36:* 36–46.

McBride Stetson, D. (2002). *Abortion Politics, Women's Movements, and the Democratic State. A Comparative Study of State Feminism.* Oxford: Oxford University Press.

McCafferty, N. (1985). *A Woman to Blame: The Kerry Babies Case.* Cork: Attic Press.

McCann, E. (2016). People have the Power. *Hot Press,* 5 May. Retrieved 6 June 2021, from www.hotpress.com/opinion/people-have-the-power-17224763

McDonagh, S. (1992). *The Attorney General v. X and Others: Judgments of the High Court and Supreme Court. Legal Submissions made to the Supreme Court.* Dublin: Incorporated Council of Law Reporting for Ireland.

McRobbie, A. (2009). *The Aftermath of Feminism: Gender, Culture and Social Change.* London: Sage Publications.

Meaghar, A. (2009). McCarthy – Community Sector Takes to the Streets. *Changing Ireland, Winter:*14–15.

Moore, A. (2020). Overreach of Power: Intimidation and Harassment in the Social Welfare System. *Irish Examiner,* 19 October. Retrieved 18 November 2020, from www.irishexaminer.com/news/spotlight/arid-40067073.html

Muldowney, M. (2015). Breaking the Silence: Pro-Choice Activism on Ireland since 1983. In J. Redmond, S. Tiernan, S. McAvoy & M. McAuliffe, *Sexual Politics in Modern Ireland.* Dublin: Irish Academic Press.

Mullally, U. (2018a). If You Think The Movement Is Going Away You Have Not Been Listening. *Irish Times,* 4 June.

Mullaly, U. (2018b). *Repeal the Eighth.* London: Unbound.

Murphy, D. (2020). Repealed the 8th: Self Care for Reproductive Rights Activists in Ireland. *Interface: A Journal for and about Social Movements,* 12(1): 420–436.

Murray, A. (2021). Toxicity in Irish Activism. *Quare, 10.* Retrieved 3 January 2021, from https://quaremedia.com/toxicity-in-irish-activism/

Najambadi, S. (2021). House committee advances anti-abortion bills, including ones aimed at outlawing the procedure in Texas. *Texas Tribune,* 15 April. Retrieved 16 April 2021, from www.texastribune.org/2021/04/07/texas-house-abortion/

Naughton, G. (2013). Misadventure Verdict in Hospital Death. *Irish Independent,* 6 November. Retrieved 9 March 2021, from www.independent.ie/irish-news/courts/misadventure-verdict-in-hospital-death-29730405.html/

Ní Fhloinn, E. (2018). The Case of Travellers and Traveller Voices. In C. Florescu, E. Balboa, S. Juliana, & P. Rivetti, *We've Come a Long Way.*

Reproductive Rights of Migrants and Ethnic Minorities in Ireland, 2nd Edition (pp. 105–110). São Paulo, Brazil: Editora Urutau.

Ní Shuilleabhain, J. (2015). My Story. In A. Quilty, C. Conlon & S. Kennedy, *The Abortion Papers Volume 2* (pp. 25–33). Cork: Cork University Press.

Ó Fatharta, C. (2015). Special Investigation: Government Already Knew of Baby Deaths. *Irish Examiner*, June 3. Retrieved June 21, 2021, from www.irishexaminer.com/news/arid-20334260.html

Ó Gráda, C., & Mokyr, J. (1984). New Developments in Irish Population History, 1700–1850. *Economic History Review, 37*(4): 473–488.

O'Rourke, M. (2018). *Freedom of Artistic Expression and the Referendum on the 8th Amendment.* Dublin: Irish Council for Civil Liberties.

O'Toole, F. (2003). The Sisters of No Mercy. *Guardian,* 15 February.

O'Toole, F. (2014). Why Ireland Became the Only Country in the Democratic World to have a Constitutional Ban on Abortion. *Irish Times,* 26 August.

Park, A., Bryson, C., Clery, E., Curtice, J., & Philips, M. (2013). *British Social Attitudes the 30th Report.* London: NatCen Social Research.

Pembrook, S. (2019). Foucault and Industrial Schools in Ireland: Subtly Disciplining or Dominating through Brutality? *Sociology, 53*(2): 385–400.

Powell, R. M., & Nickolson, J. (2019). Disparities on Child Protection Services: Commentary on Kaplan et al. *Psychiatric Services, 70*(3): 209–210.

Raftery, M., & O'Sullivan, E. (1999). *Suffer the Little Children: The Inside Story of Ireland's Industrial Schools.* Dublin: New Island.

Reddy, L. (2019). *L&RS Note: Safe access zones – What do other Countries Do?* Oireachtas Library & Research Service.

Rocca, C. H., Samaria, G. B., Fostera, D. G., Goulda, H., & Kimporta, K. (2019). Emotions and Decision Rightness Over Five Years Following an Abortion: An Examination of Decision Difficulty and Abortion Stigma. *Social Science & Medicine, March:* 1–8.

Ross, L. (2017). Concetualizing Reproductive Justice Theory: A Manifesto for Activism. In L. J. Ross, L. Roberts, E. Derkas, W. Peoples & P. Bridgewater Toure, *Radical Reproductive Justice* (pp. 170–232). New York: Feminist Press.

Ross, L. J., & Solinger, R. (2017). *Reproductive Justice: An Introduction.* Oakland: University of California Press.

Ross, L. J., Roberts, L., Derkas, E., Peoples, W., & Bridgewater Toure, P. (2017). *Radical Reproductive Justice.* New York: Feminist Press.

Rottenberg, C. (2018). *The Rise of Neoliberal Feminism.* New York: Oxford University Press.

Sanger, C. (2017). *About Abortion: Terminating Pregnancy in Twenty-First Century America.* Cambridge, MA: Harvard University Press.

Scally, G. (2018). *Scoping Inquiry into the Cervical Check – Final Report.* Dublin: Government Publications.

Schoen, J. (2015). *Abortion After Roe : Abortion After Legalization.* Chapel Hill: University of North Carolina Press.

Sheldon, S., & Wellings, K. (2020). *Decriminalising Abortion in the UK: What Would It Mean?* Bristol: Bristol University Press.

Sherwood, H. (2018). Abortion Question Divides Rural Ireland as Referendum Looms. *Guardian,* 9 May.

Silliman, J., Gerber Fried, M., Ross, L., & Gutiérrez, E. R. (2004). *Undivided Rights: Women of Color Organize for Reproductive Justice.* Cambridge, MA: South End Press.

Smyth, A. (1988). The Contemporary Women's Movement in the Republic of Ireland. *Women's Studies International Forum, 11*(4): 331–341.

Stevenson, R. (2021). Opinion: Our Baby Would Not Live, so We had to Travel to London. Our Hearts are Broken. *Journal.ie,* 21 March. Retrieved 6 June 2021, from www.thejournal.ie/readme/maternity-care-5381970-Mar2021/

Sweeney, R. (2019). *The State We Are In: Inequality in Ireland Today.* Dublin: TASC.

Sweetman, R. (2020). *Feminism Backwards.* Cork: Mercier Press.

Taylor, J. (1998). Feminist Tactics and Friendly Fire in the Irish Women's Movement. *Gender and Society, 12*(6): 674–691.

Thompson, B. Y. (2017). Centring Reproductive Justice: Transitioning from Abortion Rights to Social Justice. In L. Ross, L. Roberts, E. Derkas, W. Peoples, & P. Bridgewater Toure, *Radical Reproductive Justice.* New York: Feminist Press.

Ui Bhriain, N. (2018). *Our Hearts Are Broken. But We Will Fight On, Because No Referendum Can Ever Make Abortion Right.* Retrieved 21 June 2021, from https://thelifeinstitute.net/blog/2018/our-hearts-are-broken-but-we-will-fight-on-because-no-referendum

United Nations (2005). *Convention on the Elimination of All Forms of Discrimination against Women Concluding comments: Ireland.* United Nations. Retrieved 25 June 2020, from www.un.org/womenwatch/daw/cedaw/cedaw33/conclude/ireland/0545060E.pdf

United Nations (2019). *A Human Rights-based Approach to Mistreatment and Violence Against Women in Reproductive Health Services with a Focus on Childbirth and Obstetric Violence.* UN General Assembly. Retrieved 17 December 2020, from https://undocs.org/A/74/137

Valiulis, M. G. (1992). Power, Gender, and Identity in the Irish Free State. *Journal of Women's History, 7*(1): 117–136.

Valiulis, M. G. (2011). The Politics of Gender in the Irish Free State. *Women's History Review, 20*(4): 569–578.

Wade, J. (2012). Simon Harris Responds to Criticism Over Abortion Position. *The Journal.ie,* 22 July. Retrieved 5 June 2021, from www.thejournal.ie/simon-harris-responds-to-criticism-over-abortion-position-529520-Jul2012/

Wade, K. (2017). Caesarean Section Refusal in the Irish Courts: *Health Service Executive v B. Medical Law Review, 25*(3): 494–504.

Ward, M. (1983). *Unmanagable Revolutionaries: Women and Irish Nationalism.* Dingle, Co. Kerry: Brandon Press.

Women's Aid (2019). *Unheard and Uncounted: Women's Domestic Abuse and the Irish Criminal Justice System*. Dublin: Women's Aid.

World Health Organization (2012). *Safe Abortion: Technical and Policy Guidance for Health Systems, 2nd edition*. Geneva: World Health Organization Press.

World Health Organization (2018). *WHO Non-clinical Recommendations to Reduce Unnecessary Caesarean Sections*. Geneva: World Health Organization.

Index